GLENCOE

D1220821

...ings

Ballachulish Ferry, 1692

Duncanson's H.Q.

Glenlyon's H.Q.

Invercharnan, where MacIain signed a treaty of friendship with Campbell of Inverawe

•••••••• Hamilton's march

—·—·— Duncanson's march

——— Tracks to Fort William

⟶ Probable flight of survivors

Kinlochleven

Devil's Staircase

Little Herdsman

Big Herdsman

RANNOCH MOOR

BREADALBANE

BLACK MOUNT

GLEN ORCHY

Achallader

Glencoe

By the same author:

WHERE THE SEA BREAKS
THE EDGE OF DARKNESS
AGE WITHOUT PITY
THE MATHER STORY
THE BRUTE STREETS
MY GREAT AUNT APPEARING DAY
THE BUFFALO SOLDIERS

History:

THE HIGH GIRDERS
CULLODEN
THE HIGHLAND CLEARANCES

Glencoe

THE STORY OF THE MASSACRE

by John Prebble

"Let it be secret and sudden"

Holt, Rinehart and Winston

New York   Chicago

San Francisco

FOR JOHN ROSS PREBBLE

Contents

List of Plates

Maps

I HAVE written this book because its story is, in a sense, a beginning to what I have already written about Culloden and the Clearances —the destruction of the Highland people and their way of life. The Massacre of Glencoe is commonly thought to have been a bloody incident in a meaningless feud between Campbell and MacDonald, which it was not. On a higher level, it is also thought to have been incidental to the political events of its time, an accident of judgement almost, whereas it was the product of them. It can be understood only within a knowledge of the Highlander's resistance to an alien southern government. The quarrel between Clan Donald and Clan Campbell was a rivalry for the leadership of Gaeldom, embittered by the Campbells' growing support for that government.

The Highland people were once the majority of Scotland's population, a military society that had largely helped to establish and maintain her monarchy. This society, tribal and feudal, could not change itself to meet a changing world, nor did it wish to. Its decline became more rapid in the second half of the 17th century, and within a hundred and fifty years its people had been driven from their mountains. By 1690 the Highlanders were already regarded by many Lowlanders as an obstacle to the complete political union of England and Scotland, and their obstinate independence of spirit—expressed in their customs, their clothes and their language—had to be broken and humbled. The MacDonalds of Glencoe were early victims of what the High-landers called *Mi-run mor nan Gall,* the Lowlander's great hatred.

Lowland leaders naturally despised what they wished to destroy, and therefore that destruction seemed to be a virtuous necessity. No Scots or English statesman would have thought of ordering the extirpation of a lowland or English community, but a Highland clan, particularly one of the Gallows Herd, was a different matter. One of the principals involved in the Massacre said afterwards, "It's not that anybody thinks that the thieving tribe did not deserve to be destroyed . . ." It was only regrettable that the murder of men, women and children should have been carried out in a dishonourable way.

The same contempt for the Highlander was responsible for the brutalities that followed Culloden in 1746, and the same indifference to his way of life was shown when the Clearances began fifty years later. In the end *Mi-run mor nan Gall* was triumphant.

The story has a relevance for us. Our age has seen a monstrous attempt at genocide, and we have had to determine the moral responsibility of those who carried it out under orders.

JOHN PREBBLE
October, 1965

1

THE GALLOWS HERD

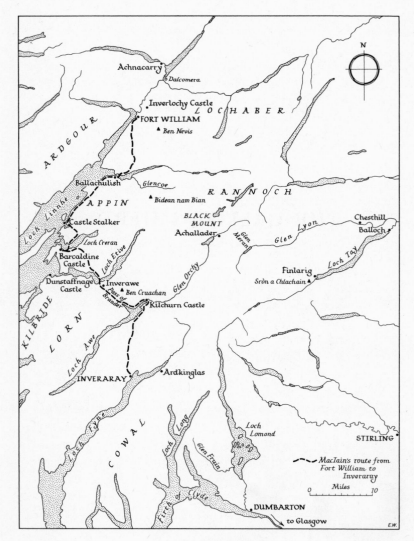

N

Achnacarry

Dalcomera

Inverlochy Castle

LOCHABER

FORT WILLIAM

▲ Ben Nevis

ARDGOUR

Ballachulish

Glencoe

RANNOCH

APPIN

▲ Bidean nam Bian

BLACK
MOUNT

Castle Stalker

Achallader

Glen Lyon

Chesthill

Balloch

Loch Creran

Glen
Meran

Loch Linnhe

Barcaldine
Castle

Loch Tay

Loch Etive

Finlarig

Dunstaffnage
Castle

Inverawe

Glen Orchy

Sròn a Chlachain ▲

Pass of
Brander

▲ Ben Cruachan

KILBRIDE

Kilchurn Castle

LORN

Loch Awe

INVERARAY

Ardkinglas

STIRLING

Loch Fyne

COWAL

Loch Long

Glen Fruin

Loch
Lomond

━ ━ ━ *MacIain's route from*
Fort William to
Inveraray

Miles

0   10

Firth of Clyde

DUMBARTON

to Glasgow

E.W.

The Western Highlands.

"It will be a proper vindication of the public justice"

THERE WERE boats on Loch Leven when John Forbes reached the
narrows at Ballachulish. They lay like curled leaves on the dark
water, high at the stem and stern, and almost motionless as the
oarsmen pulled against the drag of the tide and the tug of the
wind. They were ferrying soldiers across from Carness, and when
Forbes saw the slant of pikes and the burnished barrels of muskets
his memory stirred uneasily. At first there was nothing by which
he could identify the soldiers, only the scarlet of their coats in the
winter's grey light. Riding closer to the ferry he saw the boar's-
head badge on their bonnets, the green plaids in which some them
were wrapped, and he recognised them as men of the Earl of
Argyll's Regiment of Foot. When the first files waded through
the shallows and formed up with their faces toward Glencoe he
felt more uneasy still.

Tired, and anxious to be at Fort William before nightfall, he
waited impatiently for an empty boat to take him over to the
north shore. The sky promised more snow. Bad weather had
already delayed his passage from Edinburgh to the lonely garrison
in the Great Glen. In the best of seasons it was not a ride he
enjoyed. In winter it meant eight days or more in the saddle and
was "the most troublesome journey that I ever take". Wild men
in the Central Highlands, outlaws or Rebels, made the shortest
route hazardous, and he was forced to travel by way of Glasgow
and Dumbarton, then northward across Loch Long and Loch
Fyne, coming through Appin to Fort William like a tinker to the
back door. Even thus, when he brought the garrison its pay (too

infrequently, the semi-mutinous soldiers were always complaining), he had to rely upon the armed protection of Argyllshire lairds to see him safely through those glens infested with broken men of Clan Gregor or Clan Donald.

An eager and ambitious man, with a beaked nose and pale, proud eyes, John Forbes was bitterly resentful of service in the Highlands when other young men had the good fortune to campaign in Flanders. For the most part he kept this hurt to himself, and when he did speak of it to his brother, the Laird of Culloden, he tempered it by adding "I pay my pains with the satisfaction of serving my King and Country." Three years earlier, in the summer of 1689, there had been some substance to this satisfaction. Then, as a captain of an independent company, he had commanded Ruthven Castle for King William III and the Protestant Revolution. Besieged there by an army of Jacobite clans under Viscount Dundee he shouted boyish defiance from the walls, though probably in words less theatrical than those put into his mouth later by a classical-minded contemporary: "I, a Forbes, hold this castle for the Prince of Orange, and for him will I hold it while the gods permit!" The support of the gods was no stronger than the slender resources of his garrison, but he enjoyed three days of such heroics before surrendering to Dundee's cannon and the scaling-ladders of the MacDonalds. Since that was a year when most of King William's Scottish soldiers were running in panic before those of his father-in-law King James, this brief stand at Ruthven was regarded as highly creditable. Yet it had required all the strenuous influence of the Laird of Culloden, and of John Hill the Governor of Fort William, to squeeze from the King a commission in Hill's Regiment. Now, as he dismounted by the ferry and frowned at the Argyll men, Forbes wore a major's crimson sash and white shoulder-knots beneath his blue cloak.

There were, he estimated, a hundred and twenty of the Campbell soldiers: a grenadier company in fur caps, and a battalion company in bonnets. There was a piper, and there were Lowland sergeants shouting in English above the Gaelic of the private men.

Stepping toward Forbes, and lifting his hat in greeting, was their commander, Captain Robert Campbell of Glenlyon. He was an old man but there was a curious, almost feminine youthfulness in his face, the flesh pink and full, framed in a fine gauze of fair hair. His nose was long, his lips red and thin, and above them his eyes were steady in the unnerving stare of an habitual drinker. He said that he was away with his command to find quarters among the MacDonalds in Glencoe, and what further unease this caused Forbes the major thought it prudent to keep to himself. He nodded shortly and led his horse on to the ferry.

On the north shore he rode eastward for two miles along the lochside, his head turned now and then to watch the march of the Argyll men across the water. Their red coats and yellow hose were a trickle of colour against the white wall of hills, the ordered pikes a black hedge at the centre of each company. They were behind him, and still far from the mouth of Glencoe, when he turned away northward to climb the drove road to Fort William. He felt in need of John Hill's reassurance. Because of an old friendship for the Forbes family, the Governor treated the young man with affection, calling him his "dear child" and placing trust in him. He sent him to Edinburgh three or four times a year, to plead with the Privy Council for the meal or the pay or the shoe leather which the wretched garrison always needed, and while there Forbes had the colonel's permission to open and read any dispatches that came from London, before sending them on to the Highlands. Some ten days ago he had opened two such letters, addressed to Hill by the Secretary of State for Scotland. They had come by flying pacquet in four days, and both were dated January 16, 1692. The first was a double of the instructions sent that day to the Commander-in-Chief in Scotland concerning the action to be taken against those Rebels who had failed to take the oath of allegiance within the time set, and the copy made it plain that in the original King William had signed his name at the head and the foot of these instructions. The second was a letter from the Secretary to Colonel Hill, and was concerned with the same subject in greater detail. It was the memory of the letters

that had troubled Forbes when he first saw the red coats of the
Argyll men, and echoing sentences from them troubled him still
as he rode northward over the high snows.

Towards nightfall he came down the brae to Inverlochy.
Lights pricked the frosty dusk where the fort sprawled in a dis-
torted, five-pointed star on a spit of land at the mouth of the River
Nevis, looking across Loch Linnhe to the hills of Ardgour. To the
west of the ramparts was the Royal town of Maryburgh, mean
streets of turf and wattle cottages crouching close to the earth. To
the south were the garden patches where John Hill grew summer
vegetables in the hope of reducing the disease and despair that
crippled two-thirds of his garrison. The men whose lives such
efforts had failed to save lay in regimental rows, unmarked in the
burial-ground on Forbes's left as he rode over a shallow burn of
ice, passed the brewhouse and the Mercat Cross, forded another
run of water and entered the fort by the main gate. It was full of
soldiers, men of Hill's regiment, some of Argyll's, and kilted
Highlanders of the independent companies from Clan Grant and
Clan Menzies for whom Forbes, like most regular officers, had
more contempt than respect. He rode along the rear of their
wooden barracks and dismounted before the Governor's house at
the south-east ravelin.

The old Englishman was seated at his desk in the green-panelled
drawing-room he used as an office. His skin was yellow from the
fever that had plagued him since he came to the fort eighteen
months before, and his face was a map that charted the weary
struggles and disappointments that each had brought. But he
smiled with warm pleasure, rising to embrace the young man and
to welcome him back as a son. Forbes had no patience for the
small-talk of reunion, and he told Hill that he had seen Glenlyon
and the Argyll companies marching on Glencoe from Ballachulish.
The smile on Hill's face faded, and he began to complain bitterly.
He was the Governor of Fort William and the King's representative in the Highlands, but in the past few weeks it had become
plain that His Majesty's Ministers had less than full trust in him.
The Secretary for Scotland was writing to his deputy, Lieutenant-

Colonel Hamilton, asking his advice and giving him instructions and thereby violating common courtesy as much as military procedure. Hamilton made no secret of the fact that he had the Secretary's confidence. He showed the letters to Hill, deferentially, but knowing, perhaps, that the old man's pride would be wounded by the warm tone of them, by their promise that Hamilton could not be more certain of preferment were he the Secretary's kinsman.

The reason for this soft wooing of Hamilton's conceit was now plain. Orders about the Glencoe men had come to Hamilton, and the Deputy-Governor had already arranged the whole affair with Major Duncanson of Argyll's. Like a man avoiding guilt by rejecting responsibility, Hill told Forbes that he had left the matter to the management of these two men, and when he saw the shock in the young officer's face he lifted his voice in protest against a crime he could not prevent and in which he must finally participate "I like not the business. I am grieved at it!"

What that business would be both men knew as they faced each other in the candle-light. It was stated bluntly in Article Four of the King's instructions to the Commander-in-Chief: *If M'Kean of Glencoe, and that tribe, can be well separated from the rest it will be a proper vindication of the public justice to extirpate that sept of thieves.*

"They bound their appetites by their necessities"

GLENCOE HAS no melancholy except that which men bring to it, remembering its history.

Running east to west along the northern border of Argyll, and eight miles in length, it is a deep scar left by the agony of Creation. It is an arm bent at the elbow, with sinews of quartz and muscles of granite. It is both fortress and trap, for the only natural entrances are at either end—across Rannoch Moor in the east and by Loch Levenside in the west, and the high passes to the north and south lead ignorant men to higher hills only. Before the building of a road the Rannoch gate was itself frequently closed by winter snows and summer storms. Since pre-history the moor has been a quaking floor of moss and heather, leaden lochs and the white skeletons of an ancient forest. Only the people of Glencoe, and the broken men of Clan Gregor who hid on its fringe, knew the paths across Rannoch.

The northern wall of the glen is a rippling, saw-toothed escarpment called Aonach Eagach, the Notched Ridge. It is three thousand feet and more in height, and unbroken except in the west where it twists sharply toward Loch Leven, dips, and rises again in the black hill of Sgòr na Ciche, the Pap of Glencoe. At the eastern end of Aonach Eagach is the only path to Glencoe from the north, a narrow, crooked trail that climbs cautiously from the head of Loch Leven, flanks the escarpment for five painful miles and comes down at last to Rannoch through deer-grass and heather. It is rightly called The Devil's Staircase, and when a man reaches the foot of it he still has not entered Glencoe; he stands at the eastern door.

On the south is a loosely clenched fist of mountains, five ridges joined to the great knuckle of Bidean nam Bian, the Pinnacle of Peaks, the highest mountain in Argyll. The first of these are the lonely and austere Buachaille Etive Mòr and Buchaille Etive Beag, the Great and Little Herdsmen of Etive, so named because their lower slopes once gave rich grazing to the black cattle of the MacDonalds. Between them, and opposite The Devil's Staircase, is Lairig Gartain, the green pass to Glen Etive in the south, and this too is no escape from or entrance to Glencoe, for the Great Herdsman stands outside the valley. Westward for five miles down the glen there are gaps between the fingers of Bidean nam Bian but they lead the climber nowhere. They end in high cauldrons of mist, in weeping cliffs, in a bitter snow line that lingers long into summer. Where Bidean nam Bian ends at the bend of Glencoe there is an opening southward, a fork of two valleys each with its stream of furious water. The first, named for the legendary warrior Fionn MacCumhail, is a broad slash narrowing to an almost impassable gorge. The second, called Gleann Leac na Muidhe, twists and climbs, and here men who know the path and their own strength may cross over into Appin, though few, perhaps, would attempt it at night in the numbing confusion of a February blizzard.

A thousand small streams from north and south create the River Coe. At The Meeting of the Waters, below the Little Herdsman of Etive, it leaps westward over a wall of rock, and now the Pass of Glencoe truly begins, wild and independent in its moods. The river runs musically into black pools, or over wide shallows and rippled stones of white and pink and blue. In the middle of the glen, where Aonach Eagach rises imperially from purple shadows, there is an *urlar*, an open valley floor on which the Coe swells into the quiet loch of Achtriachtan. It narrows again in half a mile, and by the mouth of Gleann Leac it turns northward to a meadow called Achnacone, the Field of the Dogs. Within the oxbow thus formed is a conical hill, a massive outcrop from the top of which a man can see almost all of the glen, and for two and a half centuries it has been known as Signal Rock. In the two miles of the glen that are left, between Achnacone and Loch Leven, the land is wide and green, well timbered and hospitable, watched by Sgòr na Ciche and the brown hill of Meall Mòr.

Macaulay translated Glencoe's name as The Glen of Weeping, having no Gaelic and trusting to his imagination when in doubt. None can be certain what it means, except that it has nothing to do with grief. To some it is The Glen of Dogs, and so the Mac-Donald bards called it, remembering Bran and the other hounds of Fingal, who was also Fion MacCumhail. To others it is the glen of *comhan-taisg*, the common store of plunder which his followers, the Feinn, hid in the hills. Seventeen hundred years ago, according to the mythology, these long-haired Fingalian giants made their home in Glencoe, sailed their galleys to Ireland and the Hebrides, hunted with their dogs in Appin, and followed their warrior passions across Rannoch to the south. In Glencoe the land remembers them, and Ordnance Survey maps keep faith with the legends. The harsh, western spur of Aonach Eagach is called Sgòr nam Fionnaidh, the Cliff of the Feinn. At the end of Fionn Mac-Cumhail's glen is Fingal's Gorge. Above Loch Achtriachtan is a cave where Ossian, the poet son of Fionn, composed heroic verse of which no true line has survived. Along Bidean nam Bian and Aonach Eagach, on every mountain in Scotland, three thousand of the Feinn are sleeping. Their breathing is the wind, and one day they will arise at the call of Fingal's horn.

In Glencoe and along Loch Levenside the Feinn fought their great battles with the Vikings. Forty shield-lined galleys, one made from wood of the sacred yew, brought the Scandinavians to the narrows at Ballachulish, where the ship of yew foundered and sank. On a field by Laroch, now covered with man-made mountains of slate, Earragan King of the Norsemen set up his tents and ordered Fionn MacCumhail to yield. The young men of the Feinn were away hunting the deer, but being a smooth-tongued, plausible man, as were all Celtic heroes, Fionn argued with Earragan and so passed the time until his spearmen and bow-men and swordsmen came home with their dogs. He dug four great trenches on the brae between the Pap of Glencoe and Sgòr nam Fionnaidh,* filled them with his warriors, and waited for the Vikings to come. In the thousand years of telling, in the passing of the story from father to son, in the improvisation of the bards, what was probably a savage and bloody mêlée became a formalised ritual of honour and courage. Earragan, it was said, chose seven score of his best men and invited Fionn to send an equal number against them. The offer was accepted. One hundred and forty of the Feinn came down to Achnacone and defeated the Vikings. A similar contest was fought the next day, and the next, and the next for a week, and although many men were killed on both sides the Norsemen's losses were greater than those of the Feinn. On the eighth day Earragan drew up the whole of his army before his camp at Laroch, westward a mile from the mouth of Glencoe, and the Feinn swarmed down against it. The battle was fierce and merciless. Men pursued each other up the side of Meall Mòr, or stood to their waists in the red water of Loch Leven, hewing with sword and axe. Earragan was killed by a giant Fingalian called Goll MacMorna, and at this the Norsemen broke and ran. Many were stabbed, or axed, or shot in the back with arrows as they floundered towards their galleys, and the survivors were only enough to fill two of the forty ships that had brought them to Laroch. And these two ships, it was said, were lost on their way home to their fjords. The dead of the Norse and the Feinn were buried on the field of Laroch, their commanders in stone coffins beneath high cairns, and traces of these heroic sepulchres may be there still among the blue cones of slate, the bungalows and the railway line.

Fionn MacCumhail had won no real victory. Never again, the bards said, were his Feinn a band of warriors as bold and as terrible as they had been. Something endured, however, an example of bloody and savage war, a mythology that inspired. Until sheep drove out both men and their legends, a century and a half ago, a stranger was always welcome at a MacDonald fireside

* Sixteen hundred years later traces of these trenches were said to be visible on the slope of Sgòr nam Fionnaidh, and they may still be there beneath the timber.

in Glencoe, or in any township in the Highlands, if he could respond to the gentle enquiry, "Can you tell tales of Fingal?"

After the Feinn and the Norsemen came Christians, wandering saints from Ireland and the Isles who planted the Cross firmly, even though they did not succeed in blunting the Sword. The Gospels merged happily with tales of Fingal, and that was perhaps the most that any simple monk could expect. Fillan had a cell and a chapel in the east by Glen Etive. Mundus came from Iona with Columba's blessing and lived on a necklace of small islands in the middle of Loch Leven, eight hundred yards from Invercoe. His chapel was still in use on Saint Barnabas' Day in 1485, eight centuries later. MacDonalds of Glencoe, Stewarts of Ballachulish, and Camerons from the north across the water buried their dead on Eilean Munde, generation by generation. The body was brought to a traditional landing-place, and if bad weather prevented it from being taken ashore there it was rowed back to await a better day, for a man, it was said, should follow the footsteps of his father. MacDonalds, Stewarts and Camerons each claimed Eilean Munde, but did not fight over it. They cropped its hay in rotation, and what other disputes they had that were not settled by war were resolved by debate on the Isle of Discussion close by.

Glencoe was clan land before the MacDonalds came to it. It was part of the medieval lordship of Lorn and was held by the MacDougalls, but MacDougall of Lorn chose the wrong side in the quarrels of Robert the Bruce and lost what he held to Angus Og of Islay who, choosing the right side, had brought his MacDonalds to fight for the Bruce at Bannockburn. Clan Donald was a proud and contentious tribe, its chiefs claiming descent from Conn of the Hundred Battles, High King of Ireland, from Colla the Prince of the Isles, and from Fergus the first ruler of the Scoto-Irish Kingdom of Dalriada. When Angus Og's son, remembering this impressive lineage, took the title of Lord of the Isles he was declaring his superiority over all and his ultimate loyalty to none. The MacDonalds peopled the Hebridean Isles from the Butt of Lewis to South Uist, from Skye to Jura and Islay. On the mainland they held Lochaber, Ardnamurchan and Kintyre. In Ireland they filled the Glens of Antrim. Whatever compromise history forced upon them, whatever bitter defeats they suffered, they believed themselves to be the leaders and the lords of Gaeldom, and as such the inevitable rivals of the Kings of Scotland, by whom they could be persuaded or bought but never successfully ruled. Even when the title was taken from the Lord of the Isles, a hundred and fifty years after his ancestor had assumed it, the MacDonalds remained intractable in their claims, resentful of government by the south and at odds with all who represented it. They never forgot what they once had held, and never forgave those who had taken it from them. Few peoples have had longer memories or shorter tempers.

The MacDonalds of Glencoe were the smallest branch of Clan Donald, but the equal of all in touchy pride. The first of them came early in the 14th century. He was Angus Og's bastard, Iain Og nan Fraoch—Young John of the Heather, also called Iain Abrach, John of Lochaber. The land was a gift from his indulgent father, and it was from him that the Glencoe chiefs took their title MacIain, and their bonnet badge of heather. With such a progenitor the bards of Clan Iain Abrach could unroll each successive MacIain's ancestry back to Angus Og and Angus Mor, to Donald and Ranald and Somerled the scourge of the Norsemen, to Colla the Prince and to Conn the High King of Ireland. A whole winter's evening at Invercoe could be pleasantly passed listening to such a splendid genealogy.

Having been given one of the sweetest glens in the Highlands, John of the Heather had then to impose his right to it upon the MacEanruigs, the Hendersons, who were already living there. According to one tradition he did this in the old manner, by beating the fact into their heads, and according to another in a manner equally old, by marrying the daughter of their chief. MacDonalds and MacEanruigs lived amicably together and, in the solacing way time has, there were Hendersons in Glencoe long after MacIain's power was gone.

Though the MacDonalds held Glencoe it was not theirs in free holding. When the Lord of the Isles lost his title in 1493, the power of Clan Donald began its slow decline. The King of Scotland distributed MacDonald lands among those more inclined to respect and defend his authority, and the life-rent of Glencoe went to Duncan Stewart of Appin (though the King charitably acknowledged MacIain as the possessor thereof, provided the feu-duty was paid to the Stewarts). MacDonalds and Stewarts occasionally fell out, settling their differences with lively sword-play, or by feasting and debate on the Isle of Discussion, but for most of the time they lived in amity, it being the sensible opinion of a Highland chief that no matter how strong might be the natural defences of his property, they were all the stronger with good neighbours.

Half a century later, during the minority of Mary Queen of Scots, the Earl of Argyll became the feudal superior of Appin and the Campbell writ began to run in Glencoe. This was the age of Clan Campbell's growth. It had already profited from the forfeiture of the Lordship of the Isles by acquiring Clan Donald land in Kintyre, Colonsay and Ardnamurchan. What it did not get by force it got by guile or by bargaining with the Crown, and all it got it held by Law. With each step forward taken by the Campbells of Argyll, Clan Donald took one step back. Enmeshed by their own dreaming, relying on mythology when their opponents were employing lawyers, the MacDonalds' resentment of southern authority grew more and more bitter, and with it their hatred of the Campbells who were frequently the Highland arm of that authority. What legend has presented as a senseless blood-feud was more properly a long civil war for the leadership of the Gaels. This rivalry lay beneath all the political, religious or dynastic issues over which Campbell and MacDonald clashed.

In the resistance to a central government and to the house of Argyll, the MacDonalds of Glencoe were as steadfast as any branch of Clan Donald, and more enduring than some. For nearly two centuries after the burial of John of the Heather on Iona in 1338, they lived an unrecorded life in the shadows of Aonach

Eagach. When they emerged again into history it was in opposition to the Campbells and in defence of the ancient claims of the MacDonalds. In 1500 the lords of Argyll, making their first cautious move into Appin, tried to evict "John of the Ilis, utherwyis Abrochsoune" from his land in Glencoe. Although the Campbells had the support of the Lords of Council in Edinburgh, the attempt was probably no more than paper-thin, but it was a warning to the Glencoe men. The next year they broke down the doors of Argyll's castle at Innischonnell and liberated Donald Dubh, the claimant to the Lordship of the Isles, thus making it plain that their only loyalty was to the line of Angus Og. This stubborn view, and authority's reaction to it, was to make Glencoe's proud or squalid story for the next two hundred years.

In the seventeenth century the Highland way of life reached its zenith and began its bright fall to extinction. The people of Glencoe, like most in the mountains, felt no sympathy with the outside world. Though they would range far to steal cattle or sell their own, to fight as mercenaries or join in wars that promised but never brought a return of Clan Donald's power, the Valley of Dogs was enough for them. It was the country of the Feinn and the home of the Saints. If wild boar and wolf were now gone, it was still the land of marten and wildcat, of fox and badger. Eagle and kite swam in the currents above Aonach Eagach. There were red deer on Rannoch. Linnet and thrush sang with blackbirds in the oaks at Achnacone, and larks climbed above the stillness of Achtriachtan. On the meadows in spring were primroses and hyacinths. By the river grew cherry and willow, elderberry and briar. The west winds brought swans from the Outer Isles to feed on water weeds in the river pools. Herring were silver-bright in Loch Leven, and above them hung the sails of ships from Ireland and France. "Traveller, you are welcome here," was the people's greeting to those who came in friendship.

In the last year of the century William Sacheverell, onetime Governor of the Isle of Man, made a voyage to Iona and the Western Highlands, and published his impressions for the diversion of England and the Lowlands.

I thought myself [he said] entering upon a new scene of nature, but nature tough and unpolished, and (if I may be allowed the expression) in her undress. I generally observed the men to be large-bodied, stout, subtle, active, patient of cold and hunger. There appeared in all their actions a certain generous air of freedom and contempt for those trifles, luxury and ambition, which we so servilely creep after. They bound their appetites by their necessities, and their happiness consists not in having much but in coveting little. The women seemed to have the same sentiments with the men; though their habits were mean, and they had not our sort of breeding, yet in many of them was a natural beauty and graceful modesty which never fails of attracting.

The greatest number of swordsmen sent to war by Clan Iain Abrach was a hundred and fifty, and from this it may be assumed that the population of the glen was rarely more than five hundred, and frequently less. The people lived in little townships between Achtriachtan and Loch Leven, at Carnoch on the mouth of the river where MacIain had his winter house, at Brecklet westward where Fingal slaughtered the Norsemen, at Inverrigan below Meall Mòr, on the field of the dogs at Achnacone and at Leacantuim by the Cliff of the Feinn. The most easterly of the townships was on the loch beneath Aonach Eagach, although over Lairig Gartain in Glen Etive the tenant of Dalness and his people also acknowledged MacIain as their chief. The thickest settlement was at the entrance to Gleann Leac na Muidhe, creamy water and slopes as smooth as stone giving it its name of the Valley of Slate and Churn. Deep in the higher folds of Gleann Leac was MacIain's summer home, where the hills hold back the wind and bright insects spin in the heavy heat. In winter it is a funnel of snow and the wind makes up for summer idleness.

The land at Carnoch and in Gleann Leac was MacIain's and his sons'. The tacks, the leases to the remaining townships were granted at MacIain's will to others of his kin, all of them descendants of John of the Heather, and they paid their rents in kind or by bringing out their sub-tenants in arms when the chief demanded, when his summons flamed on Signal Rock. It was a

cattle economy and a warrior society, and MacIain counted his
wealth in those hundred and fifty fighting-men.

The appearance of the people matched their background.

The usual habit of both sexes [said Sachervell] is the plaid; the
women's much finer, the colours more lively, and the squares larger
than the men's, and put me in mind of the ancient Picts. The
men wear theirs after another manner, especially when designed for
ornament, it is loose and flowing, like the mantles our painters give
their heroes. Their thighs are bare with brawny muscles. Nature has
drawn all her strokes bold and masterly. What is covered is only
adapted to necessity, a thin brogue on the foot, a short buskin of various
colours on the legs, tied above the calf with a striped pair of garters.
What should be concealed is hid with a large shot-pouch, on each side
of which hangs a pistol and a dagger; as if they found it necessary to
keep those parts well guarded. A round target on their backs, a blue
bonnet on their heads, in one hand a broadsword, and a musket in the
other. Perhaps no nation goes better armed, and I assure you they will
handle them with bravery and dexterity, especially the sword and target.

However impressed Sacheverell and other southerners were by
the carriage of Highland men and the grace of the women, they
were usually disgusted by the houses in which these heroic
figures lived, comparing them to cow-byres, to dung-hills and
the earths of wild animals. Crouching together on the slopes
of the hills, the cottages appeared to be some strange fungoid
growth, smoking with sickly heat. But they were built against the
weather. Their thick drystone walls were less than the height of an
average man, and above them was raised a roof-tree, covered with
divots of earth and thatch held down against the wind by roped
stones. Inside were comfort and protection for men, women,
children and animals. Windows, where they existed, were glass-
less. A central hole in the roof, or at one gable, sucked up the
draught for an open fire. Peat-smoke thickened the air, blackened
the dry-stone walls, and red-rimmed the eyes of men and cattle.
Each house was an expression of the people's unity and inter-
dependence. Each was built by all the township and in one day.
As the stones were passed from hand to hand, the timber raised

and the divots laid, the workers sang and told tales. At sunset the house was blessed, as much by sweat as by appeals to the saints or by charms placed at its door. A Highlander's home was made from his land and was the foundation of his spiritual strength. "To your roof-tree!" he said, wishing a man well. And the houses endured longer than the people, mute, eyeless, and open to the sky.

MacIain had no defensive keep, no black castle on an island like other chiefs. Of his house at Carnoch nothing remains, though the last stones were rolled into the river within memory. It stood below the Pap of Glencoe and, probably two storeys high, its walls washed with lime and its roof covered with blue slate from Ballachulish. Inside, its austerity was luxury compared with the cottages of the people, the light of torches and candles on un-draped stone, a council-room and rooms for privacy, books bought or stolen, a broad table for feasting, charter chests for papers and cupboards for fine cloths and foreign lace, glass to hold claret and a silver quaich for MacIain's whisky.

In Gleann Leac, on a lower brae and by a falling burn, are the ruins of his summer house, the foundations of its walls, its worn hearths, the straggling stones of outer byres. Ruder than Carnoch, it probably resembled the houses in which his sons and tacksmen lived; thirty feet long and twelve wide, three rooms below, and above them a loft formed by beams of cleft oak. A single window with four panes of glass, and others that were boarded holes. A roof of sods thatched with bracken every year, chimneys of twigs daubed with clay. A Highland gentleman asked for little comfort in his house, but much respect for his pride in it.

The land was good. "Glencoe is a garden enclosed," said one visitor. "This country," wrote another, "is very profitable, fertile, plenteous of corn, milk, butter, cheese and an abundance of fish." Both of them, perhaps, passed that way in summer. In winter Glencoe was as like to starve as most Highland glens, and the life of the people swung between gluttonous excess and bitter privation. Some seasons they existed on little more than the herrings which hung in golden rows beneath their roof-trees, cured by the smoke of their fires. Every spring, and again in July and August, shoals of herring shimmered in Loch Leven. Glencoe fishers were quick to recognise the King of the Shoal, the great fish of greater wisdom that always led the school. If it were caught in a net it was returned to the water, and a blessing was asked from it. All fish, said the men of Glencoe, needed a leader, as did all men. The days of fishing were a time of cautious amity and carefully chosen words, for if there were a quarrel in which blood was drawn, the herring would turn away in disgust and return to the open sea.

Each township farmed its land in strips, growing oats, barley and kail. The valley's sheep were small, doglike animals, giving milk and scanty fleece. There were ill-tempered, ranging goats on the braes, and chickens roosting on the roof-timbers at night. There were horses, short, close-coupled garrons, dun-coloured and sure of foot, with heads of gentle beauty. And there were grey deer-hounds of which Clan Iain Abrach was extravagantly proud, tracing their ancestry back to the hunting-dogs of Fingal.

But the real economy of Glencoe was cattle, short, black animals with shaggy hair, melancholy eyes and fearsome horns. There were nearly a thousand of these docile beasts in the valley, from Invercoe to Rannoch, and not all of them had been calved there. A cattle economy determined the people's lives and enriched their oral culture. The herding of cattle or the stealing of cattle kept the young men alert and healthy, training them for war and nurturing endurance and guile. At the beginning of the 17th century the Privy Council of Scotland, seeking some way of breaking the iron independence of the Gael, recognised that cattle were an indication of a Highlander's power and influence. It ordered that all men in the Highlands who owned sixty cows or more should send their children south, there to be taught the reading and writing of English. The clans paid no more attention to this than they did to other orders from the Privy Council.

In winter the cattle were close-herded near the townships, on the meadows by Loch Achtriachtan, at the mouth of Gleann Leac, and at Carnoch. By spring those that had not been slaughtered were little more than skeletons and often unable to rise from the ground. But they recovered quickly and their beef became sweet and tender, the flesh larded rather than separated into lean and fat. In summer, when the cattle were driven eastward for grazing, all the townships of Glencoe were emptied. Summer began with the Feast of Beltane, *bealtuinn*, the first day of May. Fires were lit in the open before every township, and from these every cottager took a brand to rekindle the fire on his own hearth. There the women made the Beltane Bannock which was broken into pieces and offered to the wild beasts of the glen. "This we give to thee, o Fox," cried the people, "spare thou our lambs!" And again, "This we give to thee, o Hooded Crow, and this to thee, o Eagle!" Other bannocks were marked with a cross and rolled down a hill, and if they broke, or came soon to a halt, or rested with the cross uppermost, then misfortune would come to the summer grazing.

The cattle were then driven between the Beltane Fires and eastward out of the glen to the slopes of the Herdsmen, or beyond to the braes of the Black Mount, to the Loch of the Cows on the west of Rannoch Moor. There men and women lived in the shielings, huts which their ancestors had built and which were repaired each summer. On the Feast of Samhain, the beginning of winter, people and cattle returned to Glencoe.

Shieling life was the happiest time of the year for the Mac-Donalds. Women and girls sat before the turf huts making butter and cheese, spinning and singing, while the men watched the cattle or drove them south for sale along the Highland Line. Younger men hunted and fished and went on forays. They ranged far on these robber raids, armed with sword and dirk, round shield and musket, and they sang a braggart song about themselves.

> We'll get cows from the Mearns
> and sheep from Caithness.
> We'll stall the herds
> in the shielings of Rannoch.

The animals they stole they brought back to the Black Mount or, if pursuit were hot, to Glencoe itself. High on the southern wall of the valley, between the nippled peak of Gearr Aonach and

Beinn Fhada is a small saucer called Coire Gabhail, the Hollow of Capture. The climb to it is almost sheer, and the opening to the corrie is narrow enough to be closed by the trunk of a tree. Here the young men hid the cattle they stole, or drove their own when other clans came hungrily to Glencoe. Young boys waited impatiently for such days of manhood to begin, for the time when, at the age of eight or nine or ten, they would be allowed to wear bonnet, shoes and hose. During the summer months they attended simple military schools in the open, learning how to use bow and musket, to carry a bull-hide shield studded with metal, practising cut and parry first with wooden sticks and then with the broad, basket-hilted swords of their fathers.

During the evenings the people danced and sang and told tales. They listened to the pipers and to the many poets of Clan Iain Abrach, enriching their spirits and refreshing their hearts. Though they commonly drank ale, whisky was the fierce inspiration of good fellowship. They made it from corn, and Martin Martin of Skye (who wrote a dispassionate account of his people at the end of the 17th century) warned all simple southerners against it. There was, he said, one kind of whisky that was three times distilled, and this was strong and hot. Another was four times distilled and this was most powerful. "At the first taste it affects all the members of the body; two spoonfuls is a sufficient dose, and if any man exceed this it would presently stop his breath and endanger his life."

Drinking was not self-indulgence, though it could last from sunset until dawn. Drinking gave no pleasure unless it were accompanied by conversation, by songs and story-telling, and a good companion's ability to hold his liquor was matched by his power to entertain. But there was no love for a temperate man.

Among persons of distinction [said Martin] it was reckoned an affront to put upon any company to broach a piece of wine, ale or aquavitae and not see it all drunk out at one meeting. If any man chance to go out from the company, though but for a few minutes, he is obliged on his return, and before he takes his seat, to make an apology for his absence in rhyme; which if he cannot perform,

Glencoe

he is liable to such a share of the reckoning as the company think fit to impose, which custom ... is called *beanchy bard*, which in their language signifies the poet's congratulating the company.

Among a people depending upon memory and oral traditions for their history and self-respect, the Orator and the Bard of the clan were men of almost mystical importance. In their heads they preserved the genealogy of the chief, repeating it in rolling cadences or involved rhyme at births, marriages and deaths. Their way of preparing for such occasions amused Martin, for all his Highland blood. "They shut their doors and windows for a day's time, and lie on their backs, with a stone upon their belly, and plaids about their heads, and their eyes being covered they pump their brains for rhetorical encomium or panegyric; and indeed they furnish such a style from this dark cell as is understood by few."

But Martin, like other Highlanders, believed in the Second Sight, and sensibly made no jokes about it. The more remote and self-contained a community, like Glencoe, the stronger was the belief. It was easy to recognise a man or a woman upon whom the Second Sight had come. The body became rigid, the eyes wide and staring, and this cataleptic state persisted until the vision passed. To see a chair empty when a man was in fact sitting upon it meant his death, as did the sight of a shroud about him, or fish-scales in his hair, a glow-worm above his head. A spark that was no spark, falling upon the arm or breast of a woman, foretold the death of her child. Blood on the face was death by terrible wounding. But there were happier visions, if not so entertainingly frequent, and if a lone man were seen with the vision of a woman at his right hand she would become his bride (if on his left, she would not). When the vision was seen early in the morning then it would happen before noon, if at noon before evening, if in the evening that night, and if after candles were lit it would take place before dawn. "Children, horses and cows see the Second Sight," said Martin, "as well as men and women in advanced years."

Superstition was woven intricately into the practical life of the people of Glencoe. They believed in moon-struck men who suddenly acquired lunatic powers, in the great black cats that gathered to plot mischief on All Hallows Eve, in the water-bull of Loch Achtriachtan and the water-horses in the Coe. Sporting in the hills were malevolent goblins, and by the willow and oak at Achnacone were kindly fairies. If disaster was coming *An Duine Mor*, The Big Man, walked at night by Ballachulish, cows broke from pasture and ran up the brae, bellowing mournfully, and the voices of men who were to die were heard crying in the darkness outside, though their bodies were there by the fire. There were trout in the river that could dry up the milk of a cow, and there were men and women with the Evil Eye who would wither corn and shrivel a woman's womb. There were men who could see through earth and space and say with truth what was happening that moment beyond the mountains. There was the Oracle who could boil mutton from a shoulder-blade and read the future in the markings on the clean bone. Men who wished to know more of that future would wrap the Oracle in cow's hide, covering all but his head, and leave him in the open for the night, during which his friends from the past and from the world beyond the world came to him, and sat about him, answering his questions.

And the people of Glencoe were also Catholics.

"All of gigantic mould, all mighty in strength"

ALASDAIR MACDONALD was the twelfth chief of Glencoe. The number may well be inaccurate, for none can say with certainty how many MacIains there were between him and John of the Heather. More is known about him than any of his ancestors, and what is known divides itself into three major scenes that are close to melodrama: He stands in the sun before a hundred and fifty of his clan, ready for war. He weeps before a Campbell sheriff and pleads for his people. He is pistolled in the brain as he struggles to pull on his breeches, calling for wine to be brought to his murderer.

He was born late in the third decade of the century, with the red hair of his family, and he grew to an extraordinary height, six feet seven inches it was said. In his youth he went to Paris, where the sons of Highland chiefs were frequently sent to lacquer their splendid savagery and pride. A treasured relic of this visit was a drinking cup of French silver which probably disappeared from Carnoch one February night in 1692. The death of his father brought him home in 1650, and perhaps he led his people south with other MacDonalds the next year, when the Scots invaded England under Charles II, and were butchered by Cromwell in the streets of Worcester or in the ditches outside the city. Thirty-eight years later MacIain's hair, beard and great moustache were white, but his back was still straight. He was described as "strong, active, and of the biggest size, much loved by his neighbours, blameless in his conduct . . . a person of great integrity, honour, good nature and courage". This, however, was the opinion of his friends and allies. There were others, in Argyll and Breadalbane and the Lowlands, who thought he was a thief and a murderer. Among all men he was easily recognised by his height and his white mane of hair, by the fine buff coat and brass blunderbuss which he had looted in Strathspey. A young man* who saw Clan Iain Abrach drawn up for war in 1689 wrote of them

Next came Glencoe, terrible in unwonted arms, covered as to his breast with raw hide, and towering far above his whole line by head and shoulders. A hundred men, all of gigantic mould, all mighty in strength accompany him as he goes to the war. He himself, turning his shield in his hand, flourishing terribly his sword, fierce in aspect, rolling his wild eyes, the horns of his twisted beard curled backwards, seems to breathe forth wrath wherever he goes.

He took a wife from among the Keppoch MacDonalds who, living to the north of Loch Leven, were the Glencoe men's constant companions in raiding and war. By her he had two sons, John who would succeed him, and Alasdair Og, Alexander the Younger, a man of eager spirits and a hot temper. There was also at least one daughter, of whom little is known but her existence. John's wife was the daughter of the tacksman of Achtriachtan, but Alasdair Og's came from outside the glen. She was Sarah Campbell, daughter of Campbell of Lochnell, great-grand-daughter of a Breadalbane Campbell, and niece of the Glenlyon Campbell who would one day come to cut her husband's throat.

This marriage of his son to a Campbell may have been a love-match, but was more probably the result of MacIain's canny knowledge that his people, of all Clan Donald, were the most exposed to Campbell ambition. Marriage was frequently the best insurance to be taken out by a Highland chief, and sometimes more enduring than a treaty with his enemies. Twice in his lifetime MacIain wrote his name beside a Campbell's, below promises of friendship and mutual protection, and he did so to

---

* James Philip of Almerieclose, the author, in Latin, of the *Grameid*. The translation is from the Scottish History Society's edition of 1888. In this is also recorded John Forbes's defiant stand at Ruthven, see p. 16.

guard the southern marches of his land. The eastern gate of Glencoe could be reached by way of Loch Etive and Lairig Gartain, and Loch Etiveside belonged to Campbell of Inverawe, to whom MacDonald of Dalness paid tack. In 1669 MacIain and Archibald Campbell of Inverawe swore to their friendship in peace and adversity. Ten years later they met again for the same purpose. MacIain rode on his little garron to Invercharnan in Glen Etive, with his tail of Piper, Bard and Sword-bearer, his gillies and his bodyguard of mettlesome young men. By the blue run of the River Etive he and Inverawe scrawled their spidery signatures to another deed, acknowledging the warm feelings that had existed between their ancestors and promising "to live in all good neighbourhood and friendship, and to assist and succour one another in all our lawful affairs in so far as it lies in us both, in protection and defence of one another's persons". Though there is no record of either coming to succour the other, in 1685 when Inverawe may have needed it, or in 1692 when MacIain certainly did, at least the cattle of one was safe from the forays of the other, and MacIain could feel that there was a lock of sorts on his eastern door, albeit with the key in the hands of a Campbell.

The tacksmen of Achtriachtan and Achnacone, of Laroch, Inverrigan and Dalness, were all MacIain's cousins, descendants of Black John, the prolific second son of the eighth chief of Clan Iain Abrach. By this ancestry each was a *duine-uasal*, a gentleman of the blood of Angus Og, called not by his name but by the title of his tack, as his chief was called Glencoe. Their dress distinguished them. They wore tartan trews and plaid, instead of the simple kilted plaid of the common people, and buckled shoes rather than brogues of deer-hide. A gentlewoman, a *bean-uasal*, wore a linen kerchief on her head, her hair plaited in a single lock, tied with ribbons and hanging down one cheek to her breast. Her sleeves were scarlet, buttoned with gemmed plate, and her arisaid, the white plaid of Highland women, was belted with leather and silver. The arisaid reached from her throat to her feet, said Martin Martin, "and was tied before on the breast with a buckle of silver or brass, according to the quality of the person. I have seen some of the former of a hundred marks value. It was broad as any pewter plate, the whole curiously engraven with various animals."

The tacksmen were bound to MacIain by tradition, by kinship, and by the terms of their leases. They paid him rent or quit-rent, brought him their sons as officers and their people as swordsmen, made his quarrels theirs, shared his grief and love, his joy and hatred. And, as inexorably, they took their rents in kind from their sub-tenants, demanded those swordsmen when needed, and gave in return their protection and loyalty. The word *clann* means children, and MacIain was the father. A bard spoke the thoughts of all the people of Glencoe when he said that MacIain was like a peacock's tail in his splendour, like a serpent's sting in his power to destroy. His rights and privileges were almost absolute, and were described by Lowlanders as the power of "pit and gallows". He was among the last of the Highland chiefs who stubbornly maintained that they, and none other, had the right to judge and condemn their own people, even to the thrust of a dirk or the singing of a hangman's rope. Upon the death of any of his dependants he could take the best beast from the dead man's byre. If a clansman's cow calved twice, his ewe produced two lambs, then one was given to MacIain. If a woman bore twins, one child could be taken into the family of the chief or tacksman and there nurtured as their own. These rights were willingly offered rather than despotically demanded, and the custom of promising the best animal from the byre after death was known as giving *calp*. A broken man, a Highlander outlawed by his clan or by the Crown, would quickly offer his *calp* to another chief, and consider himself fortunate if it were accepted. The safety and happiness of MacIain came before all things, for he was Clan Iain Abrach and while he prospered none would want. His clansmen concluded each meal with a grace in which the Almighty was asked to give particular attention to his welfare. His honour was the pride of his people, his disgrace would be their shame. "May your chief have the ascendancy!" said a Highlander, wishing another good fortune.

Though a chief inherited his rank and privileges by birth, from an early age he had to convince his people that he deserved them, to prove his valour and his talent for leadership. This he could best do in war, or in cunning and successful cattle-raids. Long before his father's death he gathered about him a band of hot-blooded, quarrelsome young men from gentry and commons, each anxious to earn an enduring stanza of encomium in the Bard's next composition. The earning was frequently bloody. "It was usual," said Martin Martin, "to make a desperate incursion upon some neighbour or other that they were in feud with, and they were obliged to bring by open force the cattle they found in the lands they attacked, or die in the attempt." When the heir became chief, these young men formed his *luchd-tagh*, his bodyguard, which among the MacDonalds had its origin in the house-carles who once surrounded Angus Og in war. From his *luchd-tagh* the chief chose his officers, and such body-servants as his armour-bearer and henchman, usually a foster-brother whose privilege it was to enjoy a double portion of meat at table, and to take upon his own shield or body any blow in battle that the chief was too busy to deal with himself.

Though the custom was obsolescent by the end of the 17th century, MacIain the Twelfth had probably been acknowledged as chief in the old way of the hills, set atop a great pyramid of stones while his bodyguard stood about him with bonnets cocked and weapons in their hands. When MacIain was given his father's sword and the white rod of leadership, the Bard began a lengthy recitation of his family's honour, courage and liberality, to impress the people and to remind the new chief that as much and more would be expected of him.

It was believed in the Highlands, and particularly by the MacDonalds themselves, that all men of Glencoe were poets from birth, and it was said that if one of them could not readily put his tongue to verse when invited then his paternity was open to doubt. In a country without any substantial written culture, where oral traditions jealously preserved were the inspiration of life, this glorious claim probably had some truth in it. The spirit of man is instinctively poetic, seeking expression in imagery, and only an age that has abdicated its emotions to professionals has forgotten this. If Glencoe in the 17th century was not a nursery of poets, they were certainly made welcome there, and paid for their board with the rich coin of their verse. Ordinary men touched poetry in the names they gave to the land in which they lived. A rock on the north wall was The Anvil of the Mist, a black tarn where they once fought over the division of cattle was The Little Loch of Blood, and a burn rising musically from the earth was The Water of Singing Birds. For all things in their way of life, the savagery and the sweetness, they sought an immortality in verse, but most of it died when their voices were stilled.

The best remembered of Glencoe's bards lived in the time of MacIain the Twelfth, and Achtriachtan was their birthplace and home. Like other poets of their age, they found the stuff of their inspiration in what they dimly recognised as the beginning of the end of their society, in the self-destructive feuds, the dragging civil wars, the invasion of Lowland authority. There was Angus the son of Red Alasdair MacDonald of Achtriachtan, and there was John the son of Ranald the Younger, but the greatest of them was Ranald of the Shield, the author of a sad and elegaic lament for the execution of Charles I. He is said to have been still alive in February, 1692, though by then he must have been a very old man. He was not only a fine poet, with an unashamed admiration for his own talent, but also a skilled and cunning fighting-man. He fought at Inverlochy in 1645 when the "grey blades of Clan Donald" cut down the Campbells, and six years later he was wounded in the bloody hedgerow fight outside Worcester. He earned his name during those wars. A captured English dragoon, looking at the Highlanders who surrounded him, said that if his sword were returned to him he would be happy to fight any one of them for his life. Ranald accepted the challenge and, although the Englishman was the better swordsman, the Highlander had the advantage of a bull-hide shield and triumphed. Ranald had two sons, both of whom lived almost as long as he and were as ready with verse and sword.

Most of the common people of Glencoe who were MacIain's children are now lost in an empty anonymity. There were Rankins and MacColls toward Ballachulish, MacPhails by Laroch, and Hendersons at Carnoch and Achnacone. Where they are remembered as individuals—like Big Henderson of the Chanters, MacIain's hereditary piper—all that is known of them can be told in as brief a sentence. But the remembrance of one man lasted until sheep drove men from the glen of the dogs. He was *Gilleasbuig Mor*, Big Archibald MacPhail, and generation by generation the people of Argyll continued to talk of him as if he had passed by their doors that morning. A hundred years ago a woodsman of Argyll, John Dewar, spent the last years of his life putting such Highland memories to paper,* and thus saved Big Archibald MacPhail from oblivion.

There was more brawn than brain to Big Archibald, and it was probably the humour of the man's adventures that kept his memory alive. "He was a very strong man," says the story recorded in the Dewar Manuscripts, "he was very expert at the sword, and he had no fear of any person whatever. He went frequently with others on a cattle-lifting raid, and in consequence of being so strong, fearless and expert at the sword, he was highly esteemed by the people of Glencoe, and they did not often go on a raid without Big Archibald being with them. Notwithstanding, Archibald MacPhail was but a foolish, inconsiderate man in many respects."

This was a gentle understatement. He once met a Lowlander by Achnacone and greeted him in the Highland way: *"Beannachd Dhia dhuit, a dhuine!"* God's blessing on you, sir. The Lowlander, having no Gaelic, but seeing that some response was expected, replied that it was indeed a fine day. "Foolish man," said Big Archibald, "do you despise the word of God?" Before the Lowlander had time to decide what this might mean, he was struck down by MacPhail's sword. Big Archibald took the dead man's shoes, musket, and a guinea from his coat pocket, and walked on to Ballachulish. There he told the Stewart laird what had hap-

---

* The Dewar MSS are in the archives of Inveraray Castle. The first volume, in English and edited by the Rev. John MacKechnie, has now been published by William MacLellan, Glasgow.

pened, adding that to his mind it had been a profitable morning. Stewart sent men to bury the Lowlander and they, being less simple than MacPhail and knowing more about southern tailoring, searched the breeches pockets where they found sixty more guineas. No one thought of hanging Big Archibald for this wayside murder, and he was not troubled much by it himself, except at night, when he expected to meet the Lowlander's vengeful spirit.

At the approach of his own death, some years before the Argyll men came to Glencoe, Big Archibald spoke the heroic feelings of all his people at such a sobering moment. He was lodging with his son in Glen Orchy to the south of Rannoch Moor, and he was roused to a black fury by the suggestion that he would be buried there. "When it is death to me," he told his son, "if it happens here, strike a blow of the dirk in my back, put me across the piebald mare and she will carry me to Glencoe, and the people of Glencoe shall bury me on Eilean Munde. By all that you have ever seen, dare not lay me but beside the MacDonalds. Put a sword in my fist and my face to the Camerons. I have never turned my back on them!"

In his youth, MacPhail's close friend and partner in cattle-lifting was Iain MacAllein, who was also remembered long enough for recording by John Dewar's pen. He was a nephew of the tacksman of Achtriachtan, and a young man delicately aware of his honour, his descent from John of the Heather, and of the niceties that should be observed between gentlemen even when they were bent on letting each other's blood. One summer's day he and Big Archibald, with three companions, went raiding in Strathspey, where they relieved the Laird of Grant of some of his cattle. On their way home they stopped for the night by a lake, put the cows on a promontory, and went into a shieling to eat, to boast, and to sleep. They were roasting the meat of a calf when sixty men of Clan Grant appeared on the brae above, led by the Laird's son. Big Archibald decided to pray. He informed the Almighty that he had never troubled Heaven with his prayers before, and if he and his friends could have some prompt assistance from that quarter now he would never trouble it again.

Meanwhile Iain MacAllein had gone forward to meet the Grants, holding out his broadsword by the point in a gesture of surrender. As the Laird's son reached for it, MacAllein spun the weapon in the air, caught it by the hilt, and cut down the Grant with one blow. Now Big Archibald and the others came up, seeing in this, perhaps, the proper intervention of God, and although some of the Grants made a stand, most of them ran. Since those who remained were not very expert swordsmen (according to the Glencoe story), they were quickly defeated, and the MacDonalds joyfully drove the cattle toward Rannoch. They had not gone far, however, before Iain MacAllein was worried by a chivalrous concern for the Laird of Grant's son. He turned back to the lochside and brought the boy some water in his brogue, upon which the Grant shot him with a pistol, breaking his thigh-bone. MacDonald and Grant lay in their blood, watching each other like animals, until MacAllein pushed himself up on one knee, grasped his sword, and suggested that they continue the fight. Grant agreed, but when he saw that he could stand on both feet and MacAllein could only kneel, he proposed friendship instead. And so in friendship they rested until morning, when the Grant clansmen returned and carried them both to the Laird's house in Strathspey. There MacAllein lived pleasantly for a year until he was well enough to return to Glencoe. This, all Highlanders would have agreed, was a very civil way of behaving.

Beyond the Highland Line, most Lowlanders cared little when the clans fought among themselves and stole each other's cattle, for it was no more than was expected of them, and men sensible of their own virtues see themselves best against the vices of others. But the thought that these armed and ferocious tribesmen could be persuaded to move south in times of stress (if all were got to agree), was never a happy one for the people of the Lowlands. Nor did the Highlanders always need some high political motive for carrying their broadswords down to the Sidlaw Hills, the Ochils or beyond. Small bands of them were always foraying there, robbing byres or demanding blackmail, chattering about their honour and their valour, and most of them, it was said, without a shirt to their backs. Lowlanders called them the herd-widdifous, the Gallows Herd, and were happy to pay them to be on their way without molestation. An old Aberdeen ballad sang the general feeling:

> Gin ye be gentlemen, light and come in,
> There's meat and drink in my hall for every man.
> Gin ye be herd-widdifous, ye may gang by,
> Gang down to the Lowlands and steal horse and kye.

Action taken against the Gallows Herd was usually ineffective, though the threat of it was fearsome enough on paper. When complaints were made to it, the Privy Council could summon the accused to Edinburgh, there to answer the charges and there to suffer punishment if they were proven. If this order were ignored, and it frequently was, the raiders could be put to the horn, declared broken men and outlaws with every man's hand against them. In more serious and persistent cases, where a whole clan was accused, and where too much blood had been let and too many cattle stolen, the Council could issue Letters of Fire and Sword against them. In the absence of a standing army, the Crown granted the execution of these Letters to a powerful laird whose land lay closest to the offenders, or whose eye for gain was keenest. With his own clansmen at his back (or with others attracted by the chance of pillage), he fell upon the Gallows Herd, burning, killing and driving cattle, harrying men, women and children into the hills, hoping that the land he was now invading with the sword he might later secure for himself with parchment. As a remedy, the issue of Letters of Fire and Sword was understandably often worse than the malady. It led to bitter feuds, to bloody reprisals, and to the involvement of other clans drawn in by common fear or ties of blood. Great men became greater, small men were diminished. Private greed was cloaked in the Crown's authority, young men dreamed of combat and immortality in death, and blood ran into the ink of charter, deed and treaty.

In the last terrible extent of its power the Crown could place a

whole clan under proscription, and this was done to the Mac-
Gregors, one of the earliest attempts at genocide in modern
history. In 1603 it was first enacted that no man, under pain of
death, might call himself MacGregor, nor his children and his
children's children unborn. If he did so use that name he could be
killed like a beast of the wayside, with all his lands and possessions
forfeit to his killer. An outlaw could earn a pardon by coming
before the justices with the severed head of an obstinate Mac-
Gregor, and MacGregors already under proscription were invited
to atone for their past offences by murdering each other. Death
was the sentence if more than four of Clan Gregor met together,
if they possessed any other weapon than a blunt knife to cut their
meat, but only, said the Law in its clemency, if they obstinately
persisted in calling themselves MacGregor. Within a year thirty-
six men of Clan Gregor were brought to trial and death, and six
hostages in the hands of the Government were hanged without
trial. Many others died in brutish killings, or of starvation, cold
and despair. Later Acts dealt with the branding and transportation
of MacGregor women, and the Lords of the Privy Council discussed and finally abandoned (after protest) a proposal to send all
their children to Ireland. Clan Gregor was driven from Glen Strae
and Glen Lyon to a life of banditry and bitter resistance on Rannoch Moor, and the lands they once held passed to the Campbells
of Glen Orchy who had been most active in executing Letters of
Fire and Sword upon them. Nearly two centuries later the penal
Acts against Clan Gregor were still on the Statute Book, in the
adult lifetime of Tom Paine, Edmund Burke, and William
Wilberforce.

The Crown, in its efforts to reduce the ferocity of the Highlanders and the anarchic disorder of their way of life, usually
succeeded in making matters worse. James VI,* who was nause-
ated by the sight of blood, laudably wished to get rid of family
feuds, but like many men who are repelled by violence he
attempted to stop it by measures of greater brutality. He approved
an Act which, by authorising reprisals against any members of an

* James I of England after the union of the kingdoms in 1603.

offender's clan, helped to perpetuate the blood-feud and indiscriminate murder. Later, the General Band of 1587 was designed to make great men responsible for their dependants, but it largely resulted in the persecution of the weak by the strong. The Band was based on the feudal principle that a landlord was answerable to the Crown for the behaviour of his tenants, was obliged to hand over the accused to the justices, and was in duty bound to make reparation to the injured. The Band also demanded that troublesome chiefs should supply hostages against their good behaviour, or else be "esteemed public enemies to God, the King and his true and faithful subjects, and to be persecuted with fire and sword wherever they may be apprehended, without crime, pain or danger to be incurred by the doers thereof". Since the hostages could be executed if the chief failed to deliver an offender demanded by the justices, few Highlanders obeyed this part of the Band, and even fewer were naïve enough to travel down to the Lowlands without first getting the Privy Council's promise that they would not be thrown into the Tolbooth of Edinburgh as a hostage. All these measures deepened the clans' bitter resentment of government by an alien race to the south, and even when they were enacted their success depended on those who were chosen to bell the cat. The Crown had to rely on the great Highland lairds to enforce them, and such men differed from the offenders only in the degree of their power and nobility. The blood feud, the foray, and the bloody struggle for land continued.

Safe within the walls of Aonach Eagach and Bidean nam Bian, Clan Iain Abrach usually thumbed its nose at King and Council. By the end of the 16th century it was agreed that the men of Glencoe were the most incorrigible and troublesome of the Gallows Herd, and had their land been as desirable and as accessible as Clan Gregor's they too might have come under the Crown's proscription. They had no enduring friends but men of their own name. They raided where their quixotic fancy took them, and were so successful that more powerful clans, like the Camerons of Lochiel and the Grants of Freuchie, signed treaties of mutual assistance against them. Clan Campbell, Stewart, Ogilvie,

Menzies and Colquhoun all lost blood and cattle to the Mac-
Donalds, and all urged the Lords in Council to burn out this nest
of thieves, from Rannoch to Loch Leven. In 1591 MacIain the
Eighth was accused, with his brother and son, of lifting the cows
of one John Drummond of Blair. They were ordered to appear
before the Justices in the Tolbooth of Edinburgh, under pain of
rebellion, an order which they lightly ignored, if indeed anybody
had the courage to convey it to them. They were called again the
next year, and again refusing to answer they were declared rebels
and fugitives. The King appointed two Commissioners (Fraser
and Mackintosh lairds) to root out MacIain and prosecute him,
but Glencoe was a far cry from Edinburgh and it must have been
a relief to the Commissioners when the Privy Council persuaded
the King to relax MacIain and his kin from the horn.

If the Lords in Council hoped that this conciliatory gesture
would make the Glencoe men more tractable, they were of course
mistaken. MacIain was soon raiding again, stealing seven great
cows and a bull worth £140 Scots from a laird called Craig. In
Perthshire he was accused of "hership and stouthreif", of murder
and fire-raising. In Argyll another charge was "reif, houghing of
cattle and purpose of murder" when, as a reprisal for some real
or fancied slight (or perhaps for the simple joy of it), the Glencoe
men swarmed down on the glens of MacAulay of Ardincaple.
They chased MacAulay into the hills one night, spoiled his house,
and moved on with several of his clansmen as prisoners. In the
lands of the Duke of Lennox they pillaged and burned more
houses belonging to his Grace's tenants, stole thirty-two horses and
twenty-four cows and returned well content to the shielings of
Rannoch. Less content was the Earl of Argyll who, under the
General Band and as feudal superior of Glencoe, was compelled
to pay the Duke of Lennox £1,000 in compensation. The thought
of this undoubtedly seasoned the MacDonalds' enjoyment of the
foray.

During the first forty years of the 17th century, until the civil
wars in England and Scotland offered greater fuel for Clan
Donald's warring nature and smouldering resentment of the

Campbells, the Glencoe men frequently appeared (in name at least) before the Privy Council on charges of robbery, burning and killing. This was the period of their savage squabbling with the Stewarts of Appin. In 1609, Alasdair MacIain Og, brother to the chief, was accused of being "a common and notorious thief and sorner and oppressor, for many years a fugitive and outlaw", guilty of murdering two men of Appin. What was murder in Edinburgh, was probably the settlement of an affair of honour in the Highlands, and Alasdair MacIain Og declined the Council's invitation to come to Edinburgh for a sober discussion of his behaviour. A Campbell laird, however, caught him one day and sent him there just the same. He was released from the Tolbooth on a surety placed by two of his kinsmen, whereupon, having their own ideas of the purpose of bail, all three at once left for the Highlands and never returned.

In a short feud with the people of Appian the Glencoe men are said to have dirked and shot more Stewarts than any other clan, and included in the number was a surprised burgess of Inverness. When a large raiding party of MacDonalds relieved Stewart of Strathgarry of all the cattle he pastured on eastern Rannoch, killing some of his clansmen as well, a meeting of Stewart chiefs was called—Appin, Athole and Balquhidder, and they entered into a written bond to avenge the death of their clansmen and the rape of their property. They asked Edinburgh for Letters of Fire and Sword against Glencoe, reinforcing the request in the customary way by sending one of the widows of the slaughtered men, with her husband's bloody shirt.

The Letters came with understandable promptness, and the Stewarts gathered on Loch Levenside by the mouth of Glencoe. It was high summer, and the MacDonalds were away in the shielings of Rannoch and the Black Mount. The Stewarts marched unmolested up the length of Glencoe, surrounded the shielings, and fell upon Clan Iain with sword, dirk, axe and matchlock. Some versions of the story say that the battle took place by Carnoch, and that the Stewarts never entered Glencoe, but wherever it occurred there is general agreement on the result: the

MacDonalds lost. The Stewarts lopped off the heads of MacIain and his brother (neither of whom had survived the fight), put them in a barrel and sent them south to the Privy Council on the back of a simple-minded messenger. He stopped on the way to give Stewart of Strathgarry's lady a sudden and stunning sight of his burden, and he entertained himself now and then by knocking the heads together in the barrel and crying out "Why are you making such a noise in there? Aren't you friends?"

In the manner of things this should have made any reconciliation between Glencoe and Appin impossible, but by the middle of the century they were amiable friends and firm allies. Their common fear of Clan Campbell was stronger than their own quarrels.

In 1635 the Privy Council got its hands on the animate head, trunk and limbs of a MacIain—Red Alasdair, the 11th Chief. He was accused of raiding far across country into Aberdeenshire, burning, robbing and killing in the lands of the Crichtons. The foray was the work of broken men who had brought MacIain their *calp*, though he was indeed responsible under the General Band, and perhaps it was this that he went south to explain, having more faith in the moderate temper of the Council than his predecessors. He was lodged comfortably enough in Edinburgh, and had the Council's permission to travel a Sabbath day's journey beyond the capital, on promise to return. But in July, having exhausted their Lordships' patience, no doubt, he was thrown into the Tolbooth and there he stayed until he promised to obey the relevant Acts against his like.

To the south-east of Glencoe, twenty miles across the bogs and black pools of Rannoch, was the district of Breadalbane where the Campbell lairds of Glenorchy, Glenlyon and Lawers enjoyed the valleys and meadows that had once been Clan Gregor's. The Glencoe men were always hungry for the rich meat of Breadalbane, but never felt strong enough to lift it on their own. They raided in company with the MacDonalds of Keppoch, and the records of the Privy Council refer to them both as "the Lochaber men", and this pejoratively. The first great raid which Glencoe and Keppoch made upon Breadalbane was a terrible failure, and one which they never forgot. Mad Colin Campbell, the Laird of Glenlyon, captured thirty-six of them, more than half the party, and hanged them in rows outside his castle of Meggernie. He was as independent a spirit as any MacIain, and as reluctant to acknowledge any authority but his own. When he was asked by the Privy Council if he would put his hand to a deed swearing that he had executed the MacDonalds in defiance of proper justice, he said that he would not only put his hand on the paper but his foot as well.

The next time the Lochaber men came to Glenlyon, in the summer of 1583, it was with more cunning and success. They came, said Mad Colin in his complaint to the Council,

. . . with bow, quiver and other weapons invasive, upon the 24th of June last by the break of day, and masterfully reft, spulzied and took away from the said complainer and his servants, four score head of kye, eleven horses and mares, together with the whole insight and plenishings of their houses; and also not satisfied with the said oppression committed by them as said is, struck and dang the women of the said lands and cutted the hair of their heads.

When the great wars between King and Parliament spread to the Highlands in 1644, Clan Donald fought for the King, not so much out of a selfless loyalty to the Stuarts (whose attitude to the Gaelic way of life was rarely sympathetic and frequently brutal), as from the belief that the struggle for the leadership of the Gael between them and the Campbells might here be finally settled in their favour. The Glencoe men, with others of their name, joined the clan army which the Marquis of Montrose raised for Charles I against the English Parliament's allies in Scotland. The campaigns which Montrose conducted in the mountains and the Lowlands appealed to the clans. He was one of the most skilful and intelligent of the world's great captains, and he used the Highlanders in the only way they could be effectively employed, in the sudden shock of the charge.

It was a war of brilliant forced marches, of clan banners above

the tartan of belted plaids, of pipes ranting in the rain, and sunlight like watered silver on the blades of terrible swords. When
the clans were put to the fight in the only way they knew, they
were always victorious. It would be a century before Lowland
and English troops found the courage and learnt the simple skill
to stand against the rush of screaming, half-naked Highlanders.
The ancient way of clan fighting, said Martin Martin of Skye, was
by set battles,

. . . and for arms some had broad, two-handed swords and headpieces,
and others bows and arrows. When all their arrows were spent they
attacked one another sword in hand. Since the invention of guns they
are very early accustomed to use them, and carry their pieces with them
wherever they go. They likewise learn to handle the broadsword and
target. The chief of each tribe advances with his followers within shot
of the enemy, and having first laid aside their upper garments, and
after one general discharge, they attack them sword in hand, having
their target on their left hand, which soon brings the matter to an issue
and verifies the observations made of them by our historians: *ut mors
cito, aut victoria laeta.*

The Glencoe men joined Montrose after his raid on Inveraray
in December, 1644, when clansmen who had old and unhealed
reasons for hating Clan Campbell exulted in the streets of its
hitherto inaccessible capital. Returning northward, Montrose's
army came by Glencoe. A MacIain guided it over The Devil's
Staircase and the high passes to Kilcumein on Loch Ness. Hearing
that the Earl of Argyll was in pursuit with three thousand Campbells, Montrose turned southwards in a brilliant flanking march
over the mountains and met them at Inverlochy. He was out-
numbered two to one, but his MacDonalds—from Antrim,
Keppoch, Glencoe and Glengarry—fell upon the Campbells in
fury, driving them into Loch Linnhe or over the drove road to
Ballachulish. The fields at Inverlochy, said Iain Lom the splendid-
tongued bard of Keppoch, were thereafter not manured by the
dung of sheep or goats but by the congealed blood of Clan
Diarmaid. He asked for damnation if he felt any pity for the
Campbells, their children, or their lamenting women. In his song

there was no mention of Montrose. Victory was won by the blue, well-balanced swords of Clan Donald.

It was a time for scourging the Campbells. In December 1645, the MacDonalds of Keppoch and Glencoe raided Breadalbane again, this time with the MacNabs and MacGregors. They killed every man they found in arms, burned houses and corn-stacks, lifted the cattle, and carried away the baptismal font from the Kirk of Kenmore. It was said that one house only was left standing on the south shore of Loch Tay, and this because it was hidden by trees. When the Kirk Session of Kenmore met to consider a visitation like unto the plagues of Egypt it reported that there were "many poor people who were burned and spoiled and have nothing to live on". The Laird of Glenorchy had to borrow great sums, £5,000 from Parliament, to buy food and seed-corn for his people that spring.

Montrose, realising that the King's cause could only be harmed if the clans used it for the settlement of their private grievances, gave the lairds of Breadalbane his word that their lands would in future be free from pillage. But a promise made by their captain was not one which the Lochaber men felt bound to keep when it ran counter to their pride and their ever-eager hunger. Early in June, 1646, some young men of Glencoe and Keppoch were on their way home from a foray into Stirlingshire, under the leadership of Angus Og, son of the Chief of Keppoch. They heard that Campbell of Glenorchy was celebrating the marriage of his daughter to a laird of Clan Menzies, and that all the gentry of Breadalbane were gathered at Finlarig Castle on Loch Tay, with "whisky in their heads". So they came down like locusts and were driving their stolen cattle over the brae of Sron a'Chlachain, a big hill to the west of Finlarig, before the Campbells got news of them. Whisky in their heads or not, the Breadalbane gentry ran out of Finlarig with swords in their hands.

Below the knob of Sron a' Chlachain, the hill of stones, the MacDonalds turned, swinging their swords and crying their slogans as they ran down the slope. Thirty-six Campbells were killed and twenty-one were wounded, in less than ten minutes, and among the dead were fifteen cadets of the house of Glenorchy. Big Archibald MacPhail was there, taking time before he charged to make a brief call upon Heaven. If God, he said, could not join the MacDonalds at this time would He please stay out of the fight altogether and "let it be between ourselves and the carles". He then ran on, stringing his bow and firing his arrows into the Campbells as they struggled up the heather. When they broke he followed them down to the lochside, and boasted afterwards that he shot an arrow into the groin of the Menzies bridegroom, thus ending any hope the gentleman might have had of siring an heir that evening.

But the MacDonald losses were also heavy. The fight was made in the shallow Corrie of the Bannocks, and the stream that ran crimson from it was known thereafter as The Bloody Burn. Carrying their wounded on stretchers made from withes, the Lochaber men hurried up Glen Lyon toward Rannoch. Another party of Campbells set out after them, and there followed a straggling, running fight in which Menzies of Culdares (not, it would seem, too much hindered by Big Archibald's arrow) cut down young Angus of Keppoch. The boy was carried to "the little house of Coire Charmaig" and there he died, while Iain Lom wept beside him, and compared himself in his grief to a tree stripped of its bark without sap and without fruit.

In 1655 Clan Iain again raided Breadalbane in strength with their friends from Keppoch. They burned byres and lifted cattle from the pastures about the castle of Cashlie, and then they turned away quickly for Rannoch. Swept up with them in the retreat was a girl called MacNee who had been tending the milch cows. When the raiders reached Glen Meran, the narrow pass to the safety of the Moor, she broke the legs of some of the calves and delayed the MacDonalds long enough for the pursuing Campbells to come up with them. There was a bloody little struggle on the shore of Loch Lyon in which the girl was killed, but she had saved some of her people's cattle, and the Lochaber men went back over Rannoch with less booty than they had taken from Cashlie. Birth and death, victory and defeat, lesser men as well as the great, all found their way into Highland song, and although the girl called MacNee had died in the stamping, slashing fight by Glen Meran she lived on for two centuries in an air which Breadalbane women sang to their children. The words were meant to be hers—*Crodh Chailean mo cridhe, crodh Iain mo ghaoil* . . .

> Colin's cows of my heart, John's cows are so dear,
> They'll give milk on the heather with nothing to fear.
> Colin's cows of my heart, Colin's cows of my love,
> Like the wing of a moor-hen, brown-speckled above.

The chief of Glencoe was now the red-haired giant Alasdair, twelfth of the name MacIain. And the laird of the valley from which his people had taken Colin's cows was Robert Campbell of Glenlyon.

"The cruelty of thieves, sorners, and broken men"

THEY WERE by nature reivers and cattle-lifters. If the prize were attractive enough, they could be mercenaries too. The only people they would never rob or fight belonged to Clan Donald. On at least two occasions they helped Clan Campbell in its little wars of aggrandisement, and if their services at these times were demanded as a feudal right by the houses of Argyll and Glenorchy, the Glencoe men became the condottiere of their traditional enemies from a simple desire for pillage and gain. It is unlikely that they argued the ethical point among themselves, for what they were willing to do on behalf of the Campbells today they were as ready to do against them tomorrow.

In 1563 they were used by the Laird of Glenorchy to clear eastern Rannoch of some rebellious remnants of Clan Gregor. They delivered the leader of the MacGregors to Glenorchy, saw his head lopped from his body, and heard his wife cry out that only by drinking a cup of her husband's blood could she endure her terrible grief. In 1591 they were employed by the seventh Earl of Argyll in his family's calculated feud with the Ogilvies of Glenisla. The cause of the feud was as melodramatic as the Campbell's motives in pursuing it were unsentimentally practical. A Campbell gentleman attending an Ogilvy wedding got drunk enough to insult the bride and dirk her protesting father. He was disarmed and tolerantly kicked beyond the bounds of Ogilvy land. The Campbells, coveting Glenisla, decided to avenge what they declared to be an offence against their house, but they had no intention of using their own clansmen. They called out the men of Glencoe and Keppoch, with any others willing to join, and unleashed five hundred raiders upon the Ogilvies. So violent was this foray, Lord Ogilvy complained to the Privy Council, that he was not "able to resist, but with great difficulty and sore advertisement he, his wife, and his bairns escaped".

Cutting MacGregor throats for Campbell paymasters did not prevent the Glencoe men from becoming Clan Gregor's allies in the next generation, and here too, if indirectly, they were serving the Campbells. The circumstances beg the mind's patience for understanding. The seventh Earl of Argyll, known to all as Archibald the Grim, was quarrelling now with the Colquhouns of Luss, and he invited the MacGregors to "commit both hership and slaughter" upon them. Clan Gregor gladly welcomed any great man's protection, for since the General Band no landowner had wanted its troublesome presence. Alasdair MacGregor of Glenstrae, with his kinsmen and followers, went down to the rich Colquhoun lands between Loch Lomond and Loch Long and drove off 420 cows, 400 sheep and goats, and 100 horses. They also killed some men, of course. Since the seventh Earl of Argyll was Justice-General of Scotland, and therefore hard to picture in the dual role of judge and defendant, Colquhoun of Luss wisely decided to ignore the Campbells' part in the raid. He sent the customary bloody shirt to Edinburgh and asked for Letters of Fire and Sword against Clan Gregor.

But Alasdair of Glenstrae was a rare man, who took the advantage before his opponent had the wit to seize it, and he prepared to hit the Laird of Luss before he was himself harried. He gathered four hundred men "arrayed in arms, with halberts, pole-axes, two-handed swords, bows and arrows and other weapons". Among them were some Camerons, Campbells, and an eager detachment of MacDonalds from Glencoe. They left the braes of Balquhidder in the bitter February weather of 1603, crossed Loch Lomond from Glen Arklet to the Pass of Arrochar, and swung down the eastern shore of Loch Long to come up on the rear of the Colquhouns. The Laird of Luss had an army of 500 foot and 300 horse, formed from his own people, from Buchanan levies, and from the alarmed townsmen of Dumbarton. In open country his cavalry could have ridden down the Highlanders with ease, but he placed them and his foot across the marshy floor of Glen Fruin. His Lowland infantry broke at once before the charge of the clans, his horses were hamstrung and slaughtered in the bogs. MacGregors, Campbells, Camerons and MacDonalds of Glencoe ran over the dead to fire every house and stack in the lands of Luss, and to take their share of two thousand head of cattle, sheep, goats and horses.

Forty prisoners were left behind in the charge of a Glencoe man called Allan Og MacIntuach, and he saw no profit in this work when others were enjoying themselves. So he cut the forty throats of the Colquhouns and rejoined his kinsmen. When Alasdair of Glenstrae asked him where the prisoners were, he was momentarily uncertain about the propriety of their disposal. He held out his bloody dirk. "Ask that," he said, "and God help me!" The Privy Council was more outraged by Allan Og than by all the "odious, barbarous and detestable butchery and slaughter committed by Clan Gregor upon His Majesty's good subjects at Glen Fruin". It ordered his arrest but it was six years before anyone was able to put a rope about his neck. "In the whole course of his by-past life," said the Privy Council, dispatching him to further and higher judgement, "he has so exercised himself in theft, murder, reif and oppression, and he is most unworthy to be suffered any longer to breathe the air of this country."

For his work in suppressing disorder in the Highlands (which was to include the near-extermination of his former bully-boys, the MacGregors), the Crown gave the seventh Earl of Argyll all the lands in Kintyre. Since these were taken from Clan Donald, the men of Glencoe were reminded of old rivalries and older loyalties, and thereafter drew no blood and robbed no byres for any Campbell.

There was profit enough to be got from helping new friends, in the raid which Duncan Stewart, chief of Appin, made upon Glenorchy. Stewart was the third husband of Jean Campbell,*

* For the relationship between this remarkable woman and the Campbells of Glenorchy and Glenlyon, the Stewarts of Appin and the MacDonalds of Glencoe, see pages 210–11 and the Genealogy.

daughter of a laird of Glenorchy, and he discovered one day that
the dowry that should have gone to her second husband had never
been paid. Believing that this was arguably his by rotation, he set
off to collect it in cattle. With him went some Glencoe men under
MacDonald of Dalness, and according to the story told in the
Dewar Manuscripts the boldest and bravest of these was Big
Archibald MacPhail. The Laird of Glenorchy put his people and
his cattle inside the castle of Kilchurn at the end of a marshy
peninsula on Loch Awe. He mounted cannon on the walls and
advised the Stewarts and the MacDonalds to go home. Duncan
Stewart was ready to take this advice, but his men took hold of
some calves that had been locked out of the castle, and held them
over a fire. The cries of the animals were answered by the lowing
of cows inside the walls. MacDonald of Dalness looked at the
Glencoe men and said that were there a man among them to open
the castle door now, they would all see some sport. Away went
Big Archibald MacPhail, through an enfilade fire from cannon
and matchlock. He broke down the gate, and when the maddened
cows rushed out to their calves they were driven off to Appin.
MacPhail's brother asked him why he had put himself in such
danger, Dalness had not meant him more than any other man.
"When he said the word," replied Big Archibald, "and was it not
the same as if he had asked me to go? It were all the same to me to
be dead as to refuse the gentleman."

All clans that were neighbours to Glencoe knew that with the
right opportunity to plunder, and upon the proper appeal that
should be made by one Highland gentleman to another, MacIain
would be quick to aid them in their quarrels. Glencoe men fought
beside Camerons and Keppoch MacDonalds in their feuds with
the Mackintoshes, and they helped the Macleans in their long
defensive struggle against the Earls of Argyll. By the time Red
Alasdair MacDonald, Twelfth MacIain of Glencoe, had reached
middle age, all men outside the narrow perimeter of his friendship
considered him a pestilence and a curse, despite the handsome curl
of his French moustache and the fine French silver of his drinking-
cup. Nowhere was this opinion stronger than in Inveraray, the

only town in the Western Highlands, the stronghold of the Camp-bells and the seat of the Crown's authority. Here, power was manifest in a great black castle, and wealth was apparent in the merchant shipping on Loch Fyne. Here was a Tolbooth gaol, and a Court House in which the Earl of Argyll sat as Justiciar for the kingdom. Here was Gallows Hill where robbers, reivers and murderers were hanged after one arm had been torn from its socket and impaled on a pike. Here adulterers were whipped and witches were scourged by the Mercat Cross, drunkards were fined £10 Scots if they were gentlemen, and twenty shillings if they were not. Here were lodging-houses and inns, a school of sorts and places of worship. Inveraray was a sea-gate to France, Spain and the Low Countries, but no MacDonald of Glencoe would go there alone of his own free will.

When members of his clan were summoned to appear before the Court at Inveraray, MacIain ignored the call if he thought it safe to do so. When he obeyed it, on one occasion at least, he tried to outwit the Campbell justices. The Justiciary Records of Argyll show that in October, 1673, Donald MacRankin from Achtriach-tan stood before Justice Ayre, the Laird of Aberuchil, and the awful figure of the ninth Earl of Argyll, charged with imperson-ating John Dow Beg MacDonald of Achnacone, his fellow clans-man. John Dow was wanted in Inveraray for some unstated offence against the peace, but it would seem that being considered too valuable a man to MacIain he had been kept at home, and that Donald MacRankin, obviously of lesser worth, had been sent to take his place and punishment. The Earl and his justices, not hav-ing MacIain's elastic interpretation of individual responsibility, ordered that MacRankin "be scourged through the town by the hangman, and his tongue to be bored by a hot iron at the Mercat Cross on Wednesday next, the twenty-ninth instant, by ten hours in the forenoon, in example of others to commit the like". In their absence, fines of 800 marks were imposed on old MacIain, John MacDonald the tacksman of Achtriachtan, and John Mac-Allan in Laroch, all three of whom, in the Court's opinion, were responsible for the impudent attempt to deceive.

It is probable, though impossible to prove now, that John Dow MacDonald of Achnacone was wanted for his part in a bloody crime charged against Glencoe. Within six months, MacIain himself was a prisoner in Inveraray on this charge, shackled by Campbells and thrown into the Tolbooth. How he came there, whether he surrendered or was dragged from his glen by armed men, is not known, and all the information there is can be found in a letter from the Privy Council and a single sheet of undated paper in the archives of Inveraray Castle.

Toward the end of his lifetime one of the most damning accusations made against MacIain was that he slaughtered some of his own clansmen, from caprice or for rebellion. The evidence which may support the charge is that sheet of paper at Inveraray. It is written in the nervous, angular hand of the ninth Earl of Argyll, disjointed notes set down one spring morning, in the Court House, perhaps, or in a room of his castle as witnesses were brought before him:

John M'Donald son to John Dow M'Allan Roury was killed in the pursuit by Angus M'Donald cousin germane to M'Ean in the morning
John M'Donald son to Alexander M'Donald brother to M'Alan Rory was taken out of the house after it was fired and killed after dinner in cold blood and stabbed and cut to pieces
The principal murderers were: John M'Donald in Achaterachane . . . to M'Ean
Archibald M'D cousin germane to M'Ean
Alexander M'D another cousin germane
John M'D another cousin germane
Jo M'D brother to Achaterachane
Ar. M'Do of Achatriachtans family with some others
besides common people about twenty
James Campbell of
and his friends   and several others saw
Robert M'Ewen   the first man killed
Ar. M'd
John Campbell Alan Cameron

For such crimes laid against MacIain, his kinsmen and his people, he could have been hanged from the great tree on Gallows Hill, or sent to Edinburgh for more public but equally effective dispatch. Never before had a Glencoe chief been held by the Campbells, and it must have seemed to them that nothing could now save the impenitent old rogue from just punishment. But something did. In April, when the snowline was retreating up Bidean nam Bian, when the Coe was in spate and the valley was preparing for the Beltane Feast, MacIain the Twelfth was back in his house at Carnoch. Across the water on Skye Sir James MacDonald of Sleat, who was held responsible for Glencoe's behaviour under the General Band, received an angry letter from Edinburgh:

It being represented to H.M. Privy Council that Alexander M'Donald in Polvig* in Glencoe being committed prisoner in the Tolbooth of Inveraray by order of the Earl of Argyle, as justitiar in these bounds, for certain crimes, he had broken prison and made his escape; and since he and John M'Donald in Auchtriatin, with diverse of their peoples, have committed several murders and depredations whereby the country in these parts is like to be casten loose and exposed to the rapine and violence of these persons; and the Council considering that by your bands you are obliged for the peaceable deportment of the foresaid persons and to present them before the Council when they should be called for, whereupon you might be summarily charged to produce them, yet the Council has thought fit only at this time to recommend to you, as you would prevent further trouble to yourself, to concur with and assist such as shall be appointed by the Earl of Argyle to apprehend them, and that your care and diligence in this will be answerable to the obligation that lies on you is expected by the Council.

How MacIain, in his sixth decade, was able to break out of a stout prison in the heart of Campbell country remains an exasperating mystery, like too much of his people's story. There does not

* MacIain is frequently described in contemporary records as being of Polvig, or Polveig in Glencoe. It was the site of his house on the north bank of the River Coe. The word comes from the Gaelic *Poll à mhig*, the hollow of the whey.

seem to have been any attempt to retake him by force from Glencoe. Despite the Privy Council's peremptory order, Sir James MacDonald did little, not liking, perhaps, the suggestion that he should deliver one of his own name to the hangman. The Earl of Argyll was suddenly busy that summer with a more pressing matter, and one that needed all his wits and swordsmen: his open war with the Macleans of Duart, a savage affair of slaughter and plunder that was to last six years, cost both sides more than £250,000 Scots, and ended with much of Maclean land in the hands of the Campbells. For the next few years MacIain trod gently, though he did give the Macleans some help when asked. He stayed at home, like most MacDonalds, when the Highland Host went down to the Lowlands in 1678. This was no foray but an army of 4,500 clan levies from Atholl, Perth, Breadalbane and Moray, called up by the King's Ministers and quartered on the western shires of the Lowlands. It was hoped that their wild presence and arrogant readiness for war would persuade the Covenanting Presbyterians to accept Episcopacy with all its religious and civil obligations. It was as if several thousand Afghan hillmen were to be billeted in Sussex.

The use of Highlanders for this dragonnade was the decision of the Duke of Lauderdale, President of the Privy Council and the bullying dictator of Scotland. In his youth he had been a commissioner for the Solemn League and Covenant, whereby most Lowlanders declared their determination to extirpate Popery and Prelacy in the united kingdoms, but he was now a bitter opponent of its present adherents. He believed that their conventicles were armed camps, that their preachers were plotting rebellion. Since one of them told a congregation that "Kings, nobles and prelates are the murderers of Christ", Lauderdale's fear was not entirely a nightmare. He gave the clans virtual freedom to do as they wished among the Whigs of the West, but though they looted at will, and frightened old women into a decline, they killed no one. The only fatality reported was one of the Host itself, a MacGregor from Breadalbane who was beaten to death by a mob on his way home. The Highlanders stole everything they could carry, and any stock they could drive, going back to the hills after a month laden like pedlars with pots, pans, girdles and fire-irons, clothing, furniture and furnishings. Physically unharmed, the Lowlanders watched them go with hateful derision, though they kept their smiles behind their hands until the clans were out of sight. A young student of St. Andrews, William Cleland, wrote "A Mock Poem upon the Expedition of the Highland Host" into which he put his countrymen's ridicule of the clan gentry "who led the van and drove the rear . . .

> With brogues, trews, and pirnie plaids,
> With good blue bonnets on their heads;
> Which on the one side had a flipe,
> Adorned with a tobacco pipe.
> With dirk, and snap-work, and snuff-mill,
> A bag which they with onions fill,
> And as their strict observers say,
> A tup-horn filled with usquebay.
> A slashed out coat beneath her plaids,
> A targe of timber, nails and hides;
> With a long two-handed sword,
> As good's the country can afford.
> Had they not need of bulk and bones,
> Who fights with all these arms at once,
> It's marvellous how in such weather,
> O'er hill and hop they came together,
> How in such storms they came so far,
> The reason is they're smeared with tar,
> Which doth defend them heel and neck,
> Just as it does their sheep protect.
> But least ye doubt that this is true,
> They're just the colour of tarr'd wool. "

Ten years later, William Cleland showed himself as courageous in arms against the Highlanders as he was merciless in his doggerel.

When the Host was withdrawn, the western lairds examined the reckoning. Their financial losses were high, and because the raid had taken place in winter the suffering of their people was

2. "A Generous Air of Contempt for Trifles"
A Highlander at the beginning of the 18th century, the Laird of Grant's
Champion painted by Richard Waitt.

1. "A Garden Enclosed . . . Fertile, Plenteous"
The mouth of Glencoe from across Loch Leven, with the Cliff of the Feinn
on the left, Meall Mòr on the right, and the Bidean range in the background.
MacDonald dead are buried on the largest isle.

severe. In most shires the Highlanders had "pillaged, plundered, thieved and robbed night and day, even the Lord's day they regarded as little as any other". The value of the property they had taken and the damage they had done in Ayrshire alone was estimated at £200,000 Scots. They began to plunder Kilmarnock on the Sunday before they left, despite their officers' protests, and were only bought off at last by large sums of money collected by the citizens. As they passed Stirling on their way home, wrote one Covenanter, "every man drew his sword to show the world they had returned as conquerors from their enemy's land, but they might as well have shown the pots, pans, girdles, shoes, and other bodily and household furniture with which they were loaded". He said that the Earls of Airlie and Strathmore, who had led their levies, "sent home money not in purses, but in bags and great quantities".

Lowlanders never forgot the Highland Host. Their old fear of Gaeldom was now strengthened by hatred and contempt. They became indifferent to any punitive measure, however savage, that was used against the clans, and this indifference lasted for two centuries until the mountains were empty of men. And fourteen years after the quartering of the Host, the MacDonalds of Glencoe were to be the victims of one great western laird who never allowed himself to forget it.

The intoxicating days of the Highland Host, when authority seemed to sanction reiving and blackmail, had their inevitable effect. Feud and foray, slaughter and reprisal increased. And in 1681 the iron hand of the Campbells was suddenly lifted. The ninth Earl of Argyll, who had objected to the raising of the Host, now opposed the Test Act which barred Covenanter and Catholic from civil, military or ecclesiastical office. The Earl fumbled his way through a prevaricating acceptance of the Test, and then, with lonely courage, refused it entirely. He was tried for treason and condemned to death, but his step-daughter took him out of Edinburgh Castle in the unlikely guise of her page, and he escaped to Holland.

The clans, however, had no opportunity yet to profit from the

fall of Mac-Cailein-Mor. In the spring of that year Charles II had
sent his brother James, Duke of York, to Edinburgh for the second
time as High Commissioner, with the particular duty of pacifying
the Highlands. As a Catholic, James had his own problems of
religion, and he may have felt that the English were merely getting him out of the way while they decided whether he should or
should not succeed his brother. He proceeded against the clans
with a harsh lack of sympathy, and it would be impossible to
believe that any of them, certainly the MacDonalds, were ready
to die for him eight years later, were it not for the fact that their
loyalty was less to him than to their own way of life.

Some of the most powerful barons in Scotland sat in Holyrood
House with the Duke of York as members of the Commission for
Pacifying the Highlands, and until his disgrace the Earl of Argyll
was naturally one of them. In the King's name they drew up new
measures for enforcing the Law in the mountains and isles,
declaring that a large part of the kingdom was now "subject to the
incursions, depredations and the barbarous cruelty of thieves,
sorners and broken men" from those parts. A proclamation of
intent was ordered to be printed and published at market crosses
throughout the country, and read in parish churches after divine
service on the Sabbath. It said that soldiers of the standing forces
would be stationed throughout the Highlands and maintained by
cattle and corn taken from disaffected men. Landlords and baillies
would be held responsible for the peaceable conduct of their
dependants. All landlords and chiefs were ordered to appear before
the Privy Council in Edinburgh on the second Thursday of July,
1681, and there sign a bond promising to "exhibit and produce
before His Majesty's Privy Council, or the Justices, any of my
men, tenants, servants, indwellers upon my lands, or any person of
my name, descended of my family who shall commit murder,
deforcement of messengers, reif, theft, depredations, open and
avowed fire-raisings upon deadly feuds, or any other deeds
contrary to the Acts of Parliament".

The list of the chiefs and lairds whose presence was demanded
in Edinburgh for the signing of this bond is a long roll-call of

Highland gentry, names and titles like the brassy blare of trumpets, and included among them were MacDonald of Glencoe, of Achtriachtan, Achnacone, Brecklet and Laroch. Had MacIain been at home it is possible that he would have ignored the proclamation, as many did, but he was in Edinburgh that July on some private business for MacDonald of Sleat, having first obtained the Privy Council's promise that he would not be arrested for the "slaughters" charged against him, or for his insolent escape from the Inveraray Tolbooth seven years before. It is impossible to believe that he would have been allowed to leave Edinburgh without first putting his name to the bond.

The new measures were only as strong as the garrisons set up to enforce them, and these do not seem to have frightened the clans. Eight months later John Murray, commander of a small detachment at Inverlochy, complained bitterly that he and his men had been "cruelly beaten, wounded and robbed of their clothes, and His Majesty's arms taken from them, hardly escaping with their lives, and brought to the extremity of starving in their wounds before they could get any relief". The offenders were not ordinary men but Ewen Cameron of Lochiel, the chief of his clan, his brother, his uncle, his kinsmen and their followers. Charles II amiably called Lochiel "the king of thieves", and had knighted him the year before, but the Council was outraged. It sent a herald in a flaming tabard to the Mercat Cross of Inverness and the castle at Inverlochy, there "by sound of trumpet to command and charge [the Camerons] to appear before the Council". Lochiel tolerantly sent his brother, and a few of his kinsmen, promising their good behaviour against a fine of 1,000 merks, but he did not think it within his dignity to go himself.

The MacDonalds also broke out. Keppoch resumed his interminable feud with the Mackintoshes, and when he refused to withdraw from the land he had taken from them, Letters of Fire and Sword were issued against him and his allies. But, for the moment, nobody felt inclined to execute them.

In 1683 a special Commission was sent on a tour of the Highlands, to hold sederunts for the hearing of complaints, and to exact bonds of good behaviour. It was led by Lieutenant-General Sir William Drummond of Cromlix, a tired old man who had once served the Tsar as Governor of Smolensk, and who was popularly supposed to have introduced the thumb-screw as an instrument of judicial persuasion. There were eight others on his Commission, including some Highland lairds such as Robertson of Struan, Campbell of Lawers, and Ewen Cameron of Lochiel, the last apparently appointed on the belief that a poacher can make the best bailiff. They travelled slowly from Perth to Crieff, and in June they came to Achallader, a Campbell castle to the south of Rannoch Moor. They stayed there for two months, said Drummond, summoning MacIain and his neighbour who showed a willing "inclination to comply and concur with any means that could be proposed for suppressing theft and robbery". Drummond did not say he was surprised to discover such a willingness in MacIain, a man generally believed to be the worst thief and robber in the Highlands, apart from the MacGregors. Perhaps the old soldier was pleased to see him there at all. More people had answered the Commission's summons, he said, "than it reasonably could have expected". Alasdair MacDonald also had a certain rough charm, and his splendid carriage, his mane of white hair and his fierce moustache, may have moved General Drummond to nostalgic memories of Muscovy. Since MacIain sensibly realised that he could not ignore a Royal Commission that was sitting on his doorstep, he probably chose to disarm it. He invited it to Glencoe, "which was a very tedious journey", wrote the Commission clerk unhappily. In deference to its chief, Clan Iain Abrach was hospitable, even no doubt to Campbell of Lawers whose cattle they had more than once stolen. "All the inhabitants of those parts," reported the clerk, "did meet the Lieutenant-General in their best order, and attended him during his abode there." And then the Commission went back to Edinburgh.

Two years later, having done what it could to subdue the clans, the government appealed to them in its own defence. Argyll was back from Holland, and in arms. James, Duke of York, had succeeded his brother Charles without the unanimous approval of the English or the Scots, the majority of whom would have preferred a Protestant king. His bastard nephew, Monmouth, landed in Dorset to unseat him. Four hundred miles to the north, Argyll had already raised three thousand Campbells for the same purpose. Both men were too early by three years, they were defeated and executed. Monmouth died horribly, his neck butchered by five strokes of the axe, but Mac-Cailein-Mor walked calmly to the guillotine machine which the Scots called The Maiden.

The army which the Privy Council had raised to oppose Argyll included levies from most of the clans with a long hatred of Campbells, particularly the Macleans and the MacDonalds, and when the Earl was dead the Marquis of Atholl took them into Argyllshire for the fruits of their loyalty to James II. The Atholl Raid was the greatest foray ever made. It was not a punitive campaign against rebels, but a time for collecting old debts. The clans came in three columns, from the north, the south and the east. They hanged some of Argyll's kinsmen on Gallows Hill, and would have suspended his sick son there too, had the Privy Council not stopped them. From the Earl's lands alone they took booty worth £60,000 sterling. They looted, burned and killed in all the glens, and although many of the Campbell lairds had actively supported the Crown against their chief, they too were pillaged. The raiders filled the Tolbooth of Inveraray and the common gaols of southern Argyll with their prisoners, whether these had or had not been out with the Earl. The Privy Council, concerned for the safety of the prisoners while the clans remained their gaolers, ordered them to be sent to the Lowlands. It was a brief mercy. With their ears cropped, most of them were later transported, and those who survived the voyage worked out their lives in bondage on the plantations of America.

MacIain of Glencoe was with the raiders, coming to Inveraray for the second of the three times he was to visit it. He divided his clansmen into several parties for better profit. One, under his son Alasdair Og, went north-west with some Appin Stewarts to the green and ragged coast of Kilbride. There, according to a meticulous accounting made some years later in the hope of compensation, they took from the lands of Ivor Campbell of Asknish "the full and whole soumes* of the said lands, being 48 cows with their followers, three plough-horses and two mares with their followers, which were totally robbed away in full bulk". Including what they later took from Archibald Campbell of Barbreck, their plunder in Kilbride was worth £868 Scots.

John MacDonald, MacIain's heir, crossed Loch Fyne to Cowal. From Campbell of Carrick and his tenants he took a cow, three steers and two horses, all of high value and worth £388 Scots. From the house of John Campbell of Ardintennie he looted "pewter plates, whole glass windows, a great house Bible, Josephus his *Works*, Turk's *Historie*, *Polybius*, the Countess of Pembroke's *Arcadia*, with several other great volumes, together with several small grammar authors". Ardintennie was obviously a scholar of some discernment, and he bitterly lamented the loss of these books, saying they were worth £100 Scots. Just as plainly, John MacDonald had a good taste for literature, unless his father's clansmen stole the books to make cartridges from their leaves.

A small band of Glencoe men under Alexander MacDonald of Dalness raided Kenmoir and took cattle worth £104 Scots. From the land of Colin Campbell of Dressalch, Sheriff-clerk of Argyll, twelve cows worth £240 Scots were driven over to Glencoe, a loss which he may have remembered too well some years later. In both of these small forays the MacDonalds were helped by followers of the Laird of Lochnell, who was himself a Campbell and related by marriage to MacIain's family. His assault on men of his own name was not uncommon. The Atholl raid offered a rare opportunity for some Campbells to enrich themselves at the expense of their neighbours.

One of the greatest lairds in Argyll was the Sheriff of the county, Sir Colin Campbell of Ardkinglas, who held sweet glens across Loch Fyne from Inveraray. The Glencoe men joined with Keppoch and Appin in plundering these. Together they stole 500 horses, 1,500 cows and over 2,000 sheep and goats. They burned

* *Soume*—the number of sheep or cattle grazed on a particular pasture.

or stole all goods and crops, houses and barns, boats and nets, and the total loss to Ardkinglas and his people was £63,630 18s. Scots.

Old MacIain, selecting the sweetest fruit for himself, went down to Rosneath. This narrow peninsula on the Firth of Clyde was well stocked and well cultivated, fat with good living. From the property and tenants of Donald Campbell of Knockderrie, MacIain and those Appin men who went with him took milch-cows and beef-cattle, horses, sheep and goats, clothing, furnishing and household goods (including one copper kettle) to the value of £998 1s. 4d. Scots. What they could not take with them, they destroyed.

Campbell of Knockderrie was astounded, and rightly so, for like MacIain he was "in His Majesty's service the whole time of the troubles".

"We scorn your usurper and his government"

It was the spring of 1689, in the beginning of May. Old MacIain was in his house at Carnoch, "the hospitable house," said a bard, "of wine-cups and panelled walls." That winter, with his hunting-dogs at his feet and his valley still rich with the loot of Argyll, his leisure hours had been pleasantly passed with George Tooke's inspiring history of the expedition against Cadiz in 1625, or the Countess of Pembroke's edition of her brother's pastoral and chivalrous romance. But for rumours of war he would by now have gone with his women and his servants to his summer home in Gleann Leac na Muidhe, and his people would have been eating the custard cake of Beltane before driving their cattle to the shielings on the Black Mount. But Ewen Cameron of Lochiel had come over the ferry from Carness, leaving word with Stewart of Ballachulish that the clans were to gather in defence of James Stuart.

That obstinate man's reign had lasted three years and ten months. In November his son-in-law, William of Orange, had landed at Torbay with 15,000 men, three divisions of English, Scots and Dutch, distinguished from each other by the white, blue and scarlet of their banners. They advanced on London, enlisting those sent to oppose them, and by Christmas Day James II was an exile in France. He went to Dublin in the New Year, raising an army of Irish Catholics, and sending an appeal to the loyal clans of the Highlands. Nine months before, when still a king at St. James's, he had declared that some of them, particularly the MacDonalds, were thieves and robbers, murderers and assassins, and he had granted the Laird of Mackintosh Letters of Fire and Sword against them. He had further expressed his will that "all Our good subjects will concur in suppressing and rooting out the said barbarous and inhuman tratitors, to their utmost power, which We will look upon as most acceptable service". Now he asked the MacDonalds, and all others, to help him against "the oppression of antimonarchial and ill men". This no doubt far more acceptable service would be rewarded by his special favour.

John Graham of Claverhouse, Viscount Dundee and butcher or hero according to the way one's religious notions went, had James Stuart's commission to raise the clans. This appointment must have quickened the blood of the MacDonalds, for they had memories of that other Graham, the Great Marquis of Montrose, who had led them against the Campbells forty years before. The cause he proposed was one easily understood by the clans. It was in defence of a Stuart and therefore a Scottish king. It was, or seemed to be, in defence of Episcopacy and the toleration of Catholics. It was, or seemed to be, in defence of their own way of life against Lowland authority. To Clan Donald it was all this and more. The Campbells, under the heir to the earldom of Argyll, had declared for William and the Protestant Revolution, and the leadership of the Gaels was once more in dispute.

In the third week of May the Jacobite clans gathered in the Great Glen to meet Dundee, by the River Lochy on a low green field called Dalcomera. It was twenty-five miles from Glencoe and five from Lochiel's splendid fir-wood house at Achnacarry. Ewen Cameron was first on the field with his men. He was sixty years of age, but still with a healthy thirst for battle (in his youth he had bitten the throat from a Cromwellian officer with whom he grappled). Though his mother was a Glenorchy Campbell, and the seventh Earl of Argyll had been his guardian, his attachment to the Stuarts was strong. The wardship of Argyll had prevented him from fighting with the Great Marquis, but it was said of him that "Montrose is ever in his mouth". He was the archetype of a Highland chief, arrogant, emotional, stiff with pride and extravagantly brave.

The weather was sweet and fresh, the spring sun strong, and it was a time to stir a man with thoughts of honour, battle and pillage. Dundee's young standard-bearer, James Philip of Almerieclose in Angus, was particularly affected by the brave colour and wild music, by the savage men who stood about him in arms like classical heroes. In later years he wrote an heroic poem in Latin, *Panurgi Philocaballi Scoti Grameidos*, describing the gathering and much of the campaign that followed. "We tell of warlike deed for time to come," he said hopefully, remembering the saffron shirts and blue bonnets, the vivid tartan plaids and red feather plumes. In his poem all the clansmen are giants, and what he learned of their barbaric customs filled him with awe and admiration.

These are they who under the frozen waters of the Roy, like the redhot iron plunged into the flowing river, dip their new-born babes and teach their offspring in their tender years to despise the hailstorms and tempests of the North, and to harden them against wounds. The infant is plunged in the wave by a midwife, skilled to unfold the future of the babe in mystic mutterings. Suspended in the air, he is turned thrice round a fire, mid Stygian murmurs and words of incantation.

One by one, the Lowlander Philip described the chiefs as he remembered them at Dalcomera, or as they came later to Dundee's army. There was Ewen Cameron of Lochiel at the head of a thousand men, riding a grey horse and wearing a cuirass of leather, his tartan hose gartered below the knee. There was the great Keppoch, Coll of the Cows, "whom love of plunder would impel to any crime". Less than a year before, and with the Glencoe MacDonalds, he and his people had fought twelve hundred Mackintoshes in a bloody affray at Mulroy. He was wrapped in a tartan plaid, carried a great target studded with brass on his left arm, and walked at the head of eight hundred men. Black Alasdair MacDonald of Glengarry, heir to his frail and aged father the chief, was also richly dressed in fretted tartan, his plaid held by a brooch made from "the grinning head of some wild animal". He brought with him his brother, his son, and the best men of his clan, "their brawny shanks enveloped in scarlet hose. Bristling with arms, afar they shone, their shields covering their bodies, their loins begirt with the terrible claymore".

From the western coast and the Hebrides came the Clanranald MacDonalds, "all whom Moidart and Knoidart nurse, all who embark from the black isles of Uist and Benbecula". From Skye came Donald MacDonald of Sleat, "in the first flower of his years, with five hundred youthful warriors armed with sword and spear". There were Macleans, brought by a fleet of long-boats from the isles of Mull, Coll and Tiree, led by the chief of Duart, a young and well-favoured boy of nineteen with an undying hatred of the Argyll Campbells. Beneath a yellow-crossed banner of blue came two hundred Stewarts from Appin, "huge men carrying huge arms, with rough bonnets on their heads". The old chief in Appin was too ill to leave his home, and his son Robert, "so young that the yellow down covers not his cheek", was hurrying from college to be with his people.

MacIain brought a hundred men or more to Dalcomera, and was one of the first to arrive at the gathering. Small though his contribution was, his influence for the moment was strong. He was among friends, and although all except the other MacDonalds had at one time lost cattle or blood to Glencoe, he was welcomed today as a man of honour and integrity, blameless in his conduct. He was the oldest chief there, tall and erect in his buff coat and tartan trews, a broadsword on his hip, a bullhide target on his back, and his blunderbuss in his hand. The spikes of his great moustache curled up to his ears, and his white hair fell to his shoulders. At one elbow was his son Alasdair Og, at the other his piper Big Henderson of the Chanters. And behind him, serving as his officers, were the tacksmen of Achtriachtan, Inverrigan, Laroch and Achnacone.

Into his breathless account of the gathering Philip crowded portraits of all the chiefs of the Jacobite clans—MacNeills, Mac-Leods, MacLachlans, Grants, Frasers, and MacMillans—whether or no they were at Dalcomera. His enthusiasm, if not the tortured allegories of his prose, recreated a forgotten day when the grass was covered with steel and tartan, when the air was filled with the sound of pipes, and Graham of Dundee stood his horse before his army, with green leaves in his hat, a scarlet coat on his back, and a glass of wine in his hand. He drank a toast with the chiefs, said Philip, "the crash and clang of the pipes rose to the skies, and the flaming faggots lighten up the whole camp. Said the Graham, Generals, raise your standards . . . !"

But not all was unity and comradely love. Before Dundee could get his touchy army to march, he had to give it its head in private matters. There were raids on neutral clans, and Keppoch went off to harry the Mackintoshes again. There were also family feuds to settle. The Camerons fell upon those Grants whose sympathies were with the Protestant Revolution, and they killed a Glengarry MacDonald who was married to a Grant and living with his wife's people. MacDonald of Glengarry demanded revenge, telling Dundee that by the arithmetic of his pride "One MacDonald is worth two Camerons".

Finally the army moved southward, skirmishing and man-œuvring to meet the forces which had been sent against it under Hugh Mackay of Scourie, a hard old veteran of the Dutch wars. On July 27, both armies met in the Pass of Killiecrankie. From the brae of Craig Eallaich, half an hour before sunset, the clansmen came down in the old way upon Mackay's unnerved, unhappy troops. They came at the cry of "*Claymore!*", throwing off their plaids and running half-naked, with heads down behind their targets, dirks in their left hands, broadswords in their right. Within range of Mackay's volleys they halted, discharged what fire-arms they had, threw the pieces away and then ran on to a hacking, stabbing slaughter before the redcoats could screw their bayonets into the muzzles of their muskets. Mackay's men broke. Most of them were Lowland levies, and even his regular battalions had recently been made up with untrained recruits. Nobody had told them what to expect, screaming faces with black, open mouths, white swords that could whistle through an arm or a leg, or split a man's body from his scalp to his waist. Their volley-fire had killed six hundred Highlanders in the onset, but it had not stopped the charge. Though Mackay rallied four hundred men in a hasty retreat, the rest ran in panic into the dusk. "In the twinkling of an eye," said their general sourly, "our men as well as the enemy were out of sight, being got down pell mell to the river where our baggage stood."

Where the Glencoe men were at Killiecrankie is not known, perhaps in the centre with the Appin Stewarts, but more probably with Clanranald and Glengarry in Clan Donald's traditional place to the right. Iain Lom, the bard of Keppoch, saw it as a Mac-Donald victory, of course, a hard tussle for the seed of Conn, King William's forces brushed away like flies, and blood flowing in waves across the grass. But, he said, though they had driven away the enemy they were under a great load of sorrow. Dundee had been mortally wounded as he led his few horse against the centre of Mackay's line. The clansmen carried him away in their plaids and buried him in the old kirk of Blair. Not an enemy would have lived between Orkney and the Tweed, said Iain Lom, had not that bullet struck Dundee beneath the skirt of his coat.

His death ended any real hope that James II could have had for an influential rising in the Highlands. An army of clans, for ever quarrelling like children, needed a superlative leader to knit and hold them together. Only a Graham, or a Stuart Prince, had the genius or the charm for this. Lochiel went home, and although he left his clan regiment behind under his son, it was plain that he now thought little of the campaign's success. Others went too, to take their booty home, or to foray in Breadalbane and Argyll. But the MacDonalds remained at Blair, to serve Dundee's successor Colonel Alexander Cannon, a man of little charm and meagre ability. Three weeks after Killiecrankie, the remaining chiefs addressed a swaggering letter to Mackay, ribaldly refusing his offers of pardon and indemnity. "That you may know the sentiments of men of Honour," they said,

... we declare to you and all the world, we scorn your usurper and the indemnities of his government; and to save you further trouble by your frequent invitations, we assure you that we are satisfied our king take his own time and way to manage his dominion and punish his rebels. We will all die with our swords in our hands before we fail in our loyalty and sworn allegiance to our sovereign.

They then marched upon the city of Perth, thirty-five miles to the south. Between them and this ambitious objective was the cathedral town of Dunkeld, held for Mackay by a single regiment, the Earl of Angus's Foot. But this was no ordinary battalion of men. They called themselves Cameronians, being devoutly attached to the teachings of Richard Cameron, a Covenanting field preacher who had been killed when the Episcopacy harried the West, nine years before. Their young Lieutenant-Colonel was William Cleland, student of St. Andrew's, writer of doggerel verse, and now a soldier of the Lord. When the Cameronians heard the screaming of Clan Donald's pipes, and saw the flame of banners on a hill to their north, they sang a psalm, blew on their matches, and waited in quiet courage.

With rare foresight, Cannon sent two troops of horse about the town to block any retreat across the River Tay. Cleland had no intention of retiring, however. He posted his men in ditches, in the cathedral and steeple, behind the walls of parks and gardens. At seven o'clock on a Sunday morning, the Highlanders advanced. The MacDonalds were fiercely eager to avenge their kinsmen who had died on the redcoat line at Killiecrankie, although one of them, Donald of the Blue Eyes, the son of Black Alasdair of Glengarry, had taken payment for his own death by killing eighteen of Mackay's men before he was cut down. They drove in the Cameronian outposts without difficulty, but a town was no battlefield for the clans. Against the entrenched ditches, the stone of the garden walls and the cathedral, their broadswords and their bows, their dirks and axes were useless. They stumbled through the musketry, fired their own weapons, and then rushed on to be impaled by pikes or hewn down by halberds. Dying from a bullet in his liver, and another wound in his head, young Cleland tried to reach Dunkeld House so that his men might not see him die, but he was dead before he got to the door. This loss,

however, strengthened the stubborn resistance of the Cameronians. The battle lasted three hours, and then the clans retreated
sullenly before the advance of the Angus pikemen. Some took
shelter in the houses, but the Cameronians turned the keys in the
doors and set fire to the buildings. In this way the whole town
burned. Though they had gathered at Dalcomera like giants of the
Feinn, and had been an irresistible wave at Killiecrankie, the
Highlanders were driven from Dunkeld by one resolute regiment
strong in the righteousness of the Lord. That afternoon, as the
clans looked back at the burning town, they heard the voices of
the Cameronians singing psalms.

Among the three hundred dead the Jacobites had left in the
streets were many men of Glencoe.

Six days later, twelve chiefs met at Blair Castle, still firm in their
resistance to William of Orange, but uneasy now about the future.
They wanted to go home but, as if ashamed of this, they promised
to gather again when any one of them needed the protection of all.
"We do all solemnly promise," said their bond, "to assist one
another to the utmost of our power. . . ." Five MacDonald chiefs
signed the bond, including MacIain, and the other seven signators
were the chiefs of the Camerons, Stewarts and MacGregors,
MacNeills, Robertsons, Farquharsons and Macleans. Against their
names were set the number of men whom each promised to bring
into the field should their common safety or King James's cause
require it. The total was no more than eighteen hundred. Lochiel
offered two hundred only, Keppoch and Maclean a hundred, and
MacIain could promise less than half the hundred or more he had
led to Dalcomera. Their losses in the brief summer war had been
bitter, and all were reluctant to risk more on an uncertain future.

The MacDonalds of Glencoe travelled home with their friends
of Keppoch. They went westward through Breadalbane, determined to take their soldier's pay from this Campbell country. The
Earl of Breadalbane had played a cautious game since the fall of
James II, watching how the wind took great men's loyalties, and
keeping his own to himself. His kinsmen, like Robert Campbell of
Glenlyon, waited with him. The Jacobite leaders, knowing that

the Earl coveted his nephew Argyll's leadership of Clan Campbell, believed that he would in time declare for King James, but the Glencoe and Keppoch men had no time for such political subtleties. That October they raped the valley of Glen Lyon, from its narrow mouth at Fortingall twenty-five miles on to its last twist into the southern wall of Rannoch Moor. After a summer spent in arms, they said, this was the way to gather their winter mart, the cattle customarily killed and salted at Martinmas.

It was the greatest raid the Lochaber men ever made into Breadalbane. It was also the safest. There was no bloody opposition as there had been at Sron a' Chlachain and Glen Meran in their fathers' youth. The Glen Lyon women were scarcely home from the shielings, and the men were still dispersed at the harvest. The MacDonalds pillaged and burned without let. They drove off fifteen hundred head of cattle, horses, sheep and goats. From the houses and cottages they took everything that could be carried, even, said a Glen Lyon chronicler, a blanket and cradle from beneath a child. The value of their plunder was said to be over £8,000 Scots.

Robert Campbell of Glenlyon, crippled by bankruptcy, owned nothing in the glen now but the house and policies of Chesthill, but what he did have was taken from him by the Glencoe men in one afternoon: six great English mares and three plough-horses, 208 cows, 169 sheep, 10 goats, and a splendid brown stallion worth £200. His pleasant, grey-stone house was plundered of "several plenishings such as rack-spits, plates, trenchers and candlesticks, and other things estimate to £40 Scots". His full loss was just under £3,000 Scots. The Keppoch men looted Cambuslay, the house and estate belonging to Glenlyon's brother Colin, taking stock and goods worth £2,283 Scots.

Slowly the MacDonalds went home through the golden October days, by Loch Lyon and Glen Meran, round the brown shoulder of Beinn a' Chreachain to the Water of Tulla on Rannoch Moor. They turned westward along the shallow stream for five miles to Achallader. Here, where MacIain had charmed old General Drummond six years before, was one of the Earl of

Breadalbane's holdings. Fearing that it might be used as a garrison by Mackay, Alexander Cannon had given the MacDonalds orders to destroy it. They pulled down what they could of the castle, burnt the roof-trees of the cottages and drove off all the stock. And this they would have done, no doubt, without Colonel Cannon's order.

Parting company with the Keppoch men, MacIain gathered his women from the shielings on the Black Mount, passed through the shadows of the Great and Little Herdsmen, and came home to Glencoe. It was the Feast of Samhain and the end of summer. Within a week or two snow fell on the Highlands, and the world was white, and black, and silent.

It was a hard winter. In November, News Letters from Edinburgh to London reported that "the Highland rebels, according to their ancient custom and practice in this season of the year, have been to make a visit to some of their neighbours in the Lowlands". Six hundred clansmen had come down as far as Glasgow, at the invitation of Jacobite sympathisers inside the city, it was said. They were boldly encamped six miles outside the gates, molesting travellers, robbing the Post, and terrorising farmers.

The Glencoe men were not with them. Content with the booty of Glen Lyon, they stayed at home. There were proclamations out against them, as there had been at every Mercat Cross since July, declaring them to be murderers, traitors and rebels. But a word is only a word, and in Clan Donald's opinion those who called them traitors were quite plainly rebels themselves. If the true King were to return, said Iain Lom, just men would think no more of cutting off William's head than they would of slicing an ear from a rat.

2

THE BLACK GARRISON

"The time is short, the time for action is near"

IN MARCH, 1690, Colonel John Hill arrived in Edinburgh from Ireland. He lodged himself modestly in one of the wynds, close to the houses of the great gentlemen whose influence he earnestly desired. It was at the invitation of some of them that this old English soldier had returned to Scotland after thirty years, and his wish to be of service to the new régime sprang as much from honest zeal as it did from a too-slender purse. He was a simple, uncomplicated man with no impressive claim to blood or lineage, and nothing is known of his ancestry or his descendants. He was skilled in soldierly diplomacy, strong in the Protestant faith and well versed in the classics and the Scriptures, both of which he found a comfort in trouble and adversity. He was approaching his seventieth year and his health was poor, but he had two spinster daughters to support in London, and no income except that which his wits and experience might still earn him.

As a young man he had been a foot-soldier in the army of the Commonwealth, one of those plain, russet-coated captains who knew what they fought for and loved what they knew, according to their Lord Protector. A major of Colonel Fitch's Regiment, he served in Ireland against the Papists, and in June, 1654, was one of the thousand men sent to the Highlands to garrison the forts which General George Monck intended to build there, now that all support for the monarchy had been crushed. Hill probably welcomed this service. The great wars were over, and only in the mountains might a young and ambitious officer find opportunity for action and advancement. These Cromwellian soldiers were members of the finest army ever created by England. They did their work well, with firmness, common sense, and a rough compassion. "A man may ride all over Scotland with a switch in his hand and £100 in his pocket," reported Monck proudly, "which he could not have done these five hundred years." The pacification of the Highlands by the Commonwealth was done without stripping the clans of their dignity and sense of race, without the hanging and burning, the proscription of dress and tartan, and the deliberate attempt at extermination which later British governments thought necessary.

Monck placed his most important fort on the shore of Loch Linnhe below Ben Nevis, and the Highlanders called it *Gearasdan dubh nan Inbhir-Lochaidh*, The Black Garrison of Inverlochy. It was built by those thousand infantrymen from Ireland, under the direction of Colonel William Brayne and Major John Hill. It was protected on three sides by the water of the loch, and on the other by marshy ground. With more concern for present security than future needs, Brayne cut down all the timber in the neighbourhood to build his ramparts and ravelins, and to give himself a clear field of fire. His successors were to complain bitterly that they had to rely on seaborne ships for their fuel.

In the beginning the strength of the garrison was formidable, ten companies of Foot drawn from every regiment in Scotland, with Brayne as Governor and Hill as his deputy. Monck, the good soldier, insisted that there should never be less than seven days' provision and ammunition in the fort, and that every man should carry with him at all times his Twelve Apostles, a dozen tubes containing powder and ball for his matchlock. There was sense in this. The land about the fort was Cameron country, and young Lochiel, with Montrose ever in his mouth, was anxious for sport and battle. Now and then he and his clansmen attacked woodparties and patrols, and it was on one of these occasions that he tore the throat from an English officer with his teeth. It was, he said, the sweetest bite he had ever taken.

By 1656, when John Hill succeeded Brayne as Governor of Inverlochy, soldiers and clansmen lived side by side in amiable, if watchful, peace, Hill's garrison now consisted of 250 men, a gunner, a store-keeper, and a preacher. With only this handful to support him as Lieutenant-Colonel and Governor, he had full civil and military power over Lochaber, but he must have used his powers wisely, for he had no serious trouble with the clans. Both Lochiel and MacIain became his friends, though the attachment of one to the Episcopacy and the other to Rome must have troubled his Nonconformist conscience. His officers hunted and fished with the Cameron and MacDonald gentry, and it was on a stag-hunt that Hill persuaded the yellow-haired Lochiel to acknowledge the authority of the Protectorate. With his growing understanding of Highland pride and vanity, perhaps it was Hill who suggested that the Camerons' submission should be made in a flattering and tactful ceremony. Led by his pipers, Lochiel brought his clan into the fort one morning and surrendered his arms as a servant of Charles II. The Camerons then marched once round the parade-ground and picked up their weapons as peaceful citizens of the Commonwealth. Thereafter Englishmen and Highlanders met freely, but on Hill's strict orders, and on pain of flogging, the soldiers were not allowed to drink with the clansmen.

The most gratifying friendship which John Hill made in those days of his youth was with the Forbes family of Culloden. He met them first when he waited at Inverness for orders to go to Inverlochy. John Forbes, the laird, was a Member of Parliament and a supporter of the Commonwealth, and he warmly welcomed the young Englishman to his home on the Moray Firth. On furlough from the spartan life of Inverlochy, Hill was grateful for the hospitality and comfort of Culloden House, and enjoyed the gentle arguments he had with John Forbes on the precise interpretation of the Scriptures, or the particular reference which the classics might have to their times. He also became affectionately attached to the laird's sons. He called the Forbes family "the House of Duncan, my good friends", and meant it deeply.

When the news reached Inverlochy in 1658 that Oliver Cromwell was dead, John Hill proclaimed his son, Richard, as the new Lord Protector. He stood in the square with his red-coated garrison drawn up behind him, and before him a great gathering of the

Lochaber chiefs and their followers—Lochiel and Glengarry, Keppoch and Glencoe. The October day ended with a banquet, with songs, piping and dancing, but nobody can have truly believed that the Commonwealth would now endure. Within a few months John Hill was a Governor of nothing, and a Lieutenant-Colonel in no army. On the same parade-ground he handed the keys of Inverlochy to Ewen Cameron of Lochiel, who accepted them on behalf of King Charles II. When Hill was gone down Loch Linnhe, the exulting Camerons pulled the Black Garrison to pieces, stone by stone, and they burned its timber in a joyful celebration of the Restoration.

For the next thirty years little is known of John Hill. Commonwealth officers who had done their duty, who had not had the wit or guile to change their coats when the wind blew strongly from another direction at Oliver's death, could not hope for position or preferment in the King's army. George Monck was now Duke of Albemarle, having changed his coat most handsomely, but he still had some loyalty to his old comrades, and it may have been his influence that secured for Hill the return of sixty pounds which the Governor had advanced from his own pocket to pay the preacher at Inverlochy. And that was all that Hill got from the Restoration. He married, his daughters were born. He went to Dublin and there secured the favour of the Capels. He became Comptroller of the Household to the most powerful member of the family, the Earl of Essex, Lord Lieutenant of Ireland. In Dublin Castle his life was comfortable and his duties not too burdensome. But he grew old, and his health changed from robust good feeling to an endless succession of nagging maladies. His eyes troubled him with incessant soreness, his limbs with persistent aches and stiffness. His greatest comfort was his memory of the Highlands and his correspondence with John Forbes of Culloden. "I am sorry to hear you tell of growing crazy," he once wrote to the Laird, "God grant our elder may be our best days (though not in reference to this world, yet as to a better)."

Having no sons of his own, he fussed with concern for Culloden's, Duncan the heir and his brother John. He offered to use what little influence he had with the Capels on their behalf, should Forbes wish to send them to Ireland. And all the time he longed to meet his friend again. "What joy it would be to see you; but the distance being so great, and the sea intervening, puts me to great doubt of being made so happy. I commend you to the care of our good God, and remain in the old manner your truly loving and humble servant." But old John Forbes died before they might have been re-united.

When the Earl of Essex became the victim of his many enemies and was removed by Royal command to the Tower of London (where he was found one morning with his throat cut), Hill was not without other friends in Ireland. Six years later, in 1689, a widower and well over sixty, he was Constable of Belfast, defending this very English town against the wild Irish of the south who came to destroy it for James II. The Protestant Revolution must have seemed like a miracle to the old Cromwellian. Not only did it represent, to him at least, a triumph for the causes of his youth, but it also offered him a real opportunity to return to a career that had been abruptly ended by the Restoration. He was not the first, or the last, old soldier to believe that a new war was but a resumption of the last, or that a long interbellum did nothing to a good officer's wits and arteries. At the beginning of 1690 he moved himself busily to obtain what he most desired: a return to the Highlands in a position of authority, and a regiment to give substance to his long-empty title of Colonel. To help him with his petitions, he asked the burgesses of Belfast for a Certificate of Recommendation. Though these gentlemen had not thought of paying him the money he had taken from his own purse to buy off some of the Irish kerns, they gave him his certificate with the paper-gratitude of men who had lately expected to be paupers themselves.

Colonel John Hill hath for several years late past resided in this place in the station of Constable of the Castle, in which station he acted to the great satisfaction of all concerned, and to the advantage and benefit of this Corporation; and more especially in March last when the Irish came down into the North and possessed themselves on this country and town, he did appear zealous for the interest of their now Majesties King William and Queen Mary, in giving advice and direction to the inhabitants how to behave themselves with the enemy; and by his great expense upon their officers, and prudent converse with them until the arrival of their Majesties' army from England, did (under God) prevent the firing and ruin of this place and country adjacent. . . .

Hill sent the original of this recommendation to King William, and fair copies to some of the Lords in Council in Edinburgh. Within two or three weeks he got some reply, some reason to hope, and he sailed at once for Glasgow, posting from there to Edinburgh. Now he waited impatiently in his lodgings, husbanding what little money he had left, and writing more letters in which he mixed dogmatic assertion with shrewd good sense. He knew more about the state of affairs in the Highlands than might have been expected in an old man so long absent from them, but the clans had not changed in thirty years. When he sent the burgesses' Certificate to the King he had enclosed with it a letter containing his "apprehensions concerning some preliminaries to the settlement of the insurrection in the Highlands". He repeated these doubts now in a letter to the Earl of Leven. He did not believe that the political issues of the moment, a preference for this king or that, were of significant importance to many chiefs. Some were disaffected "by having their judgements imposed on by others more subtle than themselves; some for interest, because they get not what they desire; and others out of a vindictive temper, all preferring self and private before public interest".

He was worried by a fear that French ships, hovering off the Irish coast, would any day bring five thousand men with arms and supplies to the Highlands, encouraging the clans to gather again as they had done at Dalcomera the year before. It was, he thought, foolish to hope that the Highlanders would tamely accept the King's offer of grace and indemnity. They would have to be forced or bribed. And if force were to be used, then the Council must look to the readiness of General Mackay's army. This was suffering from the customary meanness of all governments. "I find that these forces are much in arrears [of pay], which puts them out of heart; but I hope the Parliament now sitting will supply that want; but the time is short, the time for action is drawing near."

The days passed to the end of March, and although John Hill's advice was politely acknowledged, and occasional audiences with great men kept his hopes warm, no one as yet authorised the commission he wanted. It was well known in Edinburgh why he was there, and it was assumed that his services had already been accepted. An English journalist who sent twice-weekly News Letters to London, to be published from the Rose and Crown in St. Paul's Churchyard, reported that "it is now a thing certain determined, that Col. Hill has received a commission from His Majesty to be Governor of Inverlochy in Lochaber, which puts us in hopes that the rebellious Highlanders in those parts will soon be reduced to civility and obedience". And then again, four days later, "Colonel Hill is come to Town from Ireland, and is to have the command of the garrison at Dunstaffnage until Lochaber is reduced".

By mid-April John Hill was assured by the two men from whom he expected most, and to whom he had first addressed himself, that when matters could be put in order he would get what he desired.

They were at this moment two of the most influential men in Scotland, having the ear and confidence of the King. The first was the Earl of Melville, Secretary of State for Scotland, a sadly ugly little man in his middle fifties. By some miracle of balance, his small body supported a large head made greater by the enormous wig that was then in fashion, from the dark curls of which his white chin jutted like the share of a plough. Though King William preferred the company of pretty young men, and was inclined to load them with honours in indirect proportion to their talents, he could recognise merit and ability behind less favoured faces. Melville's strength was his uncompromising zeal for the Reformed Church. John Macky, a Government spy who published entertaining sketches of the great men of his time, said that Melville had "neither learning, wit, nor common conversation, but a steadiness of principle and a firm boldness for a Presbyterian Government". It was these cold virtues that persuaded William to trust him with the affairs of Scotland at a moment of dangerous uncertainty.

Melville's resistance to the Stuart kings and to Episcopacy had been the sap of his public and spiritual life, and he had suffered for it. The Scots Parliament of James II had driven him from the country, declaring that he "ought to be punished as a horrid traitor, rebel and murderer, with forfeiture of life, lands and goods". In exile he became the friend and adviser of the Prince of Orange, and the Revolution brought him an earldom, the return of his forfeited estates, and the Secretaryship. His son, the Earl of Leven, became the Governor of Edinburgh Castle and Colonel of a splendid foot regiment. Another son controlled the Revenue. Between them, the Melvilles ruled Scotland in the first few months of the reign of William and Mary.

But powerful families provoke the opposition of powerful cabals. Melville had a pathological fear of his rivals, and he whined about them to William. "I know I may be probably misrepresented to Your Majesty by my enemies, or rather by yours, for I know none I have but whom I have procured by my endeavours to serve you." He believed that the barons of Scotland were for ever plotting against him, in their own drawing-rooms, in the dark chambers of Holyroodhouse, or the ante-rooms of Parliament House. And it is true that while most of them agreed that he was "a good and sober man", this did not prevent them from coveting his position and his influence. There was the dark-faced and lusty Marquis of Annandale, the fair-skinned Earl of Breadalbane who, said Macky, was as "cunning as a fox, wise as a serpent, slippery as an eel". The tenth Earl of Argyll, whose father and grandfather had died on the scaffold, was determined at all expense to keep his own head and trunk in one piece. There were the Dalrymples, father and son, the Viscount and Master of Stair, skilled lawyers, witty, wise and ambitious. They too had suffered from Stuart persecution, but the more they assured Melville of their friendship, the less he trusted them. There was the commoner William Carstares, "The cunningest, subtle dissembler in the world," said Macky, "with an air of sincerity, but a dangerous enemy because always hid." He hated the Jacobites, and distrusted men of title. Six years before, under torture, he had given evidence that sent an innocent man to the gallows in the Grassmarket, and much of his nature might be explained by this. He was the King's chaplain and unofficial adviser on Scottish affairs, and Scots visitors to the Court complained that they could not get an audience with William without first securing the approval of "Cardinald Carstares".

Beyond his fear of such men and others, Melville was also troubled by the activities of Jacobite sympathisers known as "The Killiecrankies" or "The Club". They met in Edinburgh coffeehouses to talk and plot treason, and at one time or another most great men in Scotland flirted with them.

Melville had one friend, or at least a man whom he felt he could trust, the amiable George MacKenzie, Viscount Tarbat, who was also John Hill's second hope for preferment. Between Melville and Tarbat there existed a peculiar alliance that seemed to be contradicted by their characters and their histories. Now aged sixty, Tarbat was still a handsome man, tall and aristocratic, "A gentleman of very polite learning and good parts," said Macky, "a great deal of wit, and is the pleasantest companion in the world." He had been one of the first members of the Royal Society, wrote pamphlets on literature, science and philosophy, and delighted in argument. He was lazy, fashionably foppish, and pretended to take politics lightly, but at heart he was a cynical trimmer. A serious misjudgement during the reign of Charles II nearly lost him his head, but he talked himself out of disaster, went into enforced retirement, and then charmed his way back into the Stuarts' favour. He became James II's chief minister in Scotland, where he was cordially detested and commonly believed to have falsified Parliamentary records. At the Revolution he was dismissed from office. He had the wit to see that the Stuarts were gone for ever, and he had no desire to become a shabby hanger-on in their Court at St. Germain. Since exile was not to his taste, he urbanely welcomed William and Mary, exercised his charm on Melville, and waited.

He did not wait long. Four months after the landing at Torbay, Melville obtained for him the King's exoneration. "We do further secure him," William wrote to Melville, "from all danger in his person or estate, notwithstanding any actings, writings, councils, speeches, or any crimes committed by him." But there was no suggestion of a post in the Government. This Tarbat had to earn, and the manner in which he might earn it brought him and Melville closer together in their strange alliance.

Reduced to its simplest form, William's attitude to Scotland was a determination that it should not become a recruiting ground for the Jacobites, and a second front for Louis XIV. As Stadholder, Captain-General and Admiral-General of the Netherlands, he had spent his life defending the Dutch against the French, and this was still the main purpose of his life, in which England, Scotland and Ireland could best serve him by supplying men and arms. Despite his Stuart mother and Stuart wife, he was Dutch in spirit and feeling, and the acquisition of three kingdoms meant less to him than the preservation of the United Netherlands. He had no wish to visit Scotland, and would not go there to be crowned. He had little real interest in the problems which the Revolution brought to the Scots Parliament: the proper administration of justice, the establishment of Presbyterianism by law, and the growing demand for union with the Parliament of England. He scarcely understood the deep division between the Gael and the English-speakers of the Lowlands. If he thought anything at all of the Highlanders, beyond those Europeanised members of his Scots Brigade, it was that they were troublesome savages. In this view he cannot be blamed, since it was shared by most of his Scots ministers.

Melville knew that his success as Secretary for Scotland depended on the speedy pacification of the Highlands. When he asked William for Tarbat's exoneration he suggested that the Mackenzie (who had undoubtedly put the idea into Melville's mind) should be sent to the Highlands with sufficient funds to bribe the chiefs into submission. "Since you think my Lord Tarbat can be serviceable in quieting the north," agreed William, "I hope you will encourage his going hither. A distribution of money among the Highlanders being thought the likeliest way to satisfy them, I have given orders for five or six thousand pounds to be sent for that purpose." Before Tarbat was able to ask the chiefs whether their good behaviour could be bought that cheaply they gathered at Dalcomera, fought at Killiecrankie, and were driven out of the burning streets of Dunkeld. And so the year passed into winter without any settlement being made, and with the certain risk of the clans rising again in the spring.

By March there were many voices, but no unanimous agreement, and William, concerned now with far more serious trouble in Ireland, would make no decision. Sir John Dalrymple, the Master of Stair, had already put into words what many were thinking, that if the sword must be used against the clans it would have been better employed in winter when the weather could have been the harsh ally of Law and Order. Far to the north by Inverness Duncan Forbes of Culloden, the son of Hill's old friend, drew up a Memorandum in favour of coercion by threat. He told the King that nine strong garrisons should be built in the Highlands, for garrisons "are proper for magazines in time of war, and will save the trouble of baggage horses, and are most proper for curbing thefts and depredations in time of Peace". The strongest fort, he said, should once more be at Inverlochy, and he could think of no better man to command it than John Hill, with his own regiment of twelve hundred men. This was obviously a loyal response to the old man's appeal for assistance.

Tarbat also urged the King to make use of Hill by sending him to treat with the chiefs. "I put it as an absolute condition [that he] be sent. He would do more for your service and to the enemy's detriment than all your forces have done in twelve months." It was Tarbat's (and therefore Melville's) opinion now that any money to be used in the Highlands should not be given in cash payments to the chiefs, but used to buy up the feudal superiorities of the great nobles, and thus "free the Highlanders from their worst financial and legal embarrasments".

Joining in the clamour of voices and the prodigal expenditure of ink there came the Earl of Breadalbane, whom few men trusted but all credited with a unique knowledge of Highland robbers and murderers, being descended from a long line of them himself. He had no original proposal. He blandly took Tarbat's, with this difference—he should treat with the chiefs, he should distribute the money among them. He had a plausible tongue, and he persuaded the King (who was now wondering if £5,000 were not too much) to give him a commission "to meet, treat and correspond with any of the Highlanders in order to reduce them to submission and obedience". But if few men in the Lowlands could be found to trust the Earl of Breadalbane there were even fewer in the Highlands, and for the moment his commission was no more than paper in his pocket. He had not, in any case, been sent the money, and felt no obligation to move until he was.

It may have occurred to John Hill, waiting anxiously in his Edinburgh lodgings, that affairs had been conducted with more wisdom and determination in his youth. Then the Protectorate had swept away the archaic rights of feudal landowners by one decree like the clean stroke of a sword. There had been no foolish talk of disarming the clans, and less of oaths of allegiance. The men responsible for bringing order and peace to the hills had been honest captains of horse and foot, serving God and the Commonwealth, not their own pockets. But if he could once more be sent to Lochaber, to talk with men like Lochiel, God's work might yet be done. The chiefs would not have forgotten him, nor lost their trust in him.

One other man in Scotland had no patience with the delay. Hugh Mackay of Scourie, still smarting under the defeat at Killiecrankie, agreed with Forbes of Culloden that the way to settle matters was to invade the Highlands in force, establish strong garrisons and let the clans see the strength of the King's power. The sooner this were done the better, and he could return to honest soldiering in Flanders. Though he was Highland, from the

4. "Be Earnest, Be Secret and Sudden, Be Quick"
Sir John Dalrymple, Master of Stair and later Earl of Stair.

3. "We'll Stall the Herds on Rannoch"
(OPPOSITE P. 96)

The edge of Rannoch Moor below the Great Herdsman of Etive, Glencoe on the right and Glen Etive to the left. From here the MacDonalds raided southward to Breadalbane.

west coast of Sutherland, long years abroad with the mercenaries of the Scots Brigade and a Dutch wife had left him with little affection for his fellow-countrymen at home. In his opinion they lacked zeal in religion and honesty in public life, "none minding sincerely and self-deniedly the common good". An uncomplicated man, he saw no paradox in his own military career when considered in the light of this judgement. He had received his British commission as a Major-General from James II, as a reward for his part in crushing the Monmouth Rebellion of 1685. Three years later he brought his Scots back to England with William of Orange, and helped to drive James from the throne in the name of the same Protestant cause for which Monmouth's men had died.

He steadfastly believed that rebellion could only be crushed by trailing a pike against it. For this reason the factions surrounding Tarbat, or Dalrymple, or Breadalbane regarded him as an enemy. That spring in Edinburgh Tarbat sought Mackay out, ostensibly to discuss their differences, and of the oddly matched pair it was probably the urbane Mackenzie who bent his back the farthest. He argued that the disaffection of the clans came less from their love for James or their distaste for William than from their own self-interest. This point Mackay would not have argued, but he cannot have thought it a good reason for buying their submission. Tarbat's purpose in the meeting may have been to secure the General's approval of the appointment of John Hill to Inverlochy, should a garrison to be set there. And in return he may have advised William to ask Mackay what measures he proposed for subduing the clans, for this is what the King shortly did.

Send an army, Mackay told him. Build forts, the strongest at Inverlochy. Supply them by sea with stores and provisions. Patrol the Isles and western waters with men-of-war. He got no acknowledgment from the King, and according to his Memoirs he thought of retiring in disgust. But, in the firm belief that God must have chosen him for some good work, despite his manifest unfittedness, he changed his mind and waited.

The King seemed to be agreeing with all factions, and deciding

in favour of none. Breadalbane had a qualified commission to
treat with the clans, and so did Tarbat. Cautious approval was
given to minor military moves, like the assault by the Argyll
Campbells upon the Macleans, and finally John Hill was given
something to do. It was not before time. "By staying to preserve
Belfast and the country round about it," Tarbat told the King,
"he so exhausted his small stock that he has not enough to sustain
him, suitable to his character, unless you order it". To those whom
he thought would serve him well, Tarbat was generously loyal.
Hill was given a small detachment of men and ordered to proceed
by Atholl to Inverness. He came again to Culloden House,
embraced Duncan Forbes and his brother John, and was happy.

Convinced that an army must be sent, Mackay began to plague
the Privy Council with demands for money. He wanted at least
£4,000, he said, to buy arms, provisions and materials to build a
fort. When he got no satisfactory reply, his anger exploded upon
the Earl of Portland, whom William had made the virtual governor of Scotland. Portland was a Dutchman, and one of his
qualifications for this post was the fact that as a handsome page of
honour he had shared William's bed when the Stadholder was
sick with smallpox, it being a belief of the age that an increase in
animal heat eased the suffering of the victim. William never
forgot this heroic service, nor should he have done, for the page
nearly died of the contagion. Portland's incredible wealth, his
gardens and his collection of birds and furniture, interested him
more than politics, and Mackay got little encouragement from
him. "This government," the General told him in bitter vale-
diction, "is capable of making Job lose patience with its delays and
haverings."

It was not the Government, it was the King. He was assembling
an army to defeat the forces which James had gathered in Ireland,
and the affairs of Scotland seemed of small importance at this
moment. And then, suddenly, the Jacobites themselves called his
hand.

Since February it had been known that Thomas Buchan, a
major-general in James's army, had been flitting in and out of the

Western Highlands, now with a few officers, now with supplies, urging the clans to rise again in the spring. In April he came again with Alexander Cannon and raised the Stuart standard. They gathered fifteen hundred men, but most of the chiefs took Lochiel's sober counsel and stayed at home. Some MacDonalds came out, honouring the bond they had signed at Blair, and MacIain's son Alasdair Og joined them with a party of Glencoe men.

Hugh Mackay stirred from his sick despair like a bear after winter. He sent Sir Thomas Livingstone against Buchan with twelve hundred horse and foot, and some levies from Clan Grant and Clan Mackay. The Jacobite leader was a brave and romantic fool. He made no proper reconnaissance, and posted too few sentinels. In the first dawn of May, while his army was still sleeping below the haughs of Cromdale, Livingstone's six troops of dragoons galloped out of the mist, swinging their swords. It was a rout, not a battle. Cannon escaped in his shirt, and Buchan without hat, coat or sword. Four hundred Highlanders were taken prisoner and the rest went home in disgust. Mackay's arguments had been proved. Why should one treat with or bribe an enemy that was perversely determined to resist? Seizing opportunity by the throat, he sent Captain Scipio Hill of Leven's Regiment to Chester (where William was preparing to embark for Ireland), with orders to impress upon the King the urgent need for an immediate invasion of the Highlands. The captain took with him a plan of the proposed fort at Inverlochy, and also maps of the country adjacent.

A day or so behind Scipio Hill, the Earl of Breadalbane also left Edinburgh for Chester in his big travelling-coach. Allied for the moment with Tarbat and Melville, he hoped to persuade the King that the policy of treating with the clans and buying off the malcontents might be more successful and less expensive than a campaign. But William was a skilled strategist and could appreciate a changed situation as well as Mackay. While he was in Ireland he wanted no trouble at his back. Scipio Hill returned to Scotland with orders for the Privy Council to supply Mackay with the men and supplies he needed to invade the Highlands and to build a new

Black Garrison at Inverlochy. Breadalbane went home to Loch Tay. He was able to wait.

Melville saw his once-bright future fading with William's growing lack of confidence in him. Since the beginning of the year he had been receiving nagging complaints and criticism from the King, and he had answered them more like a penitent child than a capable minister: "I must resolve to go over, if I can, what you were pleased to blame me for, in not being resolute enough, nor taking enough on me."

Mackay worked quickly. In addition to his advance on the central Highlands, he planned a diversion up the west coast. Captain Thomas Pottinger, commanding the sloops-of-war *Lamb* and *Dartmouth* at Greenock, was ordered to take aboard six hundred foot-soldiers under Major James Ferguson of the Cameronians, and to sail at once for a summer rendezvous with Mackay at Inverlochy. On his way, he and Ferguson were "to alarm the rebels' coasts, cut their communications with the islanders now in rebellion, and take away or burn all their boats, whether in the isles or along the coasts of the rebels on the firm land". Though they were not to make landings without certainty of success, they could help the Argyll Campbells in their assault on the Macleans of Mull. They were to take the surrender of any rebels who submitted, and to give them the full protection of Their Majesties King William and Queen Mary. They were also to behave themselves. "The said major shall have special care his men be kept under exact discipline both as soldiers and Christians, to hinder cursing and swearing, and all other unchristian and disorderly customs."

In Inverness, orders came to John Hill also. By the first week of July he was expected at Inverlochy, there to meet Mackay and the ships from Greenock. When the fort was built he would be its commander and the Governor of Lochaber once more, with power to accept the submission of the rebels. Few men can have been made so happy.

"I know many are against any gentle way of dealing"

IN THE second week of June, Hugh Mackay was once more in the saddle and in command of an army, but his temper was as hot and his patience as short as ever. There had been weeks of exasperating delay before his six thousand horse and foot could be gathered at Perth. He had discovered that squeezing £4,000 from a penny-pinching King might take longer than getting approval for the expedition, and not having the time for it he asked Mammon to pay for God's work. In Glasgow to superintend the embarkation of some Danish cavalry for Ireland, he persuaded the magistrates and merchants of that city to furnish most of the stores and provisions he needed. In view of the Highlanders' winter marauding outside their gates, these gentlemen may have considered the money well lent, were they ever to see it again or not. Glasgow money had also helped to get Captain Pottinger away with the *Dartmouth*, the *Lamb*, and Ferguson's six hundred redcoats.

Mackay had then to decide on his own route to Inverlochy. He could, of course, have gone by sea, but he had no hope of getting the Privy Council's speedy approval for the armada this would have needed. Instead, he chose a swinging march through the heart of the Highlands, northward first to Braemar where he paused to breathe sullen fire over his shoulder at the Council. "May it please your Grace and Lordships," he wrote, knowing that the tone of his letters gave them no pleasure at all, "I find myself so straightened with the want of provisions that I must venture forward before I have the assurance of any of our victuallers being about." This, he said, with sarcastic contempt for the ignorance of civilians, was somewhat contrary to the maxims of war. He had laboured hard to get this army on the march and now, because of the delays caused by others, he had less than two months' fair weather in which to do all that should be done. But he trusted in God's providence. Knowing how hot and then how cold a government's enthusiasm could blow in war, he entreated the Council not to recall him before his work was done.

His drummers beat the Assembly and he moved on, northward and eastward from Braemar to chastise some rebels in Strathdon, and then westward and northward to the valley of the Spey. Here he was joined by Livingstone's command, and by a flustered John Hill whom Livingstone had called from Inverness at less than a day's notice. The old man was irritated by this haste. He had been given no time to equip himself properly, nothing but his cloak and the earth to keep him warm at night, and he thought that by now someone should have sent him the £400 he had spent from his own pocket in the defence of Belfast. But he was quickly warmed by Mackay's civil and kindly welcome.

The General now drove his army south-westward up the Spey to Dalwhinnie in the braes of Badenoch. Three days march away, over the shoulder of Ben Alder, was his objective. On July 3 the soldiers came down to Loch Linnhe with pikes slanting, colours flowing, and the battalion drums beating bravely against the hills of Lochaber. There had been no serious resistance, though some clansmen had appeared on the heather in arms. "The Highlanders were all in Glen Roy," John Hill told Tarbat, "to stop the passes upon us, but we gave them the go-by in sending a party of Horse toward them, and in the meantime marching the Army through Glen Spean, so that we came without any injury, only some Highlanders that were in a hill shot at us, and our Highlanders went out and killed two of them."

Floating on Loch Linnhe under clean yards were the *Lamb*, the *Dartmouth*, and a merchantman full of meal sent by the Provost of Glasgow. Pottinger and Ferguson were in good spirits. They had burnt all the boats they could find belonging to the Macleans of Mull. Off the Isle of Skye they had a short but dignified correspondence with the MacDonald chief of Sleat before opening fire upon him. "Passing his house," said Pottinger, "I complimented the same with thirty or forty shots, sending the guards thereof to the hills." By springs and guys he then laid the *Lamb* inshore and broadside to MacDonald's house, "playing smartly upon the same for two or three hours with our best guns. Major Ferguson landed our men under the protection of my guns, burned both houses to the ground in the Highlanders' view, the whistling nine-pounders sending them scampering to the hills to overlook what they could not prevent." This, he thought, would stop the Laird of Sleat from "belching out defiance to authority and power". He was less pleased when Mackay demanded six of those whistling culverins, and six more from the merchantman, to man the proposed fort.

On a narrow spit by the mouth of the River Nevis, the green ruin of his old garrison must have filled John Hill with sad memories, though all else in Lochaber seemed unchanged. But Mackay grumbled about the site. In his experience a fort was built on high ground, and not commanded, as this was, by the rise of a hill. There was no time, however, to find a better position and on July 5 the work was started. Seven hundred clan levies, men of the Williamite Grants, Rosses and Menzies, were sent into the hills to keep the rebels away. The rest of the Army began to dig, helped by Pottinger's disgusted seamen and by workmen brought up from Glasgow in the merchantman. In the heavy heat they scooped out a deep, star-shaped ditch, palisading it with a *glacis* and *chemin couvert*. On the inner side of this ditch was to be raised a rampart of stone, earth and timber, twenty feet in height and cut with embrasures for those twelve naval guns. Around a levelled parade-ground inside the wall would be a bomb-proof magazine, kitchens, storehouses, offices, and dwelling-places and barracks for six officers and ninety-six private men. A larger garrison would have to lodge in tents and huts outside.

Mackay drove the workers relentlessly, and in eleven days he reported triumphantly to Edinburgh: "One would marvel how far our works have advanced. Any time next week I shall be ready to march and leave this fort not only palisaded round, but with most of the works at their full height." All this, he added with anger and pride, had been done by men who had nothing more than meal and water to sustain them, and now and then a little aqua vitae. Where was the meat they had been promised?

He had no illusions about the future, and mildly derided all talk of treaties and submissions. He advised Hill to burn the houses, lift the cattle and destroy the crops of all the clans within striking distance of the fort. This was the way of war as he had known it for thirty years. Hungry men did not sit down to besiege a well-fed garrison. But John Hill did not see this as his duty. In his first report to Tarbat, written the day after he arrived, he said that he had already heard from John Stewart of Ardshiel, tutor to the young chief of Appin. Ardshiel was ready to treat, promising to give up Castle Stalker to the Campbells, should proper compensation be paid to Stewart pride. Hill had also sent word to his old friend in the fir-wood house at Achnacarry, hoping Lochiel would persuade the Glencoe and Keppoch MacDonalds to "take their young men off the heather". Though the Cameron would not come to Inverlochy, he sent a friendly message to Hill advising him to let it be known that he was ready to receive any Highland gentleman and his people who wished to submit to King William's clemency. This Hill did, sending some of the Grant and Menzies officers to the glens. But, he admitted to Tarbat, "I know many are against any gentle way of dealing".

He was remembering the old days under the Protectorate, when it was thought proper to leave a man his dignity and self-respect. He was remembering too, and this bitterly, that in those days he was given civil as well as military power over Lochaber, for the one was useless without the other. He was more deeply hurt than Mackay by the lack of supplies, since he was the one who would have to deal with the results of shortage. Most of the two thousand bolls of meal which the Glasgow ship had brought would be eaten by the Army before it left. There were no beds and no blankets, and even in summer the Highland nights could be bitterly cold. There were no pots, pans, kettles, platters or spoons. He asked for coals, for butter and candles. He asked for shoes and stockings. He asked for soap, telling the fastidious Tarbat that men in unwashed clothing made bad soldiers. He asked for "a minister, storekeeper, chirurgeon and two mates, gunner and mattrosses for twelve guns, and their pay afforded, and such as may be encouraging; for who will be willing to be banished here without some encouragement?" He needed such encouragement himself. With dignity, he asked again for the £400 owing to him, and did not get it. He reminded Tarbat that when he had last been Governor of Inverlochy he had received ten shillings a day in addition to his pay as Colonel. He thought a similar allowance should now be paid. "I hope it will be rather more than before, so I hope (if God permit) to merit it." As the years passed he would merit it. He would also learn that Lord Protectors were more grateful to their soldiers than were Kings.

Mackay supported Hill in the almost daily reports he sent to Edinburgh, hoping to prod the Privy Council into a sense of urgency. "I am resolved to leave this garrison in a posture of defence, to which the speedy arrival of planks, cannon and other materials would contribute much. Your Grace and Lordships would seriously mind the speedy supplying of this important post from the west, of such necessaries as I sent you a list of, given by Colonel Hill, otherwise all the pains and expenses men have been at may prove fruitless."

Across Loch Linnhe in the Corpach woods, or on the rise of the Ardgour braes, the Camerons and the Macleans watched the building of the fort. High on the drove road to Glencoe, MacIain's men looked down on the poppy-red battalions and listened to the sound of hammers, the voices of the English-speakers, the beating of drums at dawn and noon and dusk. Now and then they fell upon the meagre supply-trains that tried to pass through Atholl and Badenoch, a brief, bloodless descent of flashing swords from which the baggage-men ran in panic, leaving their horses and packs behind. The constant threat of these raids made the supplying of the fort by sea inevitable. This had been realised from the beginning, but Mackay was angered by the knowledge that his

fine fort was hemmed in by robbers and thieves. To soothe his
pride and to get meat for his Army, he sent out patrols in force,
with orders to strip the land of cattle for twenty miles around.
None was found. The Camerons and MacDonalds had driven
their herds into the hills.

But one of the captains of the patrols, a Menzies or a Grant,
brought Hill some disquieting news which seemed to explain the
continued resistance of the clans and the failure of his gentle
approaches to them. Down by Loch Tay an old man who had
lost one move at Chester was plotting another. "I find my lord
Breadalbane hath broken all our measures with the Highlanders,"
Hill reported to Tarbat, "and hath been a means to keep them up
in arms to work out by that way some end of his own." It was
the beginning of Hill's distrust and dislike of the clever fox of
Glenorchy. But he was determined to persevere. "I shall pursue
my former methods," he said, this time in a letter to Melville, "in
case any of the Highlanders comply, though at present they seem
more sturdy than before; for I know the methods of another
nature will hardly ever do the work, nor can the arms of this
garrison reach all over the Highlands."

It was as well that Mackay was going, for he and Hill would
soon have quarrelled violently. Mackay was angry enough. He
was faced by a near-revolt in one of his battalions, the God-
fearing Cameronians of the Earl of Angus's Foot. They had been
told that they would remain as part of Inverlochy's permanent
garrison, and they had not liked the news at all. To Mackay's
disgust, the strongest protest came from the officers and from a
windy-mouthed preacher who should have been concerned with
the soldiers' eternal destination, not their present disposition.
Mackay handed the whole matter over to the Privy Council,
advising their Lordships to write to the lieutenant-colonel of the
Cameronians, telling him that their particular confidence in the
regiment was the reason why it had been chosen for the garrison.
It would not necessarily be true, but by such small vanities are
soldiers persuaded to do their duty.

On July 16, two days before he marched his army away,

Mackay appointed a deputy-governor to Hill, Robert Menzies, first son of Sir Alexander Menzies of that Ilk, Laird of Weem and Chief of Clan Menzies. Hill was disappointed, though he did not dislike this round-faced, hawk-nosed boy with the gentle mouth and black eyes. He believed it unwise to put any Highlander in such a responsible position, and his doubts were strengthened by the fact that Clan Menzies was divided in its loyalty. Though Robert Menzies had led a hundred of his father's people against Dundee, fighting well on the right wing of Mackay's army at Killiecrankie, others of the clan had come out more readily for the Jacobites. Mackay would have no argument. He told Hill that Menzies's Independent Company* could help with the building of the fort, and Hill must have bitten on his tongue at the bizarre thought of Highlanders working obediently with axe and spade. But if his own pride were wounded he kept the pain to himself when Mackay said that Menzies would be a good man to treat with the clans, being of their blood, tongue and manner. Perhaps the General was joking, for the same could be said of him.

On the eighteenth day of July, Mackay marched away. His army moved by battalions up the Great Glen to Glen Spean, making a fine show with its colours and drums. To Hill's chagrin, the troops left behind were almost all Highlanders—ten Independent Companies from Clan Grant and Clan Menzies, and four companies of Campbells from the Earl of Argyll's Regiment. The only Lowland regulars were two hundred and fifty Cameronians, whose chaplain began to complain about his exile before the rearguard of Mackay's dragoons had ridden out of sight. But the General had been in no mood to listen to Hill's protests. The news from beyond the mountains had been mixed and discouraging. Though William had defeated James on the River Boyne and was now laying siege to Limerick, a French fleet had beaten the English and Dutch off Beachy Head, and there were wild rumours of invasion.

* The first of the Independent Companies of Highlanders raised by the British Government, and thus a forerunner of the 42nd Regiment, Royal Highlanders, The Black Watch.

At least, Hill consoled himself, Mackay's constant badgering of the Privy Council had produced some results. There was another merchantman from Glasgow anchored off the Nevis, with her hold full of meal. The garrison now had fifty fat cows, eight barrels of herring, and a good supply of aqua vitae as morale and medicine. There was £500 Sterling in the Governor's chest, and that might placate the grumbling Cameronians. Mackay had also promised to send coats, shoes, breeches and stockings, and plaids to keep the men warm in the harsh winter coming. "A garrison," he said, "ought to be kept in good humour, and capable to serve well."

He might have added that it should be supplied with green vegetables and a good physician. Most of the thousand men whom Hill commanded were weak with the bloody flux, and a graveyard had already been started on the shore of the loch.

"That God may have glory, his Cause carried on"

THE HIGHLAND summer passed into autumn, brown shawls of
bracken on the mountains, oak leaves and elder in yellow bands
along the shores of Ardgour. On some days there were chill mists
from dawn until dusk. On others, a single sunlit hill glowed in-
candescently against a sky of thunder-clouds. The fort grew, its
embrasures finished and mounted, the greatest guns pointing
across the black water of the loch. But there was a serious shortage
of timber and canvas, and as the nights became colder Hill knew
that many of his men would be forced to lie in the open until
well into winter, unless he could persuade them to build crude
huts of turf. Their strength and morale were low. There was too
much aqua vitae, and although the soldiers and workmen had a
taste for the spirit, they were unwilling to take it in lieu of pay.
They were ready to mutiny over this one issue alone, Hill told
Melville.

He was sick with disgust for the men of the Highland levies, and
particularly objected to the "brutishness" of the Grants. Some of
them, refused the freedom to pillage, had already gone home to
Strathspey, and those who remained under threat were either
sick, or sullen, or rebellious. Hill was grateful to one Highland
officer, a major of the Mackay companies, who managed to keep
his clansmen in order, even getting them to work now and then.
After his earlier doubts, the Colonel had also warmed toward
Robert Menzies, finding him now to be "an honest, well-affected
gentleman, and rationally governable". If the young man could
break his habit of taking leave now and then, to attend to his

father's affairs at Castle Weem, he would be worth recommending
for the lieutenant-colonelcy of Hill's Regiment of Foot, should the
King ever have the common sense and good grace to bring that
into being.

Rumours of a French invasion of England, which Hill considered palpably absurd, still sparked across the hills and kept some
young men out on the heather. They frightened the occasional
baggage-train that risked the overland route to Inverlochy, and
sometimes they appeared on the braes of Nevis above the fort,
the wind pulling at tartan, and the sun shining on steel. A day's
march away, Black Alasdair of Glengarry was giving hospitality
to Sir George Barclay, one of James's emissaries, and he had im-
pudently appointed some of Buchan's Irish soldiers as his house-
guards. But there had been no bloodshed and no serious acts of
hostility. "I am very peaceable hereabouts," reported Hill with
hopeful exaggeration, "a single man may go all over Lochaber
untouched." Although it would have been hard to find a single
man in a red coat ready to prove this claim, it was plain that the
rebel chiefs intended no violent acts of defiance. Hill knew that
they met frequently, in Glengarry's house or Lochiel's or Keppoch's, to weigh the value of resistance against the profit in submission. Now that Mackay's army was gone they were in no
danger, and Hill's little command was more an affront to their
pride than a threat to their property. Had they all been of one
mind and indifferent to the result, they could have gathered five
thousand men and driven the undisciplined garrison into Loch
Linnhe before the fort was finished. They could afford to wait,
they thought—for a French invasion and the return of James, or
for a treaty with William that allowed them the privilege of
breaking it when their honour demanded. Hill doggedly pursued
his policy of firmness and conciliation. He sent armed patrols into
the hills as a show of force, a hundred, two hundred, three hundred men with colours and drums. He let it be known that while
he was waiting for the chiefs' submission he was ready to give his
letter of protection to any of their gentry and tacksmen who were
willing to acknowledge the authority of King William and Queen

Mary. He told the common people that they could come to Inverlochy without fear of molestation. This was a shrewd move. From the women of the glens he bought badly needed butter and cheese, eggs, milk and beef.

Hill worked hard and without mercy for himself. His moods reflected the changing autumn weather. There were days of storm and gales when he was ill in body and sick at heart, desperately aware of the long and empty years he had lived. Then nothing pleased him. Then the Highlanders were "people without any principle of religion or honour, always ready to strike a blow without caring what they have promised". If the soldiers and workmen were rotting from dysentery it was their own ignorant fault. There was too little wood to build the barracks inside the fort, but were there enough materials the carpenters would still be all rogues, the seamen thieves, and the soldiers cowards. For all their righteous psalm-singing, the Cameronians were ready to break their oath and desert. Robert Menzies was spending too much time in Edinburgh or at Castle Weem, and without his presence the clansmen of his company drifted away southward in threes and fours. Most of the officers of the Grant levies had gone home before the leaves turned, abandoning their dispirited and idle men to their own fancies or the graveyard. When Mackay got this news from Hill, he exploded like a mine. He ordered Robert Menzies back to his duty, and said that if the Grant gentlemen did not return he would cashier them all. This threat does not seem to have troubled them, for few came back.

And then there were days of sun and colour, of heat steaming from the marshy ground outside the fort, and grey-lag geese winging lazily across the loch. Then he had a good word to write of his "parcel of rogues, and the Angus men who now carry well". Then some of the small gentry of Appin and Lochaber came in to accept his letters or protection. He welcomed them pleasantly, warmed by the sight of a face that recalled his youth. He was particularly delighted to see John MacDonald of Achtriachtan in Glencoe, for if MacIain's cousin were willing to live in peace the old wolf himself might be ready to submit before Christmas. The tacksmen came less in response to Hill's appeal than on the advice of John Stewart of Ardshiel, the guardian of Appin's chief and a sober man who also took the Governor's protection. The chiefs had no objection to this apparent defection. It did not commit them or their clans, and it saved the tacksmen from any harrying by Hill's patrols.

On one memorable day Coll MacDonald of Keppoch himself came to Inverlochy, a proud and arrogant young man with a great tail of gillies in scarlet and green tartan, one to hold the bridle of his garron, another his shield and sword, a third to carry him dry across a stream if he wished to protect his shoes and hose. "He speaks better than any Highlander I know," Hill told Duncan Forbes, "and is a pretty fellow, 'tis pity but he were honest." Honest or not, Coll of the Cows had some encouraging news. He made no promises of submission himself, and asked for no letter of protection, but he said that he and Lochiel might persuade the other rebel chiefs to submit "if they can be made to live". Hill understood what that meant, and he passed on the advice to the Privy Council. "If the King would cast a little largesse upon Lochiel (who rules all the rest), Glengarry and Maclean, who are low in the world, and the rest must do as they do; and the value of five or six thousand pounds would do the work and make them the King's true servants."

But Coll of Keppoch may only have been curious to see the fort, giving any reason to explain his visit. Iain Lom, his bard, said that day and night in heaven Clan Donald's dead were calling for vengeance upon King William and his true servants.

Before the first frosts came Hill was given his regiment. At his headquarters in Waterford the King signed a warrant for its establishment. It was to cost the Crown little, for it was to be mustered from the disbanded companies of Glencairn's and Kenmure's, the latter a battalion that had been the first to break before the clan charge at Killiecrankie. If Hill thought he was getting less than he deserved in a gift of mutinous and ill-disciplined men, he stomached his disappointment. He asked for lists of the officers, and he began to think of uniforms, of facings and equipment. The same dispatches brought him news that he had been granted 12*s.* a day in addition to his colonel's pay, and the grumbling preacher of the Cameronians had his mouth stopped by the promise of 5*s.* a day. There was no suggestion when this money might arrive, but Hill was a good commander and honestly ashamed of complaining about his own empty pockets when his men were so much in arrears. "He that lives as ill as I do," he told Forbes, "has need of some encouragement, but it's necessary at present that I live as ill as others."

October scattered to their glens the few clansmen who had remained with Buchan since the rout of Cromdale, and he was left on Glengarry's ground with his handful of homesick Irish. Glengarry made no secret about his guest, rightly feeling secure behind five hundred armed men of his clan and the black walls of his castle by Loch Oich. Lochiel sent Hill some fair messages of friendship, and also a gift of venison, and while this pleased the Governor he was disappointed that the Cameron had not come in to submit. The weather had changed. There were more storms on Loch Linnhe, and flurries of snow on the high braes. Hill fell into despair again, believing that he had failed. He would have been encouraged by Tarbat's report to Melville: "This I must say, Colonel Hill has been the instrument of breaking the Highland trouble, and breaking all the conjunctions and designs. He first persuaded them to make no opposition to the settling of the garrison, and after all the army was retired he so dealt with the clans, that all were big of them were forced to render themselves at his mercy." This was an overstatement. No great chief had placed himself upon Hill's mercy, but neither had any challenged him, and all those with influence, except Glengarry, had said they were willing to consider an acceptable treaty.

By November Hill was desperately ill. He lay in his thin tent within the walls of the fort, half blind from the soreness of his eyes, shivering feverishly, his weary mind confusing past and present. There was no proper physician to care for him, and only his obstinate spirit kept him alive. The Edinburgh News Letters reported him dying, then dead, then not yet dead but certain to be

before the end of the month. Melville was distressed by the suffering of this old man who had done more to pacify the Highlands
than all of Mackay's battalions, or the chattering on the benches
of the Estates. He sent a butt of sack to Inverlochy by the next ship
from Glasgow, and the thought as much as the wine put some
strength into Hill. "It came in good time," Tarbat told Melville,
"to the old man in very hard case."

Long before he was recovered, Hill went back to his work and
his writing-desk. There were letters to write to the chiefs, appeals
to their common sense and pride, each tactfully composed from
particular knowledge of their persons and their people. There was
his regiment, and his desire to have his "dear child" John Forbes as
his second-in-command. His hand, as he wrote, was unsteady.
"Please to pardon errors and excuse frailties," he begged Melville.
And then, as anger and concern gave him the power, the strokes
of his pen were strengthened. He wanted money for his garrison.
There wasn't twopence among all the subalterns in the command
and he had had to advance them a few pounds of his own to
bring them and their platoons to their duty. Meal was running
short again, and the supply-ship from Glasgow was overdue.
There was no fresh meat to be got, nothing but rotten flour,
water and aqua vitae. But he kept the carpenters at their work, and
he hoped to have all his men inside the walls of the fort, at least,
before the worst of winter.

The weather was cruel enough already. There was frost on the
men's clothes and hair at dawn. To breathe deeply was to feel a
knife in the lungs. Mist hung like ice above the water and there
was no sun and no sky. Money . . . money . . . all success depended
on money. He thought of his regiment, which had yet to march to
Inverlochy, and he thought of money again. "I hope that the time
is drawing near that money will be coming in; and without that,
if these men come up, they will all run away."

His fever returned, but he sat upon his thin pallet in his cloak
and continued to work at his reports and dispatches. In his letters
to Duncan Forbes he sometimes wrote as if he were still serving
the Protectorate, referring to the rebel clans as "malignants", a

word that Cromwell's men had given to the Royalists. His religious zeal became fiercer, an unconscious prophylactic. *God forgive all . . . that God may have glory, his Cause carried on . . . God is the searcher of all hearts and knows who are upright, that's a good man's satisfaction. . . .*

He recovered again, enough to stand on his feet and walk. He followed the carpenters when they went to work at first light, pitying them when the icy air glued the skin of their hands to axe and adze, but driving them without mercy. He could do nothing about the lack of good timber, except complain uselessly to Edinburgh. He had been promised fir and oak, and might have got it had someone thought of authorising payment. In the evenings he went back to his dispatches, telling the Council that he would be grateful to have his regiment here, whether it had been adequately equipped or not. He wanted them to be armed with firelocks, not matchlocks, for the men of Glencairn's and Kenmure's were mostly Highlanders, and such men despised anything but what they called trigger-guns. He was not happy to have a regiment of Highlanders, for he thought little of their ability to stand and give fire, but if they were all the King could give him, he must be content. It was a relief to turn from such dispatches and complaints to his letters to Duncan Forbes. The Laird was now in London, and using what influence he had with Court and Parliament on Hill's behalf. "God be thanked," said the old man, "that has put me into a friend's hands." He hoped that Forbes would find time to visit his daughters. If not, there was a friend, an old Commonwealth soldier who lived at the sign of the Still in Holborn Conduit, who would be grateful for news of Governor John Hill, once a major of Thomas Fitch's Regiment of Foot.

And another day, colder than the last, and so much work yet to be done. He wanted a boat, with sails or oars, about twenty tons in burden. A small culverin could be mounted in its bows, and with a platoon of soldiers aboard it could be used to patrol the coast of Appin, Lorn and Ardgour. He wanted smaller boats for fetching wood, the fuel his men badly needed. He got none of these sensible requirements, but he was confident that God would reward him in time.

December began with great storms and squalls of snow. No vessels came up Loch Linnhe from the sea. The supply ships full of meal waited at Greenock for kinder weather. The Privy Council approved a grant of money for Inverlochy, £1,000 to buy materials and supplies, and £10 a week to buy Hill and his officers candles and coal. But the money did not come. He was told that until his supplies reached him he could take what he wanted, beef, meal, timber and fuel, from the lands of those clans that had lately been in rebellion, Glencoe for example. But Hill could not do this, the proposal was foolish and impolitic. The most he did was to threaten some of the common people who lived by Loch Linnhe, saying he would quarter soldiers upon them if they did not cut peat for his fires.

If the Black Garrison at Inverlochy was given too little money and too little materials too rarely, it was at least given a distinctive name. The Council decided to call it Fort William. West of the ramparts there had grown up a wretched straggling town of turf huts, and this, by a Royal Charter signed at Kensington Palace, became the Royal Burgh and Barony of Maryburgh. Thus both monarchs were honoured by a half-built fort and a squalid row of hovels. The Charter was not without other ironies. It gave Hill the right to hold a weekly market "for all manner of bestial goods, commodities, merchandise, and trade whatsoever".

John Forbes, the younger brother of the Laird of Culloden, came to Fort William at the end of the year. After some tiresome petitioning he had been given a commission in Hill's Regiment, but only a captaincy, not the majority asked for. The Governor did his best to soothe the young man, promising him the grenadier company, the best in any foot battalion. Forbes had been in Edinburgh for some weeks, organising clothing and arms for the regiment, and he was in no good humour to find himself now on Loch Linnhe. He told his brother that while he liked John Hill, and would be grateful for the majority if ever it came, "as long as I have a good and honest heart, and am able to draw my sword, I am sure I may pretend without arrogance to earn my bread in a place more desirable than Lochaber".

To Hill's delight the young man brought with him the £1,000 promised by the Privy Council. The soldiers were delighted, too, since most of it was paid to them against their arrears. Forbes also brought a list of the officers whom it was proposed to commission in Hill's regiment. That night the Governor sat in the office that had been built for him, wrapped in his blue cloak, leaning his elbows on his writing-desk as he carefully studied the list. He was approaching his seventieth year, and for more than thirty of them he had been a Colonel in name only. Most regiments were commanded by men no older than his grandson would be, and his pride needed the greedy pleasure he got from these sheets of paper. But he considered each name carefully, searching his mind for a memory of the man behind it. This officer was a pretty man, he must have a company. This captain—what was his name, Dunbar?—was no soldier and had a bad reputation for drink, ill-humour and a troublesome wife. The surgeon of Kenmure's, he too was a pretty man and deserved the appointment. No regimental commander of William's army, or of many yet to come, can have been more concerned about the officers he was given. And not only the officers. The private sentinels, he noted, could not live in an outpost like this on sixpence a day only (less twopence withheld against their clothing). They should have a penny more, and he would demand it.

Just before Christmas the regiment itself arrived, marching down the brae from Ballachulish. When Hill first saw it he must have slammed many doors in his mind, shutting out memories of Oliver's foot-soldiers. These men were a rag-taggle, undisciplined mob, and would come close to breaking his heart in the months ahead. Many had deserted on the march up from the Lowlands, and were now being hunted through Stirlingshire and Dumbarton by sheriffs, magistrates and justices. The gaps had been filled by pressed men from the "brutish" Grant levies, and by some of Robert Menzies's protesting clansmen. They were semi-mutinous before they arrived, and when they saw the half-built barracks, the ice-covered marsh on which they were to live, the black hostility of the mountains, they boiled close to open rebellion. Hill closed his ears to the whining gabble of Gaelic and Lowland Scots, handed them over to selected NCO's, and prayed God to guide them in loyalty and obedience. But when the four companies of Cameronians left him, singing psalms of joy, he must have felt that for once he had asked too much of the Almighty.

He returned to his writing-desk, to the quiet night hours when the flame of his candle seemed frozen by the cold. He composed his report on his first six months at Inverlochy. The hills were quiet under snow. Buchan had gone to France at last, but Cannon was lurking somewhere in Badenoch. Some young gentry of the clans, smarting under their chiefs' inactivity wanted to go to France to serve in King Louis' army, and he thought it wise to give them passes and have them out of the way. It would be sensible, too, to give passes to those Popish priests who wished to leave. He had heard of another meeting of the rebel chiefs, and he believed that, with God's good grace, they would decide on submission in the spring. He had got most of the firelocks he wanted, and since there had been good winds from the south for some days he hoped that ships might soon bring him bread. All but a score of the Independent Company raised from Clan Ross had deserted, and these twenty Hill had dismissed, believing himself well rid of them.

He hoped that Tarbat would come to the Highlands to see things for himself, and thus be able to tell the King what was truth and what was falsehood. But Tarbat knew without coming, and he told the King:

"One thing all the clans desire which is as much to your advantage as theirs, which is that all these superiorities be bought from the Highland lords, so that [the chiefs] may hold their estates immediately of you; and having them as immediate vassals, keeping a little garrison in Lochaber, and a man of ability, being no Highlander, to be your lieutenant-governor there, you will indeed be master of the Highlands as ever King of Scotland was."

3

GREY JOHN AND THE MASTER

"The origin and principle instrument of all misfortunes"

THE HANDSOME face on the canvas is round and well fleshed, aloof in a frame of long grey curls. The eyes behind lowered lids are alert to paradox and hypocrisy, the lips firm and humorous. The body, thickening with middle age, is poised calmly on a turn, as if the man has halted to listen to a petition, a scrap of useful scandal, or news that the sky has fallen. It is the enduring likeness of Sir John Dalrymple, Master of Stair, murderer of Glencoe.

"I love not so many masters!" John Hill had once cried in a moment of frustrated despair. In January, 1691, Dalrymple became another of them, but one who would make all others his servants within the year, and himself the supreme ruler of Scotland under the Crown. A dispatch from The Hague, where Dalrymple was with the King, informed the Earl of Melville that henceforward he would share the Secretaryship with the Master. Melville felt the first giddy movement of his own inevitable fall. He had been expecting this for months, increasingly aware that he was failing to satisfy William, and he had complained like a fretful child. Tarbat lost patience with the ugly little man. "For God's sake," he said, "take no pets! Remember your King, your country, and your friends!" His King and country were causes Melville could recognise, but who were his friends? "I have lived with you in intimate friendship for many years," the elder Dalrymple once told him, "God knows I never had a distrust of your friendship or kindness." And the son had been equally disarming. "I am extremely troubled to understand these representations that have been made of my father and myself to your lordship, as if we were discontented." The good-intentioned and conscientious Secretary would have liked to believe such bland reassurances from men who, he was told, were plotting against him. The Dalrymples' many enemies were less charitable. Not having the strength or the courage for open opposition, they attacked by lampoon.

> That slippery Stair goes unstraight, stoops and high,
> Do like his neck turn his whole course awry.
> That trap, for public place, that Jacob's ladder . . .

The Dalrymples were new to the government of Scotland, though they had held land in the western shires since the 14th century, and they came to power as many did, by way of the Law. The wry-necked father, James, was one of the greatest jurists of his time, and a skilful politician whose loyalty to his conscience under Charles I, the Commonwealth and the Restoration had made him enemies on both sides of every issue. The most passionate of these had been the dead hero of Killiecrankie, John Graham of Claverhouse, Bloody Dundee, the persecutor of the Covenanting martyrs. With the support of the Privy Council, and the open assistance of the Duke of York, Dundee drove Sir James Dalrymple into exile. Six years later he returned, landing at Torbay with William of Orange. He was restored as Privy Councillor and President of the Court of Session, appointed Commissioner for the shire of Ayr in the Parliament of Scotland, and created Viscount Stair, Lord Glenluce and Stranraer.

Sir John Dalrymple the son, now known by the courtesy title of Master of Stair, was as resilient in politics as the father, almost as skilled in Law, and more inexorable in ambition. He chose to keep most of his early life in darkness, and to care little what the groping hands of his enemies pretended to find there. An explanation of his character and his success was sought in the supernatural arts his family was supposed to practise. His sister Sarah, who was plainly an epileptic, was said to be possessed by an evil spirit that could lift her over high walls. His mother, who was probably no more than an embittered shrew, was believed to be a witch, casting spells and spinning ruin even upon her own children. When her daughter Janet chose to marry an unsatisfactory suitor, Lady Dalrymple screamed "Ye may marry him, but sair shall ye repent it!" On the bridal night, so went the story, she locked bride and groom in their room. All night screams and groans kept the house awake, and when Lady Dalrymple surrendered the key in the morning the girl was dead on the bed, drenched with blood, and the groom was cackling insanely in a chimney-corner. The facts were more prosaic.★ Janet died of a natural illness two weeks after her marriage.

John Dalrymple was knighted when he was nineteen, and one reason for this early honour is given in a suspect defence of his character published after the Glencoe Massacre. This claimed that he and a friend, visitors to London, saved a man-of-war from destruction when the Dutch fleet came up the Medway, though how two young landsmen were able to do what seamen could not was not explained. He was twenty when he married Elizabeth Dundas, who may have been grateful for the alliance since her marriage value had been seriously depreciated. According to a report laid before the Privy Council, she had been the subject of abduction and "most violent and barbarous rape" by a disappointed lover. But she was the daughter of the Lord Clerk Register of Scotland, and a young law student like Dalrymple, about to be admitted a member of the Faculty of Advocates, could have been excused for believing that influence was more important than virginity. For that matter, Elizabeth's ravisher had also been an advocate. There were nine children of this amiable and happy marriage, and two of them were victims of the black violence popularly believed to be inseparable from the Dalrymples. The second son was accidentally shot by the first. Bishop Burnet, never content with a good story when it might still be improved, said that the elder child rode his horse over his brother's head. Another son, added Burnet with relish, poisoned himself with cantharides.

★ But Walter Scott thought enough of the story to use it in *The Bride of Lammermoor*.

This Gothic elaboration of fact would follow the Master to his own death-bed. It was gutter-hatred, but even men of his own class detested him with brutish passion. To the Jacobites he was evil incarnate. "He was the origin and principal instrument of all the misfortunes that befell either the King or the Kingdom of Scotland," wrote one of them, George Lockhart of Carnwath, "He was false and cruel, covetous and imperious, altogether destitute of the sacred ties of honour, loyalty, justice and gratitude, and lastly a man of very great parts else he could never have perpetrated so much wickedness."

This was a bizarre libel, but written with the understandable bitterness of a man who believed that Stair had betrayed Scotland and the Scots Parliament to the English. It should, perhaps, be balanced by an equally emotional encomium from one of the Master's friends. But there is not one to be found, even in the pamphlet which his brother published after Glencoe. The lazy contempt in Stair's eyes, his obvious self-satisfaction and self-reliance, his cold and intelligent ambition, invited no man's love. He wanted power, he secured power, and such single-minded men do not have friends, they buy allies and attract sycophants. Yet in society he was popular. His sense of humour was alert and incisive, his mockery deep with understanding. His small-talk was facetious, and he flattered others into believing that their gossip entertained him more than politics. But, like Tarbat at such times, he was a dissembler, and he fooled the normally astute Macky who said that "he made always a better companion than a statesman, being naturally very indolent". George Lockhart was more discerning. "Had a judgement of his inside been taken from his outside, he might well enough have passed for that of which he was the least." This could be a fitting epitaph on any successful statesman, and although he was dead when it was written, the Master might have been pleased by it.

His first notable appearance at the Bar was in 1681, as junior counsel in the defence of the ninth Earl of Argyll on a charge of treason. Though his advocacy did not help the Earl, his own talents were quickly recognised, not the least by his father's enemies. But he was no coward, and he was not frightened by Dundee's bright cuirass and bloody plume, or the harassing of his tenants by the Graham's troopers. Though his father fled to Holland, he remained. He was accused of obstructing Dundee's authority, and of exacting nominal fines only from those of his people who were charged with attending conventicles. Twice the persistent Dundee secured his arrest. He was thrown into the Tolbooth of Edinburgh, and released only when he had asked the King's forgiveness and paid a fine of £500. A year later, in the middle of a September night, Dundee's dragoons pulled him from his bed in the fine house of Newliston that had come to him with his wife's dowry. He was taken before the Privy Council where he boldly refused to give evidence against the Lord Chancellor, who was accused of leniency in his dealings with the Presbyterians. He was sent to the Tolbooth again, on foot as a common malefactor and escorted by a file of musketeers, and there he remained for three months until he raised a bail of £5,000. He was then conditionally liberated within the bounds of Edinburgh, and to those few men who kept him company he smiled, and said that he was suffering for the "original sin of my Presbyterian father".

When the restriction on his movements was lifted sixteen months later, he still did not join his father in Holland. He waited and he watched and he listened for a year. He was a more sensitive weathervane than most men of his time, and when he felt the first faint change in the political wind he went to London. In three months he was back in Edinburgh as King's Advocate. His fine of £500 had been repaid to him, and he had been given another £700 for his expenses in London and to compensate him for loss of employment. He brought with him the King's pardon for all crimes alleged against him, his father, his mother, his brothers and sisters. Included in this blanket remission was a pardon for his thirteen-year-old son, the innocent murderer of a brother.

He had been bought. For the price paid, James II expected him to urge the relaxation of the penal laws against Catholics. Dalrymple's own religious views were tolerant and expedient, the original sin of conviction was his father's. He probably believed that sectarian squabbles were an improper exercise for a logical mind, and bigotry an obvious offence to reason. But the Presbyterians did not forgive him, and their resentment hardened into contempt and hatred when, as Lord Advocate, he moved against the field-preachers and the conventicles on whose behalf his father had been exiled. Within a year he was Lord Justice Clerk in the Court of Justiciary, and Judge in the Court of Session. He was forty. His neck and jowls had thickened, his body coarsened, but he was still handsome. He wore the awesome vestment of impartial justice, and what lay behind his faint smile only he knew.

At the Revolution he abandoned James with no more apparent thought than he might have given to a change of mind at his wardrobe. Before any of his enemies could move against him, and isolate him as a committed servant of the Stuart, he was the dominant member of a Committee for the Settlement of the Kingdom, representing the Three Estates. For a brief while this committee was the only voice of Scotland, and it spoke with Dalrymple's tongue. His cold logic drove it to its final decision: that James had forfeited his right to the throne, that the Crown of Scotland should be offered to William and Mary.

In these days, too, the tap-root of his political life was momentarily exposed. He argued for and forced through a vote upon a Treaty of Union, whereby the Scots and English Parliaments might be merged into one. But the English were as yet indifferent to any further ties with a country that seemed to consist of psalm singers and savages, and where the Scots were not hostile they were mostly uncertain. The proposal was not a new one, and Dalrymple must have discussed and considered it many times. It was William who made it an issue. Plagued enough by one Parliament, he could not see why he should have to tolerate two in one kingdom.

In the beginning Dalrymple may have become an advocate of Union in order to ingratiate himself with William, but it became in time his supreme objective, and one to which he dedicated the whole of his political life. All that opposed or delayed it, he attempted to destroy. If William wanted to pacify the Highlands because it was a strategic necessity in his war with France, Dalrymple knew that the English would never accept the Scots as civilised equals until their warring mountain tribes had been crushed. Like many Scotsmen in his own time, and for two centuries to come, he felt a nagging sense of inferiority to the English. Iain Lom MacDonald said they were greedy and gluttonous men, who would break the shafts and let the ox stray, who would put a halter on their country, who would treat it as a carrion bird.

On a May afternoon in 1689, Dalrymple was one of three Commissioners from the Convention of Estates who offered the Crown of Scotland to William and Mary, and administered the coronation oath. William had shown no desire to go to Edinburgh for this, and the undignified post-gallop of the Commissioners to London was the beginning of a long self-humiliation by those whom the Highlanders derisively called "the English-speakers". There was a brief ceremony in the Banqueting Hall of Whitehall, beneath the flesh-pink and sky-blue of Rubens' splendid ceiling. The asthmatic Dutch king sat under a rich canopy with his wife, facing the nobility and gentry of England. The clear spring sunlight fell through the tall windows, gently dusting the gold-and-scarlet cloth, and shining on the upheld blade of the Sword of State. The Earl of Argyll, as leader of the Commission, told the solemn King and smiling Queen that it had "pleased God to raise up Your Majesties to be the glorious instruments of relieving our religion, liberty and property from the very brink of ruin". Argyll could speak this with feeling, particularly the reference to property, and he inwardly hoped that the Revolution would bring him adequate compensation for the sack of his glens by the Atholl raiders.

He then read the oath, "distinctly word by word," said the News Sheets, "and their Majesties repeated it after him, holding up their right hands according to the custom of taking oaths in Scotland". It was read and repeated without interruption until Argyll reached the last clause:

We shall be careful to root out all heretics and enemies to the true worship of God that shall be convicted by the true Kirk of God of the foresaid crimes, out of our lands and empire of Scotland.

Here there was some solemn play-acting. William must have known the terms of the oath before this afternoon, and the objection he now raised was clearly designed to free him of responsibility for any future excesses of zeal on the part of the Scots. He could not, he said righteously, promise to be a persecutor. There was a pause, until Dalrymple accepted the cue. Neither the words of the oath nor the laws of Scotland, he said, put such an obligation upon the King. William nodded. "In that sense, then, I swear, and I desire you all, my lords and gentlemen to witness that I do." This careful public statement, the glances of understanding, may perhaps have been remembered two and a half years later when the King and Dalrymple were alone together in a room at Kensington Palace, discussing the extirpation of Glencoe.

Now that Scotland had a king again, the Convention of Estates pressed for permission to reconstitute itself as a Parliament. This was necessary, said a journalist's report of its proceedings, because "there can be no Treaty of Union without a Commission from King and Parliament, so that unless this meeting be turned into a Parliament, this Treaty must be for a long time delayed and postponed". It was necessary to recreate what it would be necessary to destroy.

Within a month of his adroit special pleading in the Banqueting Hall, Dalrymple was a Privy Councillor. A week later he was Lord Advocate again, representing the King in the new Parliament of Scotland. By the next year, when he became known as the Master of Stair upon his father's elevation to a viscountcy, he was potentially the most powerful man in the northern kingdom. He was feared by his colleagues in Holyroodhouse and Parliament Hall, and loathed by the extreme Presbyterians. The exiled Court at St. Germain excluded him from any amnesty should James return, and in Edinburgh coffee-houses Jacobite hot-heads of The Club threatened to pistol him some day as he went down Canongate in his coach. Not a mark of this was to be seen on his bland, calm face.

In January, 1691, when he became Joint Secretary of State for Scotland, nobody believed that such an ill-balanced partnership could last long, least of all the unhappy Melville. The Master was rarely in Scotland. He was at the King's elbow, in Kensington Palace or the great siege-camps of Flanders. He wrote smooth letters of instruction to Melville, telling him the King's will and the King's desire, and hinting now and then at the King's displeasure. "I do not see what ground of confidence the Jacobites in Scotland should have. . . . I hope the different measures and humours which always obstructed the alleys to do anything considerable, shall now, for this year, be entirely at the King's direction. . . ."

Any direction the King gave would now be on Stair's advice and conveyed to Melville by the Master. Having once enjoyed William's confidence, Melville had become the servant of a servant, the dog that is last kicked. Though he shared the Secretaryship, the responsibility for failure seemed still to be his, and the problem was the same as it had been when he took office—the pacifying of the rebel chiefs and the bringing of them to the oath of allegiance. Along the Highland Line, and in the garrisons of the glens, were seven troops of Horse and thirty-nine companies of Foot. Their pay alone was nearly £50,000 a year. In William's opinion, soldiers who were being paid should be campaigning, and if they were not they should either be disbanded or sent to Flanders where he could make proper use of them.

The King's first "direction" came from The Hague in February, where he was preparing his spring campaign against the French. It was ably composed, by Stair no doubt, and while it gave Melville and the Privy Council no clear indication of what action they should take, it presented William in a most favourable light —the wise and clement ruler.

We are willing to convince all our subjects of our affection and tenderness towards them by the evidence of an equal and moderate government, rather than to prosecute the failings of any with rigour, who are sensible of their errors, and return to their duty; but if any continue incorrigible or so foolish as to be imposed upon by vain suggestions to make their native country the stage of war and desolation, it will be your care to discover their designs and secure such persons that they be not in a capacity to ruin themselves and others.

By letters from Flanders, however, perhaps by a malicious note from Stair, Melville learned that the King was in a less charitable mood than this direction might suggest. His vanity had been stung by the derision of some princes of Europe who were asking why so great a captain, the opponent of the Sun King, was unable to crush a handful of half-naked savages. For hope and action, Melville looked to the hills, to the old man at Inverlochy.

And from Fort William there came word that John Hill was once again close to death.

Melville received this information from Sir Thomas Livingstone, a good-looking but mediocre soldier who had been raised from a colonel of dragoons to Commander-in-chief since the silly rout of Cromdale. His letter contained little regret for the valiant old governor of the Black Garrison. He told Melville that Hill "is feared to be dead before this time", and then went on to complain, in near hysteria, of the threat of rebellion in his army. Some troops of dragoons, in an attempt to get their arrears of pay, had locked up their trumpets and standards, imprisoned their officers, and entered into a seditious Bond of Association. Since there was a risk of this disaffection spreading to other units, equally angry about their pay, Livingstone was not much concerned about the health of an old man.

But John Hill would not let himself die. After a week or so, still feeble and light-headed, he pulled himself from his bed and went back to work. "God has the reins in his hands," he said once, "and it's He that governs the world." When the Almighty had such a heavy responsibility, men should not weaken. Since the arrival of his sorry regiment, he had had little time for treating with the clans. He was short of officers, and the men were quarrelsome and insubordinate. The morning drums, sounding the General, brought them to parade in untidy mobs, shouting for pay and food. And it was the same at Tap-to, with few good men and none willing to stand their turn at the night-watch. The Articles of War authorised fearsome punishments for the reluctant, rebellious or criminal soldier. His tongue could be bored by a hot iron, or his cheek branded. He could be shot, hanged, beheaded or burnt. He could be flogged, whipped naked through the gauntlet, or tied astride a wooden horse with bags of musket-balls at each ankle. Hill had been created by the Army, and Commonwealth officers had flogged their men as vigorously as any who followed them. But though he probably set up the halberts and flogged the thief, the deserter and the coward, Hill did his best to make a regiment out of his men by promise, persuasion and prayer, and by the superb example of his own devotion to duty.

There were daily problems and disappointments. The *Lamb* was long overdue with supplies from Greenock. The Duke of Gordon, feudal superior of the land on which the fort stood, declared that Hill should be held personally responsible for the woods destroyed, the peat taken and the moss cut by his soldiers. After their early and patriotic enthusiasm for the fort, the Glasgow merchants were now counting pennies. "Honest men are too few," said Hill sadly, "and those discouraged."

The coming of spring lifted his spirits and straightened the backs of his ragged garrison. Winds were warm, the air full of the sound of running water. Across the loch in Ardgour there was the astonishing vision of green leaf. Geese flew westward to the Isles, and the red deer moved on the braes below the fading snowline. There were other, less innocent movements. French men-of-war were reported off Skye, and the young men of the clans, said Hill, had begun to gather in small bodies. News had reached them of the surrender of Mons to Louis XIV and William's retreat, and this, Hill told Melville, had "pushed them up to a great degree, and that's much heightened by the malignants in Edinburgh and other places". Up the Great Glen, MacDonald of Glengarry was surrounding his castle with a ditch and palisades. When Livingstone heard of this he asked Hill to take some of the fort's cannon and blow Glengarry's impudent works to pieces. Hill ignored the fatuous suggestion.

He turned instead to his writing-desk, to firm letters of friendly advice, telling the chiefs that it was in their own good interest to submit while the King's grace held. He reminded the Council that he had not yet received one farthing of the pay and allowance promised him, beyond a grant of £100. He wondered what sort of men they were who acted like his enemies in denying him the just payment for his duty. "They say I am old, and would, I think, have me reduce all the Highlands myself." The passion, and the hurt to his pride tired him and his fever returned, died away, and returned again. Sometimes he was unable to move about the fort without an arm to lean upon. He had no deputy-governor yet, and no lieutenant-colonel now that young Menzies had left for good. A third of the garrison was always sick, and the grave-yard grew in the shadow of the ramparts.

In the second week of May he received another insane order from Livingstone. He was told to gather those men of his garrison who could march and fight, and to fall upon the clans who stubbornly refused to submit. Livingstone promised to send a strong detachment of foot to assist him. Hill did what he always did when his conscience or his good sense was outraged— nothing. He waited, and he hoped that someone in Edinburgh or Flanders would soon have the wit to restrain the Commander-in-chief.

While he waited, something happened to convince him that his way was best, and that in time his work would bear full fruit. On a bright Wednesday morning, all the gentry of Clan Cameron came to Inverlochy, with Lochiel's consent and to assure Hill that he would have no trouble from their people. The spring sun, washed by a drift of rain, shone on the tartan and the feathers, on muscled thighs and the steel of weapons. This was how it had been thirty-five years before. The Camerons made no promises of submission to William, or of acceptance of the oath, but their friendliness and their wish to live in peace delighted the old man. They drank his health, wished him well, left him gifts of meat from their chief, and then marched away. He looked southwards, wishing that MacIain would come in the same friendly manner.

But the old buff coat, the bristling horns of the white moustache were not seen at Inverlochy.

The Master of Stair stopped Livingstone before he could send his soldiers against the clans. From London he sent the Commander-in-chief a succession of tart, peremptory letters. "His Majesty ordered me to write to you not to meddle with them at present, for you know how little the Treasury can spare. . . . It is plain you are in a condition to raise the Highlanders who are at present quiet, and to give them a pretext to fall down and carry cattle from the Lowlands. . . . If it please God to give success to the projects to straighten France, then more may be thought fit to attempt upon the Highlanders. . . ."

Hill did not know that an empty Treasury and the success of French arms against William, not common sense and caution, had stopped that move to reduce the clans by force. But he knew that the Highlands might yet be kept quiet, with himself as the instrument for bringing all to submission and grace. His hopes were strengthened when Lochiel's men began to build a saw-mill and a corn-mill within two miles of the fort. This, he said, was scarcely evidence of hostility and disquiet. He had his little frigate, armed with eight small guns, to patrol the lochs and Isles, and it had met with no trouble. His men were looking more like soldiers, but the daily sick-roll kept steady, and deaths were as frequent as they were meaningless. If only he could have more food for their bellies, and a competent minister for their neglected souls.

At the beginning of June, in a long report to Melville, he confessed that he had not followed the strict letter of his orders in persuading some of the Highlanders to submit. If he had insisted on the surrender of all arms, he would have been given no more than "some old rusty trash". So he had not insisted. The oath of allegiance, he thought, was too much for Highlanders' pride to stomach.

I hope I have taken the better way, which is easier, viz., I sent them the form of a very strict oath, and that withal a draft of one much easier, which is never to take up arms against King William and Queen Mary and their Government, nor to suffer any of their friends, men, tenants and servants to take up arms; and to this oath most of Clan Cameron

have already sworn, and many of the MacDonalds in the Brae of Lochaber. More are coming in daily. . . .

He could not have pretended to himself that this sensible compromise would be accepted as enough by the Privy Council or
the King, but none could argue that it had not kept the hills
quiet. It was true that no chief had come to Fort William to take
any form of oath, but again it could not be said that this was
because they were stubbornly obstinate in spirit. "Lochiel sent me
word," explained Hill, "that he stood upon a point of honour with
his confederates that they should not accuse him as the first to
break the ice, but waits for some to come before him, or with
him, but saith he will not stir to rise in arms." It needed one chief
only, even the obdurate MacIain of Glencoe, to swear to Hill's
mild and considerate oath, and the others would follow, content
that their honour was safe. Of MacIain's eventual submission he
was daily hopeful. Most of the Glencoe tacksmen, with others of
Appin, had already been to see him, saying that they would
prefer to make what submission was necessary to the Earl of
Argyll, their feudal superior, and to this Hill had agreed.

All this had been done, he said, by gentle methods, to make the
Highlanders "sit quiet that the King's greater affairs may not be
interrupted, and that His Majesty may use some of the forces now
here where there is greater occasion". He was a good servant and
deserved a better master. He was kept short of food, supplies and
money. He was given a mob of rogues instead of a regiment. The
debts he had incurred on his country's behalf were churlishly
ignored, and his pay was not sent to him for eighteen months. He
fought death and despair to do his duty. The least reward that
could have been given him would have been to take his advice.
Had the King, the Privy Council, the Master of Stair and sundry
other great gentlemen left him alone to continue with his gentle
methods and artful compromise, he might have had all the Highlands at peace by the end of that summer.

But the Earl of Breadalbane was allowed to take a hand in the
game once more.

"Cunning as a fox, wise as a serpent, slippery as an eel"

He was a chief, MacCailein 'ic Dhonnachaidh, the son of Colin, son of Duncan. His clansmen called him Iain Glas, Grey John Campbell, eleventh Laird of Glenorchy, first Earl of Breadalbane, and sometime Earl of Caithness. After the Earl of Argyll, who was his nephew by marriage and with whom he shared a common ancestry, he was the most powerful man of his name, and the most ambitious. All his public and private actions, his marriages, his plotting and bargaining, dissimulation and cunning innocence, crocodile tears and surly spats of anger, were directed to one end: the leadership of Clan Campbell and a hand in the government of Scotland.

Though no one else liked him, or trusted him, his people gave him the unquestioning respect and loyalty due to a great *Ceanncinnidh*, their tribal chief and father. John Macky spoke for all others when he said that Breadalbane was "as cunning as a fox, wise as a serpent, slippery as an eel. No Government can trust him but where his private interest is in view. He knows neither honour nor religion but where they are mixed with interest, and then they serve as specious pretences. He plays the same game with the Williamites as he did with the Jacobites, viz., always on the side he can get most by, and will get all he can of both." This, like most of Macky's summations, is less than complete, and says nothing of Breadalbane's loyalty to his own gentry and people. But since he needed both to support his power and ambition, his feelings may not have been disinterested.

He was a bold-looking, impressive man, fair-skinned, thin-lipped below the prow of his nose, and Spanish in the gravity of his face and carriage. His body was robust and needed to be, for he put a tremendous strain upon it, and his constant fear of being left out of great events kept him on the move between his Highland castles, his house in Edinburgh, and his lodgings in London. During the first years of William's reign, except for one winter when he thought it wiser and safer to remain in the mountains, he was never in one place for longer than a few weeks. His chamberlain on Loch Tayside and his law-agent in Edinburgh, both Highland gentlemen of his name and following, were daily busy with letters to and from their chief and master. These could be concerned as much with the sale of cattle as the signing of a treaty.

Some great men can best be seen in perspective, down the avenue of their ancestry. The history of the lairds of Glenorchy was as violent, as bloody, and as savagely bizarre as any in the Highlands. Their land of Breadalbane was a thick knot of mountains in western Perthshire, tied to Loch Tay by the green strands of Glen Lyon, Glen Lochay and Glen Dochart. For centuries it was almost impregnable. Safe within its rock walls and many castles, the lairds defied their enemies, their neighbours, and the Crown. Only the Lochaber Men, coming over the Pass of Meran at night, or raiding from the east when the Campbell gentry had whisky in their heads, broke into it without opposition.

The first Laird was Black Colin Campbell, a crusader and a Knight of Saint John, who came from the west in the middle of the 15th century. His father, Sir Duncan Campbell,* Lord of Lochow, was the progenitor of both great families of the name. To the descendants of his first son he left the lands of Argyll, and to Black Colin he gave Glen Orchy, a narrow, twisting valley that runs south-westward from Rannoch Moor and the mountains of Breadalbane to Loch Awe. From the ruins of a MacGregor keep on the shore of the loch, Black Colin built the great castle of Kilchurn, using the smiths of Clan MacNab to make its iron bars and gate. He garrisoned it with wild kerns to subdue and drive Clan Gregor from Glen Orchy and Glen Strae. For all his

* Hence the designation of the Glenorchy and Breadalbane chiefs—Mac-Cailein 'ic Dhonnachaidh, son of Colin son of Duncan.

pious crusade and noble knighthood, he lopped off MacGregor heads as indifferently as he might brush away a fly, and thus began his family's merciless feud with the Gregarach. He was greedy for land, and jealous of his nephew who not only held a greater property in Argyll but was soon an earl as well. Black Colin could move eastward only, into Breadalbane, and there he became a tenant vassal of the Laird of Menzies. His son, Duncan, extended the tenancy by guile and threat until he made a more memorable contribution to Scotland's bloody history by dying with her King and most of her nobility at Flodden. Those who succeeded him—all known as "the Grey" or "the Black"—also did what they could to fulfil Black Colin's ambition by acquiring more holdings on the Menzies' land.

To be vassals only, however, was irksome to their pride. Toward the end of the 16th century, Grey Colin, the Sixth Laird, used his influence and his talent for bullying to make himself master in fact of what his forbears had held in feu. He enlisted a small army of broken men, many of them Stewarts from Appin, to harry the lands of Clan Menzies, to burn out the MacGregors, and to hang any Lochaber man who came over Glen Meran. One of them, called James the Grizzled, was said to be able to shoot an arrow from one side of Loch Tay to the other. Unable to resist these mercenaries by force, the Menzies chief complained to Edinburgh. He said that Grey Colin's men had stolen his cattle, killed his clansmen, burnt his houses, and vilely oppressed and imprisoned a tailor of Clan Menzies, "a common man, ready to work for every person for his living". A Crown Messenger, sent to investigate these charges, never returned from Loch Tay, and was generally believed to have abandoned his commission at the end of a rope outside Grey Colin's castle. When the Laird was ordered to appear before the Privy Council, he sent his son Duncan instead, saying that he would have come himself but for "shortness of time". Had the Council beheaded Duncan in his place, he might well have been grateful. He hated the boy and wished to disinherit him, a dangerous precedent in feudal custom that was only avoided by the disapproval of the Breadalbane

gentry and the intervention of the Earl of Argyll. Unable to see
what it could do about him, the Council lamely asked the old
rogue to behave himself. So he hanged no one, stole nothing and
burnt nothing belonging to the Menzies for some months, using
the time more profitably in persuading his friend the Earl of
Morton, Regent of Scotland, to grant him full control of his
holdings in Breadalbane.

Black Duncan of the Cowl, seventh Laird of Glenorchy,
succeeded Grey Colin in 1583. He drove out the brother whom his
father had favoured, and defrauded him of his inheritance. In the
following forty-eight years he made himself one of the strongest
and most feared men in the Western Highlands. He was a
shrewd, swarthy man with short black curls and a square-cut
beard *à la Henri Quatre*. His brow was an angry scowl, his nose
thick and brutish, but his eyes sparkled with impish intelligence.
He dressed himself richly in black clothes and rode like a centaur.
Though he was a robber baron, cast from the same mould as his
ancestors, he kept his windows open to the south and was a great
improver and builder, scattering Breadalbane with round towers
and solid keeps. The walls of Finlarig Castle, guarding Glen
Lochay and Glen Dochart at the western end of Loch Tay, were
six feet thick and surrounded by a deep moat. Above its fireplace
he put the arms of James VI whom he generously treated as his
equal. In the dungeon was a comprehensive collection of chains,
heading-axes, racks, screws and branding-irons. Beyond the moat
was an oak-tree from which he hanged those common people
who offended him. For the removal of men of gentler birth,
there was a heading-block and pit.

At Balloch, on the eastern end of Loch Tay, he built another
castle, once he had driven the MacGregors from the land. He
built a third at Achallader by the mouth of Glen Orchy, and here
too he had first to get rid of the owners. They were Fletchers, and
so far they had managed to hold their own against the Campbells,
but in Black Duncan there was a distillation of all Glenorchy guile.
Riding by Achallader one day with his attendants, he ordered an
English servant to pasture his horse in a patch of corn above the

Fletchers' house. The simple man did as he was told and, having no Gaelic, did not understand when the Fletchers warned him that he would be shot if he did not remove himself and the horse from the corn. So he was shot. Up came Black Duncan then, much concerned by the sight of the dead man and by the fact that the Fletcher laird would lose his own life when the Crown heard of the killing. He advised Fletcher to flee to France, but the man was afraid that his family would still forfeit the property to the King. That, said Black Duncan, was really no problem. He would purchase the land, by a mock deed, of course, and without the tiresome inconvenience of paying for it. When the King's pardon had been secured, he would return it. The laird signed the deed, and the Fletchers never recovered Achallader.

In softer moods, Black Duncan of the Cowl planted fine parks of timber, and some of his chestnuts still stood about Finlarig a hundred years ago. He introduced rabbits and the fallow deer to Perthshire, and he bred fine horses. He frothed in a mad rage for weeks when the MacGregors killed forty of his brood mares, and a stallion that had been given to him by Prince Henry. With Letters of Fire and Sword he drove Clan Gregor out of Breadalbane to the isles of Loch Rannoch, and he had no patience with his cousins, the lairds of Glenlyon, who not only tolerated the MacGregors but occasionally married them.

The Glenorchy chiefs who followed Black Duncan, when he finally and reluctantly died in 1631, were poor figures compared with their ancestors. The eighth, ninth and tenth lairds did little more than spend the money and mortgage the estates their predecessors had spent so much of their own time and others' blood in acquiring. Thus Iain Glas, who was to be the eleventh in line, comes almost as a reassurance. He was born in 1635, and he was five years old when his father succeeded to an empty treasury and emptier lands that were now a sporting-ground for the men of Glencoe and Keppoch. He was ten when the Lochaber Men fought the Campbells on Sron a' Chlachain, and twenty when they ravaged Glen Lyon for the first time. "*Conquer, and keep things conquered!*" had been the Glenorchy motto since the days of

Black Colin the Crusader, but Iain Glas's father had no spirit or strength for anything but marrying one wife after another. Even so, his victories here were considerable. He had twenty-seven children. Though most of these customarily and mercifully died before they could involve the Laird in any more expense than the services of a wet-nurse and a leech, those who did survive were a burden on an empty exchequer.

As seems to have been the way with the Glenorchy men, the tenth laird had no love or hope for his first son. And since he had no money, either, Iain Glas went to London to make a fortune of his own. He did this as quickly as possible, by marrying, at the age of 22, Lady Mary Rich, the daughter of the first Earl of Holland. "I have written several times to your honour," he told his indifferent father, who had marital problems of his own, "and have had no return concerning my intended marriage, which now by the Lord's blessing I have accomplished." A dowry of £10,000 Sterling may have inspired the Laird's blessing too, but nobody thought the match a wise one. This was the Commonwealth, and Lady Mary's first husband had been executed for his loyalty to Charles II. Iain Glas's strongest sense, however, was an uncanny prescience. The King would enjoy his own again, and those who had suffered most under Cromwell might profit best from the Restoration when it came. Until that happy day he took his wife back to Breadalbane. He travelled sensibly, without wasting any of the dowry on coaches and horses. He had two little garrons sent from Loch Tayside, mounted himself and his bride on one, loaded his baggage on the other, and set out thus. At the tail of the ponies trotted two fully armed Highlanders.

Once back in Breadalbane he took the management of the estates out of his father's hands. The Laird complained bitterly, telling his kinsmen that he was King David betrayed by Absalom.

If the Restoration did not bring Iain Glas the prosperity he had hoped from his marriage, his wife solved the difficulty by dying and leaving him free to look elsewhere. But before he chose another, and richer wife, he became a warrior. Far to the north of Scotland the valley of Strathnaver was invaded by twelve hundred men from Caithness, led by a Sinclair of Dunbeath. They burned and robbed and killed without much opposition until the Earl of Caithness, himself a Sinclair and the chief of the clan, asked for the Privy Council's help in subduing his rebellious subject. Iain Glas was now thirty, and had had no experience at all of warfare, but he offered to bring out his father's people and to lead any expedition that might be sent to Sutherland. Satisfied with "the ability and fidelity of John Campbell younger of Glenorchy", the Council agreeably gave him a general's commission without any troublesome insistence that he should rise to it from a lieutenancy. He was also given three hundred men of the King's Guard and some companies of Linlithgow's Regiment of Foot. The campaign was brief and unspectacular, and put no strain on Iain Glas's rudimentary military knowledge. He took Dunbeath Castle without difficulty, the laird having already abandoned it, burnt a few houses, destroyed crops, and drove the rebels into the hills.

Far more important to him than an empty victory at arms was his discovery that the Earl of Caithness was in debt and harried by dunning creditors. Though the bottom of the Glenorchy exchequer was not yet covered, Iain Glas's good management had at least accumulated enough money for a profitable investment. He agreed to pay the childless Earl a life-annuity of £1,000. In return, and upon the Earl's death, he would receive the titles, estates and heritable jurisdictions of the earldom. This one-sided bargain cost him no more than £4,000, for the Earl obligingly quit the world four years later, in 1672. Iain Glas posted in haste to London where he placed the attested conveyance before the King. Charles II was probably amused by the impudent effrontery of the claim, and he amiably approved it, adding a title or two besides. The untitled heir to a Highland laird became Earl of Caithness, Viscount Breadalbane, Lord St. Clair of Berridale and Glenorchy, with the right to assume the name and arms of Sinclair. On Loch Tayside, King David was at last filled with joy for the belated success of his erring Absalom.

Eleven months later, Iain Glas married the Earl's widow. She was a Campbell too, a sister of the ninth Earl of Argyll, and by this presumably loveless match he was saved the trouble of paying her the annual allowance that was due from the Caithness estate.

At the age of forty-three Iain Glas now had rank and position to fit the ponderous dignity of his frame and the gravity of his expression. The rents of his new lands flowed down to pay the debts that still saddled his father's, to bring the comforts of soft living to Balloch and Finlarig. *Or Ghallaibh air bòrd Bhealaich*, said the people of Breadalbane. (The gold of Caithness is on the table at Balloch.) And then, out of Caithness to spoil the pleasure came George Sinclair of Keiss, who not only disputed the Campbell's right to the earldom, but raised an army to secure it for himself. With the grudging permission of the Privy Council, Iain Glas sent the fiery cross about Loch Tay. Seven hundred of those who gathered at Balloch were chosen, only the best and the strongest, only those, it was said, who could leap fully armed across the length of a double plaid. The Earl gave the command of them to his cousin, Robert Campbell of Glenlyon, a spendthrift drinking-man who was already on his way to irresponsible bankruptcy. He marched his fine regiment away to the music of a new air composed by Finlay MacIvor, the Glenlyon piper. It jeered at the Caithness men for their custom of wearing breeches and not the kilt.

> Carles of the breeks,
> The padded coats and breeks,
> It's time your were rising.
> The bold band from the cold bens
> Is marching to Caithness
> To put the Northmen in danger.

By Allt-na-Meirleach in Caithness the Campbells and the Sinclairs fought one of the last clan battles of the Highlands, but the bold band from the bens did not rely on their valour alone. They allowed their baggage-train, loaded with whisky, to fall into the hands of the carles with the breeks, and when the Sinclairs were half-sodden with drink the Campbells fell upon them and routed them. When the squalid slaughter was over, Glenlyon quartered his men on Caithness and collected rents and taxes for his chief.

Sinclair of Keiss had escaped from Allt-na-Meirleach, and he took his complaints and claims to Court in London. He was supported by the Privy Council of Scotland, and the King, who was a fair man if occasionally impulsive, annulled the patent of earldom in favour of John Campbell and gave it to Sinclair. But since he saw no sense in losing one friend by enlisting another, he compensated Iain Glas handsomely, making him Earl of Breadalbane and Holland, Viscount of Tay and Paintland, Lord Glenorchie, Benderaloch, Ormelie and Wick in the Peerage of Scotland.

Iain Glas, like most of his ancestors, disliked his first son intensely and saw no reason why the boy should inherit the advantages of so much wit, foresight and brash impudence. He persuaded the King to grant him the right to nominate another of his sons, explaining that Duncan, the first, was feeble-minded and easily deceived through the "facility of his nature and the want of knowledge". But Breadalbane's disgust was not so much with the boy's state of mind as his independence of spirit. Against his father's orders, Duncan had eloped with Marjorie Campbell of Lawers, dressed as a wandering fiddler.*

In 1686, when his father died, the Earl became master of Breadalbane in fact as well as name. He was fifty-one, and by hard work and cunning he had removed the galling harness of debt from the estates. Beyond Duncan the eloper, and John the second son who was now his designated heir, he had many other children by both wives, and for the first time in four generations there was money to support the Glenorchy family's vanities and pretensions. Politically, Breadalbane's activities were as yet unequivocal. His splendid titles and privileges had come from the Stuarts, and he served Charles II and James II without question. He had sent fifteen hundred men to join the Highland Host, complaining only that while they were away in the Lowlands his glens had been sorely molested by raiders from Glencoe and Keppoch. He had

* Two hundred years later one of his descendants came forward to claim the disputed titles of Breadalbane.

kept himself and his people out of the ninth Earl of Argyll's rising in 1685, although several years earlier he had put his name to a bond promising upon his honour to help "in all things tending to the goodwill and standing of the said Earl's noble and ancient family whereof I am descended". Equally circumspect, and not wishing to antagonise a clan he hoped one day to lead, he had allowed none of his dependants to join in the Atholl Raid on Argyllshire.

The Revolution was the first great challenge to his loyalties, and he answered it by waiting, "living in retirement" he called it, in his castles on Loch Tay and Loch Awe. He was also afraid. Moments like this were dangerous for a man who was disliked and distrusted by all but his own kinsmen. When Dundee called him to the gathering at Dalcomera he stayed away, pleading an attack of gout, an affliction which providentially immobilised all his people too. Neither did he send swordsmen to help Hugh Mackay. "The Government expects no service from me," he told his chamberlain, Alexander Campbell of Barcaldine, "nor thanks me if I do any. Therefore cause my men preserve themselves and meddle with neither side, as they will be answerable." When the Lochaber men savaged Glenlyon and burned Achallader he raged inwardly, remembering MacIain's part with particular and venomous hatred. Yet he was determined to stomach even this humiliation for the moment, and when some of his Glen Orchy tenants made a retaliatory raid on Glencoe, stealing the cattle of a Mary MacDonald from their winter grazing by the Meeting of the Waters, he ordered Barcaldine to pay her £160 Scots in compensation. The MacDonalds' certain astonishment went unrecorded.

In the spring of 1690, Breadalbane emerged from his shell of non-involvement to play his peculiar double-game. To William he presented himself as an honest arbitrator, the only man in the Highlands who could talk and treat with the clans in a language they understood. It was probably at this time that he drew up and submitted to William his *Proposals Concerning the Highlanders*, a brief but masterly summary of the military strength of the clans and the use which could be made of them by a shrewd monarch. It was the first suggestion* of making the Highlands a reservoir of blood, to be profitably spent in Britain's wars, and during the next century and a half successive Parliaments at Westminster would drain the source until it was exhausted. "Your Majesty has these forces without any charge," Breadalbane told William, "except for a few officers, and that only when employed, and it may be asserted that there cannot be better militiamen than they are. In case Your Majesty, at any time, think it fit to employ a regiment of Highlanders abroad, they may be detached out of this body of men." He listed the names of the chiefs who, he thought, could or would contribute men to such a force. Missing from the list were the names of Coll MacDonald of Keppoch and Alasdair MacDonald of Glencoe.

He followed these proposals with pressing requests that he be allowed to treat with the rebel chiefs and bring them to proper allegiance, borrowing what he wished when he wished from Tarbat's scheme. Though he was given a commission to treat, the King's lack of decision, and the chiefs' indifference, meant that little could be done. He made his leisurely journey to Chester in the tail of Scipio Hill. Then came Cromdale and Mackay's march on Inverlochy. Breadalbane felt a chill in the air, and he went home to Loch Tay, to worry about the cutting of timber and the sale of cattle, the damming of water and the frustrating financial problems of his nephew, Robert Campbell of Glenlyon. In September he moved down Glen Orchy to winter in Kilchurn Castle, below the brown shoulder of Ben Cruachan. There he got a letter from the Duke of Hamilton, President of the Privy Council, inviting him to Edinburgh to discuss plans for bringing

---

* Earlier than similar proposals made in 1738 by Duncan Forbes, fifth of Culloden. Earlier, too, than William Pitt the Elder who told Parliament in 1766: "It is my boast that I called forth and drew into your service a hardy and intrepid race of men who conquered for you in every part of the world." But the scheme needed the willingness of the chiefs to deliver their people into the service of what had until then been considered an alien Government and an alien race.

peace to the Highlands. Surprisingly, after his anxious efforts to be involved in such affairs, he refused to go.

It is a good design, and I pray God it may prosper. I have been, and am, as desirous to have it done as any person, as I am a very great sufferer by the present dissolute conditions. I have had my house of Achallader (which your Grace has seen) burnt to the ground, and one of my vassal's lands totally burnt.

It was necessary now to remind the Lords in Council that, unlike most of them, he had lost men, money and material at the hands of the rebel clans. But this, he knew, was no reason for not answering their call, albeit so peremptory a summons.

My lord, I laid aside thoughts of travelling this winter, not expecting any such call, nor needed it to have had such a vertification, being I live peaceably and legally, and the diet is so short that I have not time to read it, much less be ready for such a journey. But the business proposed for my coming need not upon that account be delayed; for if the Council be pleased to send their instructions to me, when I receive them I shall go about their commands as diligently as I had them out of your Grace's hands.

But his refusal to leave the secure black walls of Kilchurn had nothing to do with the time of the year, or the shortness of notice. He was afraid to go. He knew that when he reached Edinburgh he would not be invited to sit in Holyroodhouse with the Lords in Council as their adviser, but would be held prisoner in a room below Parliament Hall, or at worst be thrown into the Tolbooth. The darker colour of his double-dealing had been momentarily seen beneath the purity of his allegiance to William. In August, the Earl of Annandale and some others of The Club had been arrested on a charge of plotting to restore James II "in a parliamentary way". The swarthy, handsome Annandale was sent to the Fleet Prison in London, where he made a long confession in a desperate and successful attempt to save his head. He said that members of The Club had met frequently in Breadalbane's Edinburgh lodgings that summer, before the Earl went home to the Highlands, and the wily old Campbell had been seen burning papers that might incriminate him. The Earl of Annandale, said the confession, further remembered that

. . . Breadalbane kept a constant correspondence with the Highland rebels, and that he hath shown him letters of Buchan, and that the Earl of Breadalbane delivered him a letter from Buchan, telling him he was very glad to hear he had returned to his duty, and advising him to appear in arms to give example to the rest who were well affected.

The Council made no attempt to prod Grey John of Breadalbane from his castle by Loch Awe, and no charges were brought against him on the evidence of Annandale's confession. This did not mean they could not be laid upon him later, at any time the King chose. It may have occurred to William—it certainly would have occurred to the Master of Stair—that a man who had been discovered at the double game might be more useful, in his own interest, than an honest and loyal servant like John Hill. It was more than a year now since Lochiel had let it be known that he was willing to talk over this matter of submission with his Campbell cousin, and once the Cameron chief came in, the rest would follow. In the spring of 1691 the King once more empowered "John, Earl of Breadalbane, to meet and treat with the Highlanders and others in arms in our Kingdom of Scotland, in order to reduce them to our obedience".

"If I live to have geese, I'll set the fox to keep them!"

A BASIC principle of magnetism, that opposite poles attract, may explain the psychological paradox of the alliance between the Master of Stair and Grey John of Breadalbane. Despite the warmth of their letters, their association was without real friendship and probably without trust. Each was determined to use the other, the Lowlander working for the pacification of the clans as an essential step toward the union of Parliaments, and the Highlander following his enduring ambition to make Glenorchy the dominant house of Clan Campbell. Each, too, knew the depth and danger of their unpopularity and the risks they ran by failure. "There never was trouble brewing in Scotland," Charles II had once said, "but that a Dalrymple or a Campbell was at the bottom of it." Trouble was something that neither man wanted at this moment, nor expected.

Though the proposal to treat with the rebels, and to indemnify them, was originally Tarbat's, the Master was now calling it "my Lord Breadalbane's scheme". In June, he was at Approbaix in Flanders with William's army, and early in the month he sent the Earl the King's final instructions and permission to arrange an early meeting with the chiefs. The intimate tone of his covering letter was typical of their correspondence at this time.

My Lord, I can say nothing to you. All things are as you wish, but I do long to hear from you. By the King's letter to the Council you will see he has stopped all hostilities against the Highlanders till he may hear from you, and that your time may be elapsed without coming to some issue, which I do not apprehend. . . . But if they will be mad, before Lammas, they will repent it, for the army will be allowed to go into the Highlands, which some thirst so much for, and the frigates will attack them. But I have so much confidence in your capacity to let them see the ground they stand on, that I think those suggestions are vain. I have sent your instructions.—My dear Lord, adieu.

Thus Breadalbane was plainly told that his would be the last attempt to reason with the chiefs, and if it failed there would be a return to force.

When John Hill got news of Breadalbane's commission he was sick with anger. "I should have had much more of the people under oath," he told the Earl of Crawford, a commissioner of the Treasury, "had not my Lord Breadalbane's design hindered, which I wish may do good, but suspect more hurt than good from it. For my part hereafter, if I live to have geese I'll set the fox to keep them!" The old soldier was bitterly disappointed because his efforts had been set aside, and he gathered all the malicious information he could about Breadalbane, reporting it to Melville with childish satisfaction. Now little more than a clerk to the Master of Stair, the Joint Secretary may have wondered what he was supposed to do with these stories. One of Breadalbane's outrageous promises to the chiefs, Hill told him, was that if they took the oath Fort William would be destroyed, even handed over to them. Despite such criminal proposals, the Earl was having little success. MacDonald of Glengarry was not interested in treating with anybody, and had gone raiding northward into Ross with five hundred of his men. A Cameron gentleman had stopped by Inverlochy to tell Hill that Lochiel was now coldly hostile to the Earl and did not trust him. Other chiefs did not believe that they would see much of the £12,000 Sterling which Breadalbane was said to have been given for distribution among them. "He tells them the money is locked up in a chest at London, but they believe he will find a way to keep a good part of it himself."*

---

* The belief that Breadalbane pocketed some of the indemnity money persisted for two centuries. There is no evidence that it ever left that chest in London, and the story does less than credit to the man's intelligence. It was not money he wanted, and what he wanted he would not have got had he taken it.

The truth was, Hill may have admitted to himself during those lonely evenings at his writing-desk, his friendship and protection meant less to the chiefs than the thought of handsome payments. There was talk that Lochiel would be given £5,000, and Glengarry £1,500, if they behaved themselves and took the oath.

The Governor was a good and dutiful soldier, however, and bearing his wounded pride he did what he could to help the Breadalbane scheme. "Twice or thrice a week," he reported, "I march a party of four hundred men sometimes up, and sometimes down the country, where the people (being under protection) meet them and are civil. So I let them see we can reach them if they behave otherwise than they have engaged to do." That he was able to put seven companies of his regiment on the march, and so regularly, was proof of the miracle he had worked on the rabble sent to him six months before. But so much had not changed. No pay had reached him, and his soldiers were far in arrears. There were frequent desertions, angry and desperate men taking their chance of survival in the hills rather than endure the fort for another day. Hill had recruiting officers at work in the Lowlands to fill these gaps and to replace the men taken to the graveyard. But of every three recruits sent, one was sick and another dead within a month. And all this mocked by the wild beauty of a Highland summer.

In the last week of June, Breadalbane met the chiefs at Achallader, the castle ruins still black from burning by the Lochaber Men two years before. *Achadh-fhaladair*, which means a cornfield ready for reaping, was one of the oldest settlements in the Highlands. Here, it was said, the Fletchers had been the first to kindle fire and boil water, thus establishing their title to the land in the old Celtic way. It had not belonged to them for nearly a century, but some still lived there as vassals of the Campbells. On the brae above their township was a green mound they called *Uaigh a' Choigrich*, the Grave of the Stranger, of the English mercenary who had grazed his horse in a cornfield ready for reaping, and who had died because he had no Gaelic.

The chiefs came from the north across the bog-cotton, the

skeleton trees and the flaming heather of Rannoch. Stewarts, Macleans, Camerons and MacDonalds, they came boldly, arrogantly, with pipes playing, and each with a fine tail of followers to support his dignity. MacDonald of Glengarry, back from his cattle-raid on Ross, brought his house-guests Major-General Thomas Buchan and Sir George Barclay, representing His Majesty King James's forces within the kingdom of Scotland. Breadalbane talked with them all beguilingly, not as an alien emissary from William but as MacCailein 'ic Dhonnachaidh, a chief like themselves, and now and then as a man sympathetic to the Stuart cause and wishing it nothing but good. He said that their interest was his, and if he had been forced to pretend an allegiance to William (to save himself, his family and his people from ruin) this did not mean he would not further King James's cause by whatever means and whenever he could. He knew the moment to flatter, to advise, or to warn.

In the week of talking, quarrelling and bargaining, in the idler hours of backgammon, feasting and field-games, he seems to have isolated the chiefs one by one, securing from each, when he could, a promise to accept what terms he might be able to get for them from the Government, and to live peaceably until then. One of the first to give him such an assurance was, surprisingly, young Coll MacDonald of Keppoch, who signed a bond in his own name and the names of eight of his tacksmen.

Two MacDonalds, however, were unmoved by the Campbells' soft words and measured arguments. Glengarry was surly and suspicious, and much of his discontent may have come from the fact that the £1,500 promised as his indemnity had now become £1,000 only. The second man was MacIain. He had come across Rannoch with his sons, and with no belief that any good could come from this meeting. He was stiff, cold and hostile, and the rock of his obstinacy broke Breadalbane's calculated charm. Four generations of hatred for the Gallows Herd stirred and burst from the Campbell. MacIain's sons later swore on oath that Breadalbane "did quarrel about some cows that the Earl alleged were stolen from his men by Glencoe's men, and that although they were not present to hear the words, yet their father told them". This passionate, angry quarrel worried old MacIain. "There's bad blood between our family and his," he told his sons, "I fear mischief from no man so much as the Earl of Breadalbane." He gathered his people and went home, saying he had no trust in someone who was Willie's man in Edinburgh and Jamie's in the Highlands.

The others were more realistic, less hostile to the Earl. They knew that they could not continue as they had since Killiecrankie. Hill's patrol-boat and marching companies at Inverlochy, Livingstone's army in the foothills, and the frigates sailing off the Isles were plain evidence that William was ready to turn again to force if necessary. The chiefs were no longer willing to fight alone. James must send them French help, or set them free to make what terms they could for their own preservation. They would take the oath to William if and when James relieved them of the allegiance they had sworn to him at Dalcomera and Blair. Grey John knew that their honour was the fulcrum upon which all must move. Though he had not the authority, he agreed that emissaries should be sent to get this relief from the exiled man at St. Germain, and upon this understanding the Treaty of Achallader was signed.

We, Major-General Buchan and Sir George Barclay, General Officers of King James the Seventh his Forces within the Kingdom of Scotland, to testify our aversion of shedding Christian blood, and that we design to appear good Scotsmen, and to wish that this nation may be restored to its wonted and happy peace, do agree and consent to a forbearance of all acts of hostility and depredation to be committed upon the subjects of this nation, or England, until the first day of October next, providing that there be no acts of hostility or depredation committed upon any of the King's subjects who have been, or are, engaged in his service under our command, either by sea or land; we having giving all necessary orders to such as are under (our command) to forbear acts of hostility by sea or land until the aforesaid time. Subscribed at Achallader, the 30th day of June, 1691.

In his turn, Breadalbane, gave his assurance in the name of a king and queen who had so far not considered the merits or value of such a treaty.

Whereas the Chieftains of the Clans have given bonds not to commit acts of hostility or depredation before the first day of October next, upon the conditions contained in the aforesaid bonds; and in regard that the officers sent by King James to command the said Chieftains have, by one unanimous consent in their Council of War, agreed to the said forbearance: Therefore I, as having warrant from King William and Queen Mary to treat with the foresaid Highlanders concerning the peace of the kingdom, do hereby certify that the said officers and Chieftains have signed a forbearance of acts of hostility and depredations till the first of October next. Wherefore it's most necessary, just, and reasonable that no acts of hostility by sea or land, or depredations, be committed upon the said officers, or any of their party whom they do command, or upon the Chieftains, or their kinsmen, friends, tenants or followers till the foresaid day of October. Subscribed at Achallader, the 30th day of June, 1691. BREADALBANE.

There was no mention of the oath to William, of permission from James, or the payment of indemnity upon submission. This was an armistice only, and for three months, but it was the first truce since William had landed at Torbay. Moreover, like the Treaty of Limerick signed later that year with the Irish Jacobites, it recognised the chiefs as legitimate belligerents not "rebels", and entitled them to proper treatment under the rules of war between nations. It was a distinction that would not be honoured long.

Breadalbane was delighted by his qualified success. He had done something no other man had done, not even Hill. His agents diligently travelled through Argyll, telling the people there that their chief MacCailein Mor was out of favour with the King, and that MacCailein 'ic Dhonnachaidh was now the trusted representative of Clan Campbell. He posted to London in haste. William was in Flanders, but to the Queen and her ministers the Earl gave a full account of the Achallader meeting, or at least as full as he thought politic. The chiefs, he said, had left for their homes "in good hopes to receive the money and an indemnity when they disbanded, and had dismissed all their men". He then sailed for Flanders to report to the King.

Not all the Jacobites in the Highlands were satisfied. Though Barclay and Buchan had signed in their name, Glengarry, Mac-Iain, and some Stewarts of Appin were restless and suspicious. Charles Edwards, who had been Dundee's chaplain, circulated a letter among the chiefs, saying that Breadalbane would ruin them and King James's cause. "All the fair stories he told you at Achallader against the Government were on purpose to deceive you, therefore meddle no more with him. The Pope has given a large sum of money to King James which you may expect to have a share of very shortly." This brave lie had little effect, the chiefs believed more in London's gold.

At Approbaix, Breadalbane leant heavily upon Stair's support. Though William was glad to have the truce, it was not a permanent solution. But Stair's smooth voice was at his ear, assuring him that this was a necessary stage, that my lord Breadalbane's scheme would be successful. The King knew nothing yet of the chiefs' insistence that James must first release them from their oath to him, and if Breadalbane told Stair about it, the Master kept it to himself.

Within three weeks of the Achallader meeting the truce was broken, and by the Glencoe men and their friends from Appin. A small boat carrying provisions to Fort William was tacking up the coast of Lorn when two others, filled with Highlanders, darted from an inlet and fell upon it. There was a piratical little affray, a flashing of swords and popping of pistols, in which some of the soldiers were wounded. The Highlanders stripped the provision boat of its cargo and took it to their homes.

When the boat's-crew and the bloodstained guard stumbled down Cow Hill into the fort, the Governor acted quickly. His battalions drums beat the Gathering, and seven companies formed up under Major John Forbes with full knapsacks and cartridge-pouches. They marched away in close order for Glencoe and Appin, and were so swift and resolute that they were able to arrest thirteen of the principal offenders before the Stewarts or Mac-

Donalds could think of resisting. Within a week Forbes brought all the prisoners into the fort and put them under guard. They were not broken men or disobedient clansmen, and it was plain to Hill that the raid had been a deliberate act of defiance. The leader was young Robert Stewart, Chief of Appin, and with him Forbes had taken eight of his close kinsmen. There was Ronald Mac-Donald of Auchterera, an impenitent and uncompromising Jacobite whom Hill described in his report as "a Captain of Horse, Glengarry's near kinsman and counsellor, lately come from France, and a Papist". Another was John Sinclair the laird of Telstan, a captain of dragoons in the Jacobite service, and there was a young gentleman of Clan Maclean, the son of a Glasgow merchant who preferred adventure in the Highlands with his people to service in his father's counting-house. Finally there was MacIain's hot-tempered and zealous son Alasdair Og, "a Captain of Foot in Major-General Buchan's regiment, and a Papist". All were young men, and all accepted their imprisonment with arrogant pride.

Hill informed the Privy Council that he had taken the prisoners, and he kept to himself any mordant thoughts he now had about the value of the Achallader Treaty. By return, he was told to hold the young men until a ship could be sent to carry them to the Tolbooth in Glasgow.

Since the King was still in Flanders, the Privy Council asked Queen Mary in London what her pleasure might be concerning the prisoners. Her answer came by flying packet at the end of the first week in August, and shows that her feelings about the Highlanders could sometimes run counter to her husband's. William would no doubt have let the troublesome fellows kick their heels against the Tolbooth walls until their rebellious temper was lower, but Mary was a Stuart, conscious of her Scots ancestry, and gently compassionate towards those who had fought for her father. She was also wise enough to see that here was an incident that might prejudice the negotiations for a peaceful settlement. She told the Council to set the young men free. And so they were. But Hill would have been out of character if he had not taken advantage of the time he held them prisoner to read them a parental lesson on the moral and military importance of keeping a promise made in their name.

If Hill had wondered how Breadalbane had managed to talk the chiefs into a truce after a week only of debate, when it had taken him months to bring the smaller gentry to submission, he discovered the answer that August. He got news of a secret agreement made between Grey John and the Jacobites, and it is generally believed that it was the cunning and sulky Glengarry who told him what was in these Private Articles. Hot with anger and honest disgust, pleased that his suspicions of Breadalbane's duplicity could now be proved, Hill scribbled a brief report and sent it south to John Forbes, who was now in Edinburgh, with instructions that he hand it personally to Sir Thomas Livingstone. On the morning of August 28, Forbes stopped Livingstone at the door of Holyroodhouse and gave him Hill's letter, which Livingstone took at once to the Duke of Hamilton, President of the Privy Council. The Articles, as Hill had been told them by Glengarry, made it plain that the published agreement on a three-months truce was subject to five conditions:

1. That if there be either an invasion from abroad or a rising of His Majesty (King James's) subjects in Britain, then this agreement is null.
2. If His Majesty (King James) does not approve of the said agreement it is also null.
3. And to that purpose there is a passport to be granted to two gentlemen, to acquaint the King therewith in all haste.
4. That if (King William's) forces go abroad, then we will rise.
5. That if King William and Queen Mary deny all or any of these articles, then my Lord Breadalbane is to join us with a thousand men, which he promises to perform, both on oath and honour.

It was probably the last of these articles that stuck in MacIain's throat, and turned him away in contempt for a man who was one king's servant in the mountains, and another's in the capital.

The day after Hamilton was given Hill's letter, he read it to the fifteen members of the Council at Holyroodhouse. It was start-lingly confirmed by the old Earl of Kintore who dramatically pulled a paper from his pocket, saying that it had been written by Buchan's nephew, and that it too contained an account of the Private Articles. Both letters were sent to the King with the Council's loyal indignation. This charge of double-dealing delighted the enemies of Grey John and the Master. The Duke of Hamilton, who led a faction against Stair, told his friend Melville "That Breadalbane will deny these articles sent by Colonel Hill, I put no doubt of, as I little doubt the truth of them would be found if put to exact trial."

At Balloch on Loch Tay, Breadalbane did deny them, most strenuously. He was not long back from the King's camp in Flanders, where he had been kept informed of events in Scotland by his Edinburgh law-agent, Colin Campbell of Carwhin. Carwhin's letters, written almost daily and sealed with black wax stamped by a bleeding heart, told the Earl that the Queen had expressed satisfaction with the Achallader negotiations, that Appin had been arrested and then released, that some broken men of the clans were raiding the Lowlands, and that Colonel Hill had been spreading malicious rumours about Breadalbane. Grey John called these "coffee-house stories", but he came home in haste to deal with them. He may now have wished himself back in Flanders, close by Stair and the King's elbow. He was uneasy and afraid, and he sent a letter to the Master, asking if he should write to the King, exonerating himself. Stair advised him to do nothing. With considerable distortion of fact, he said that nobody would believe Breadalbane capable of so base a thing as the Private Articles, and then he turned the compliment upside down by saying that nobody thought "there could be any secrets in your treaties when there were so many ill eyes upon your proceedings". The King's faith in the Earl was unshaken and when all was made known Breadalbane would stand even higher in Royal favour. "Let not anything discourage you," said the Master, "but believe all these devices will tend to magnify your service when you finish your undertaking."

Thus encouraged, Breadalbane turned upon Hill, not in violent protest but in well-phrased sorrow. "I could not have believed you would have been the transmitter of an accusation (yet very lame) to the Council against me, until you had first resigned that old friendship past unviolated on my side for many years." He asked for an apology, no more; with that he would be content. No doubt astonished to discover that he was the Earl's old friend, Hill refused to apologise or retract. In a letter stiffer than usual with parentheses, he stoutly defended himself. He had done his duty, he said, and his had not been the only accusation laid before the Council. Nor was Breadalbane fair in accusing him of endangering the peace of the kingdom, "for who laid the first stone in the foundation of peace and settlement?" If he had not done his duty, let the King remove him from Inverlochy and put a better man in his place, were there one to be found. Hill had earned the right to that conceit.

Breadalbane's denials, his anxious appeals to Stair for reassurance, went on into autumn. Long before then the King had dismissed the matter from his attention. A cold and imperious man, he was a realist who worried more about his asthma than he did about the moral weaknesses of other men. Rogue or not, Breadalbane was the only man dealing with the rebel chiefs, and the more his rascality was exposed the more diligent he might be in atonement. As for the Private Articles, William acknowledged that they probably existed, and gave Breadalbane's motives the expedient benefit of the doubt. "Men who manage treaties," he said with unstatesmanlike candour, "must give fair words."

Three weeks before he heard of the Articles he had decided, on Stair's prompting no doubt, to put a limit to the havering of the chiefs. From his camp at St. Gerard on August 17, he had given them four months to make up their minds.

And we, being satisfied that nothing can conduce more to the peace of the Highlands and reduce them from rapine and arms to virtue and industry than the taking away of the occasions of these differences and feuds, which oblige them to neglect the opportunities to improve and cultivate their country, and accustom themselves to depredations and idleness*—are graciously pleased not only to pardon, indemnify and restore all that have been in arms who shall take the oath of allegiance before the 1st day of January next, but likewise we are resolved to be at some charge to purchase the lands and superiorities which are the subject of these debates and animosities, at the full and just avail whereby the Highlanders may have their immediate and entire independence of the Crown.

The Crown was ready to pay £12,000 for the superiorities of the great landowners, thus relieving the chiefs of their feudal obligations and making them vassals of the King only. If there was as yet no mention of the bribes Breadalbane had led them to expect, at least an ancient and irksome yoke was to be lifted from them.

William was determined to be as reasonable as possible, from common sense if not from compassion. He was told that some Highland lairds would be reluctant to take the oath if they were still to be held responsible for crimes that had little to do with rebellion or the Jacobite cause. He accordingly discharged them from this fear, including the most notorious of the Gallows Herd. MacIain of Glencoe and his cousin John MacDonald of Achtriachtan were pardoned, indemnified, fully and freely acquitted of "a slaughter committed by them". This pardon, which William signed under the Great Seal of Scotland on August 20, gave no details of the slaughter. But there can be no doubt that it referred to the bloody incident twenty years before when, on the orders of MacIain, "John MacDonald son to Alexander MacDonald and brother to MacAlan Rory was taken out of his house after it had been fired and killed after dinner in cold blood, and stabbed to pieces".

On August 27, when Major Forbes was hurrying to deliver

---

* One hundred and fifty years later the "idleness" of the Highlander and the need to "improve" his land were used as righteous arguments to justify his removal by force from his land. When that was done the improvers replaced men with profitable herds of Cheviot sheep.

Hill's letter to Livingstone, the Privy Council put William's orders into a Proclamation of Indemnity. It was posted at the Mercat Cross of Edinburgh, and at crosses in the head burghs throughout the kingdom. It ordered all men who had been in arms against King William and Queen Mary to appear before the Sheriffs of their shires and there swear the oath of allegiance. And this, on pain of punishment to the utmost extremity of the law, was to be done before the first day of January, 1692.

The chiefs looked southward to France for guidance from James. This garrulous, weakling exile, scratching at his memoirs and pious aphorisms, shamed by the recollection of his sexual appetites, surrounding himself with priests and enjoying the melancholy tragedy of his life, as yet knew nothing of what was expected from him. The emissaries had not left the Highlands. Two men had been selected. The first was Sir George Barclay, Buchan's second-in-command and co-signator of the Achallader Treaty, a brave and determined man with a weakness for assassination plots. The second was Major Duncan Menzies of Fornooth, a fanatical Jacobite who had defied his chief and taken some of his clan to join Dundee two years before. Since the end of July, Barclay had had a pass to travel freely through England to France and back. It had been given to him by Breadalbane, and he seems to have been reluctant to test its validity at first, pausing at Achallader to discuss the matter with Campbell of Barcaldine, Breadalbane's chamberlain. At last he took the risk and got away without stop.

Toward the end of August, Menzies left Edinburgh where he had been in hiding. In keeping with his character he made an adventure of the journey. He had no pass, and for a year now it had been impossible for even the most innocent of travellers to go in or out of British ports without one. But he had friends in the city, and one of them was the Postmaster at Holyrood Palace, William Cairnes. With a commendable indifference to the safety of his own neck, Cairnes made out a pass for the Major in the name of Stewart, and under this scarcely innocent alias Menzies posted down through the Lowlands and England, and over the

Channel to France. When the Privy Council heard of the affair, it threw the luckless Postmaster into the Tolbooth, along with an advocate and a gentleman of the Palace Guard who had helped him.

Much now depended on the speed with which James II acted in response to the chiefs' appeal. In the palace of St. Germain-en-Laye outside Paris he lived a comfortable life as a pensioner of Louis XIV, rapidly becoming senile, obsessed with guilt over the pleasures he had enjoyed with his ugly mistresses, and happy only when he was hunting or working on his papers of devotion. His greatest fault had always been irresolution. It had now become a vice.

"*Look on and you shall be satisfied of your revenge*"

WITH THE approach of his second winter in the Highlands, John Hill was depressed by a sense of failure. Those whom he had trusted, Tarbat and Melville, had lost their influence in the Council and at Court. He now had Glengarry's promise to swear on oath to the truth of the Private Articles and the treachery of Breadalbane, but no one was interested. If the offer of pardon and indemnity brought peace to the Highlands it would be the result of his patient work in laying the ground, yet neither the King nor the Master of Stair had had the grace to acknowledge this. The damp cold, the mist above the marsh, brought back his rheumatism, and his eyes were sore and inflamed by long hours at his desk. He did his duty loyally. "I came not to serve myself," he told the Earl of Crawford, "by expecting to gain anything by pinching and unjust methods, but only the bare pay and salary my Master allows me; but I will always be a faithful subject and servant to the King in any station, either military or civil." Though he agreed with the poet, *Hos ego versiculos feci, tulit alter honores*, he was not too deeply hurt because others had taken the credit for his work. "Let me but live in such favour with my Master as he thinks fit to vouchsafe me. I shall therein rest fully satisfied, though I confess it would much please me to see the King's affairs, the true religion, and the public good prosper."

The old man's humility was as real as his occasional small vanities. He put his faith and energies into what he believed to be a righteous cause, and in the end it would betray him. He was never in doubt about the necessity of his work until it reached its bloody climax, and not even then did he see his world for what it was. Great men are often dwarfed by their honest servants.

That autumn his duties at Fort William were at last eased by the appointment of a Deputy-Governor, James Hamilton, who was also given the lieutenant-colonelcy of Hill's Regiment. Hamilton is a mystery, and it seems fitting that he should be. He appears late on the stage like a cloaked bravo, and what he was matters less than what he may have been sent to do. His Christian name is a common one in the Hamilton family, and it is impossible to find him with any certainty in its extensive genealogy. He may have been a Scot, and he may have been Scoto-Irish, for there were several James Hamiltons who came from Ireland to serve in the army of William III. The first record of him is in July, 1690, when he appears on the muster rolls as the lieutenant-colonel of Cunningham's Regiment of Foot. A year later, his name is on the roll of Hill's Regiment at Inverlochy. Oblique references in the letters that passed between him and Stair suggest that the Master secured him the appointment. They suggest also that there was some incident in Hamilton's recent past, some error of judgement or dereliction of duty, for which he was anxious to atone by diligent and unquestioning service.*

Hill's attitude to Hamilton, in his letters and reports, was briefly non-committal. This, too, is curious, for the Governor was a man who generously recommended those whom he respected,

---

* The "lapse" to which Stair frequently referred may have occurred two years earlier. In April, 1689, Cunningham's Regiment (9th Foot) and Richards's Regiment (17th Foot) sailed from Liverpool in the frigate *Swallow* to help the Irish Protestant garrison of Londonderry, then under bitter siege by James II. Its Governor, Robert Lundy, told Cunningham that since the city must soon surrender it would be unwise to land more soldiers for its defence. The people of Londonderry, who did not agree, begged Cunningham to stay, but he decided to take Lundy's advice. Supported by Richards, and by some of the officers of both regiments, he ordered the captain of the *Swallow* to take him and his troops back to Liverpool. Both Cunningham and Richards were later cashiered, and their officers were held in public contempt as cowards. If Hamilton were one of them, his military career would have been seriously affected.

and boldly censured those whom he distrusted. But for nearly five years Hill said almost nothing about Hamilton, little that was good or bad. For his part, when Hamilton first came to Fort William he was full of compliments for "this worthy gentleman, my Colonel", but such calculated phrases dropped from his letters as he grew more sure of his own influence. He had none of Hill's avuncular concern for the clans, or his wish to bring them to submission by reasonable persuasion. To Hamilton the Highlanders were all villains, insolent and saucy, and he was eager to take the field against them, and "to put in execution such commands as shall come for reducing them to better manners". When Hill was shown Hamilton's letters, before their dispatch to Edinburgh or London, he may have wondered why the words were "shall come" and not "*may* come".

Hamilton was a liar when it suited his interest. Hill had no illusions about the rabble he had been given for a regiment, hoping that time and God's will would eventually make soldiers of those who did not die or desert. Though they could now stand watch and march on patrol, they still did not *look* like soldiers. They wore what clothing there had been when Glencairn's and Kenmure's were disbanded, and this lacked uniformity where it was not already in rags. Some men were wearing coats, breeches, hose and shoes that had seen three or four others through to the graveyard. Hill had been sent a cap and a coat for approval, but they were of poor quality and unlike the pattern of the new uniform he had chosen. Patiently he asked for better design and workmanship, and waited. He knew that a good red coat with bright facings, stout shoes and a waterproof hat went a long way toward the making of a soldier. Until his men could respect themselves, they would continue to drink, to rebel, and to desert. More worldly wise, Hamilton saw what Edinburgh wished to see. "I do not know, nor have not known," he reported, "a regiment better composed of discreet, sober men, and am satisfied they are entirely zealous to the service." The sick and ill-clad bodies of these discreet and sober men were rungs up on which Hamilton was determined to climb. "Let what will be said of them, I shall never deserve the King's pay, nor be trusted in his service, if any in this kingdom exceed them in any point which my willing though weak industry shall never fail to be employed."

Hamilton's industry as Deputy-Governor, and his ambition, were far from weak, and Hill began to have uneasy doubts. Once more he was afraid that he was about to be replaced, perhaps by Hamilton, and he wrote to the Privy Council in protest. To recall him now, he said, would be dishonourable, and would cause more trouble than the King's affairs could afford.

By the end of October and the beginning of the winter storms, there was still no word from the vacillating exile at St. Germain. Some of the chiefs who had accepted Breadalbane's assurances at Achallader were now openly disgusted with him. Though Coll of Keppoch had been one of the first to accept the Earl's promises, he locked himself away in his hills and refused to talk about the oath. Lochiel retired in haughty silence to his fir-wood house at Achnacarry, and the Macleans, with a cautious eye on the Campbells of Argyll, were behaving as if there had been no talk of pardon, indemnity or oath. The chiefs' hostility and waywardness angered Breadalbane. "They are ruined and abused with lies that children of ten years of age could not believe," he told his chamberlain, "and they talk as if they were to give terms and not to receive them, but they will find that a great mistake in a few weeks, not withstanding my endeavours to the contrary."

They will find that a great mistake in a few weeks. . . . How much Breadalbane knew of Stair's intentions, should the chiefs ignore the Proclamation of Indemnity, it is hard to say. But that sentence indicates some knowledge, or some suspicion. What might happen to the malcontents, however, worried him less than what was happening to him. Since the exposure of the Private Articles, since his return to Balloch from Flanders, he had felt the ground moving uncertainly beneath him, and Stair had a machiavellian trick of increasing his alarm while professedly reassuring him. "There wants no endeavours to render you suspicious to the King, but he asked what proof there was for the information, and bid me tell you to go on in your business. I hope your Lordship will not only keep [the chiefs] from giving offence, but bring them to the allegiance." Breadalbane thought that the chiefs would be less like to give offence (and more willing to talk to him) if they could be given some news of the money he had promised them. Stair gave him little encouragement. "The King said they were not presently to receive it, which is true, but that he had ordered it to be delivered out of his treasury, so they need not fear in the least performance."

November, and winter had closed the glens. In one sense, John Hill was glad to see snow on Ardgour, and black ice rimming the banks of the Nevis. There had been talk again of making Glengarry surrender his castle, but winter had made this impossible, even if someone had thought of the artillery and engineers such an attempt would need. A fire burned continuously in his tiny room inside the fort, but he was never warm and never well. His age lay heavily upon him. His dear child, John Forbes, was away in Edinburgh, and he was lonely for the young man's bright company.

November, and Rannoch was white. There was snow on Aonach Eagach and the five fingers of Bidean nam Bian. Home from the shielings for more than a month now, Clan Iain Abrach waited for spring. Black cattle that had once grazed in Breadalbane and Argyll were herded close to the townships, and Glenlyon's fine stallion was warmly stabled at Carnoch. MacIain kept to his house. John MacDonald of Achtriachtan had Colonel Hill's protection in his pocket, and like the other tacksmen of Glencoe he left the oath of allegiance to the conscience of his chief. None of the rebel chiefs had as yet appeared before the Sheriff of his shire. It was twelve weeks since the departure of Menzies and Barclay, and no word had come from France.

At the beginning of December there was news from London. The Earl of Melville had been relieved of his office, and the Master of Stair was the sole Secretary of State for Scotland.

Now the pace changed. For a year Stair had worked to secure a peaceful and bloodless settlement with the chiefs. He had waited three months for them to obey the Proclamation of Indemnity and swear the oath of allegiance. There were four weeks left until the first day of January, and there was no sign that anything had been achieved. Alone in office he could not lay the blame for failure or delay upon Melville. If the entire responsibility he coveted had become his at the worst moment, perhaps he welcomed the opportunity to succeed by one bold, merciless and effective stroke. He did not believe that James would now send the chiefs a discharge from his service, or that if it came the Highlanders would readily take the oath. His impatience, his anger, his growing fear of failure were suddenly evident in everything he wrote or did. It was as if the bland, ungiving mask of his face had cracked, revealing the scars he had kept hidden—the memory of the Highland Host, the thought that these obstinate chiefs had been the friends of Dundee, the implacable enemy of the Dalrymples, and the bitter hurt of knowing that outside Scotland men saw little difference between a Lowland laird and a Highland cateran. He was now obsessed with what the clans called *Mi-run mor nan Gall*, the Lowlander's great hatred of the Highlander. From the moment he took full office he no longer talked of treaties and bargains. He spoke of force, and soon the word would spit from his pen in black venom.

Long before December he had thought of what should be done if the chiefs did not take the oath. Although he put nothing to paper, he discussed the matter with Breadalbane, filing the advice the Earl gave him in his mind. The first dark hint of the understanding they had reached is in a letter he wrote to Breadalbane from Kensington Palace on December 2. "*I repent nothing of the plan. . . .*" An instrument was needed, however, an executor of this plan, and it was to be Lieutenant-Colonel James Hamilton. By the same post Stair wrote to him, flattering him, reassuring him, and tempting him.

I am very glad you are there. And you will see that my way is not so partial, or to mind nothing but my own friends and interest. The public shall always be first with me. And therefore, though I never had the good fortune to be acquainted with you, yet you shall find me as ready to do you justice as if you were my nearest relation. You need not care that at present you are not to kiss the King's hand. He wants not a just character of you.

It was a strange letter for the Crown's great minister to write to an obscure officer of Foot, whom he had never met, but whom he was now promising preferment and recommendation to the highest power in the land. And yet Hamilton was obviously no stranger to the Master. Stair knew something about him, some past fault or omission that could be used as a lever, working the ambitious man to do all that was expected of him. Stair referred to this lightly, in one of those sentences he favoured, an expression of goodwill barbed with threat. "I do not consider the lapses of a single person so as to make me do harm to what I do know to be their Majesties' service." As for the work Hamilton might have to do, Stair was suddenly and startlingly frank: "It may be shortly we may have use of your garrison, for the winter time is the only season in which we are sure the Highlanders cannot escape us, nor carry their wives, bairns, and cattle to the mountains."

He did not explain why the children of the clans had become such a danger to the King that their escape from his punishment would be regrettable. Two days later he wrote again to Hamilton, explaining more fully what was in his mind, and asking the man's help.

I see the settlement of the Highlands is obstructed by false insinuations. Some make the MacDonalds think their part is too small. Some have emulation at Breadalbane, and do stop the work for the despite against the instrument. I am satisfied these people are equally and unthinking, who do not accept what's never again in their offer. And since the Government cannot oblige them, it's obliged to receive some of them to weaken and frighten the rest. The MacDonalds will fall in this net. That's the only popish clan in the kingdom, and it will be popular to take a severe course with them. Let me hear from you with the first whether you think that this is the proper season to maul them in the cold long nights . . . and must be in readiness by the first of January.

He wrote thus four weeks before the end of the year, with time yet for word to come from King James, for the chiefs to take the oath. He told Breadalbane that he had not changed his mind about the expediency of bringing the chiefs to submission by gentle methods, if such were possible, but he no longer believed they were. "The madness of these people makes me plainly see there is no reckoning with them; *delenda est Carthago.*" Even if some were to take the oath by the day set they deserved no kindness and hostages should be taken from them. All must be taught a harsh and brutal lesson, and the victims of it, quite plainly, should be Clan Donald, the Gallows Herd whose deaths none but their own kinsmen would mourn.

He wrote to John Hill, telling him what was proposed, advising him to discuss it with Hamilton, and warning both men to keep their mouths tightly closed upon the subject when they were not together. The old Cromwellian made no protest against this shattering end to all his hopes. He waited, and perhaps he hoped that by Christmas none of it would be necessary.

Though Stair pursued the matter with vigour throughout December, the plan was not his. It was Breadalbane's. Whether the grey fox deliberately put it in the Master's mind one day during his summer visit to Flanders, or whether he did no more than suggest that if all else failed the clans could still be brought to submission by fire and sword, is not clear. But the plan was his, and so Stair acknowledged it by the same post as he declared that Carthage must be destroyed.

By the next I expect to hear either these people are come to your hand, or else *your scheme for mauling them,** for it will not delay . . . Menzies, Glengarry, and all of them have written letters, and take pains to make it believed that all you did was for the interest of King James. Therefore look on, and you shall be satisfied of your revenge.

There would be no more money, said Stair savagely, to waste upon the chiefs or to entertain the vanities of their feudal lords. God alone could now say whether it might not have been wiser to

* My italics, J. P.

use that £12,000 on soldiers' pay for ravaging the glens. But that was past. Now the Papist rebels must be rooted out.

Breadalbane was alarmed. Perhaps his ear caught an hysterical note of insanity in Stair's letters, his nose a whiff of brimstone, for he left the Highlands at once, posting furiously south. This was no time for him to put his thoughts to paper. He paused long enough in Edinburgh for a talk with his law-agent Carwhin, and to become involved in an undignified scuffle with Lord Murray at the Palace of Holyroodhouse, over the eternal debts of his cousin Glenlyon. And then on in haste to London. He kept close to Stair in Kensington Palace, and though he was welcomed cordially, though he warmed his back against the great fire in the Master's room, their relationship was changing. Breadalbane may have felt that having handed the assassin a dagger, he was no longer able to guide or avert the stroke.

On December 21, when he was no longer expected, Major Duncan Menzies arrived in Edinburgh. He knocked at the door of Carwhin's house in the Court of the Guard and collapsed from exhaustion. He had left Paris nine days before, and had travelled from London in four. In his pocket he carried King James's discharge to the clans:

To our trusty and well-beloved General-Major Thomas Buchan, or to the Officer commanding our Forces in our ancient Kingdom of Scotland.

JAMES R.

Right trusty and well-beloved, we greet you well. We are informed of the state of our subjects in the Highlands, and of the condition that you and our other officers there are in, as well by our trusty and well-beloved Sir George Barclay, brigadier of our Forces, as by our trusty and well-beloved Major Duncan Menzies: And therefore we have thought fit hereby to authorise you to give leave to our said subjects and officers who have hitherto behaved themselves so loyally in our cause to do what may be most for their own and your safety. For doing whereof this shall be your warrant. Saint Germain this 12th day of December, 1691, in the seventh year of our reign.

The weak, irresolute man, hoping for miracles, had let three months pass before making this decision. He was deeply in debt to the clans. As Duke of York, he had been responsible for harsh, penal measures against them. As King, he had asked them to defend him and die for him. As an exile, he had kept them to their oath and they had honoured it as best they could. When he finally released them, there were nineteen days only before the expiry of the time set by William. James must have known that, in winter, even so determined a courier as Menzies could not reach Edinburgh in less than nine days. It could be another week before the news reached Lochaber, and longer still before each of the chiefs could be told of the discharge. It was impossible for all of them to take the oath before the end of the year.

The responsibility for the Massacre of Glencoe has in the past been attributed to Stair, to Breadalbane, to William, and to all three. But much of it must also be borne by James the Second of England and Seventh of Scotland.

Duncan Menzies left Carwhin's house on the morning of December 22. His strength was now gone, and he could travel no farther than his home in Perthshire, four miles from Dunkeld. From there, two or three days later, he sent messengers into Lochaber. In Edinburgh, Campbell of Carwhin wrote at once to Breadalbane's chamberlain, asking Barcaldine to inform the Argyllshire clans. It was all that could be done. Three days before the end of the year, Menzies' messenger reached Ewen Cameron at Achnacarry. Lochiel set out at once for Inveraray where, before a Campbell Sheriff in a Campbell town, he would take the oath to William and be the first to break the ice after all. He gave John Hill the news as he passed by Fort William, and the old man must have thanked God for this mercy, praying that all the malignants would be able to make their peace in time. Although there is no evidence of this, as Lochiel passed over the ferry at Ballachulish he probably sent word to MacIain, urging him to lose no time.

Since the middle of the month marching men had been moving northward in red columns from Perth and Stirling, Dundee and Aberdeen, Blair and Inveraray. On December 15, the Master of Stair had put the Army in motion. Livingstone's dragoons closed the passes from Stirling and Dunkeld. Sir James Lesley was told to send seven companies of his regiment from Perth to Inverness, where they would be joined by six more from Colonel John Buchan's Regiment in Aberdeen. All the Independent Companies of the Williamite clans were mobilised. Fifty Mackays were ordered from Badenoch to Inverness, with a hundred men of Atholl under Captain George Wishart and Captain Archibald Murray. To Fort William was sent Captain Robert Lumsden's company from Blair, and Captain George Murray's from Finlarig. To sweeten the reluctance of these Highland militiamen, and to hearten the spirits of the regulars, £800 was distributed against arrears of pay.

Eight hundred men of the Earl of Argyll's Regiment were at Inveraray. On December 29, half of them marched out under Major Robert Duncanson. "Where they design, I know not," said Campbell of Barcaldine, reporting the news to Carwhin in Edinburgh.

"I will be a true, faithful, and obedient soldier"

On the twenty-second day of April, 1689, the Estates of the Kingdom of Scotland accepted the tenth Earl of Argyll's offer to raise a regiment of his clansmen as foot-soldiers in the service of King William and Queen Mary. This the Estates said they were pleased to do because of their special trust and confidence in the fidelity, courage, and good conduct of the said Earl. Any anxious reasons he may have had for demonstrating his new loyalty so extravagantly were not considered relevant to the warrant. It was not a moment for examining men's motives too closely, but two months later he was formally restored to the titles and lands which James II had taken from his family four years before.

Six hundred men were to be enlisted from the glens of Lorn, Cowal, Knapdale and Argyll, mustered in ten companies, officered by Campbell gentry and their sons, and placed on the Scottish establishment of the King's Army for use when, where, and how His Majesty thought fit.* No other Highland chief, and no Lowland laird brought William of Orange so valuable and so welcome a gift. The Campbells were not rustics who had to be given the will as well as the training to fight. Though their military conceit had suffered bitterly at Inverlochy forty years before, when the MacDonalds cut them down and their chief deserted them in his black galley, they were still the most formidable force of the clans, and the six hundred men needed for the new regiment were less than a fifth of their fighting-strength.

* It was thus the first regular Highland Regiment raised by the British Crown, fifty years before the formation of the 42nd Regiment, The Black Watch.

Archibald Campbell, tenth Earl of Argyll and fifteenth Mac-Cailein Mor of Clan Campbell, had learnt an important lesson from the misfortunes of his father and grandfather, and he was determined that wherever he went in life he would not arrive at the steps of the scaffold on which they had died. He had more cunning and less scruples than either of them, and was agreeably amoral where they were chillingly virtuous. For much of his life his family's earldom and property had been forfeit to the Crown, and he decided that high-principled intransigence was not likely to regain or hold them. When his father raised one half of Clan Campbell for Monmouth in 1685, he was ready to raise the other half for James II and bring his father to justice. He then offered to become a Catholic if James would restore the titles and estates that had been taken away with his father's head. This too material an approach to spiritual matters only caused offence, and he left hurriedly for Holland. He returned with William in 1688, once more a good Protestant. A bold-eyed man, with a loose, sensual mouth, he was quick-witted and open-handed, enjoying horses and women with equal pleasure. When he and his wife had properly secured the succession of his line, they parted, and kept as much of the country as they could between them. His last and favourite mistress was Peggy Alison, who called him "*Ma Mion*", and for her sake he patiently endured her quarrelsome family of brothers and cousins. He was never happy when separated from her. "I am in a thousand fears when I am any time without hearing from you. I wish I could put my Peggy in my pocket as she is already in my heart. . . ."

From Edinburgh in June, 1689, he wrote less sentimentally to each gentleman of his clan. "Loving Cousin, Their Majesties' Privy Council has ordered us to cause raise six hundred men. . . . That this may be better effectuate, we ordered Sir Colin Campbell of Ardkinglas* to go from this to meet you at Inveraray upon Thursday, the 12th day of this instant, for appointing these men to be raised. We entreat you fail not to come there at that time." Clan Campbell responded loyally. The first eight companies were

* Sheriff of Argyll.

mustered at Perth in August, and five more were enrolled during the following two years at Crieff, Stirling, Cardross and Drumakill. By July, 1691, the regiment was complete to the normal establishment, and stronger than had been originally intended: 780 men formed into twelve battalion companies and one company of grenadiers. Its first lieutenant-colonel was Sir Duncan Campbell of Auchinbreck, an old soldier of the Dutch wars and head of one of the leading families in Argyll. In 1691 he was succeeded by Robert Jackson, a Lowlander who had come to England with William as a captain of dragoons in a regiment commanded by a kinsman of Argyll's wife. Similarly, the regiment's first major was shortly replaced by Robert Duncanson, a tough, professional soldier from Fassokie in Stirlingshire whose family had long been adherents of the Argyll Campbells. It was by the energy and relentless discipline of Jackson and Duncanson that the clansmen were drilled into a red-coated line regiment as good as any in William's Dutch or English army.

The company officers were almost all Campbell gentry, landowners and tacksmen of Argyll or their sons. James Campbell of Ardkinglas, brother to the Sheriff, commanded one of the senior battalion companies. There were three Campbells of Barbreck with captains' commissions, and others of Kames, Allengrange and Airds. Vassals or allies of Argyll, like Bannatyne of Kames, Lamont of Lamont, and MacAulay of Ardincaple, also sent one or more of their sons to be captains, lieutenants or ensigns. The last two companies mustered, at Stirling in April, 1691, were Captain Thomas Drummond's grenadiers and a battalion company which Argyll gave to the importunate Robert Campbell of Glenlyon. Now aged fifty-nine, Glenlyon was the oldest officer in the regiment, and the only Campbell from Breadalbane who held a commission. Grey John sourly disapproved of the appointment.

At one time or another, the families of all these officers had been robbed and maltreated, their lands despoiled by the men of Glencoe and Keppoch. They had suffered bitterly in the Atholl Raid, losing kinsmen and tenants to the rope or the transports, and most of them had some particular and unforgiving reason for hating all or any of the Jacobite clans. Thus they hoped for revenge as well as glory. It was the belief of young John Campbell of Airds, for example, that by his service in the regiment his family would regain Castle Stalker, the square black keep on the coast of Appin which the Stewarts had occupied since the gathering at Dalcomera. Who had a proper right to it, however, was arguable. Eighty years earlier, a Campbell of Airds had persuaded a Stewart of Appin (understandably called *Baothaire*, the silly-headed) to give it up in exchange for an eight-oared boat. Since the bargain had been made during a night of heavy drinking, the Stewarts had never regarded it as valid, and they had put their blue and yellow standard back above the castle walls as soon as they could, and dared the Campbells to take it down.

In the beginning the companies were raised in the old manner of the clan levy, each captain bringing sixty of his own people. Argyll's company, commanded by a captain-lieutenant, was raised from his tenants about Inveraray. Auchinbreck's was wholly recruited on his lands in Knapdale, the Barbreck brothers' from Kilbride. Ardkinglas's men were drawn from his brother's estates on Loch Fyne, and MacAulay, Lamont and Bannatyne brought sixty each from their own clans. The names of these private men endure on the fading Muster Rolls, the common names of Argyll: Campbell, MacCallum, MacDiarmid, MacKissock and MacKellar, MacIvor, MacUre and MacNichol. Later companies, raised in Cowal and Rosneath, contained some Lowland men, but the great majority were Campbell clansmen, and they too had hard memories of the Atholl Raid, the burning, the killing, and the robbing by Macleans, Stewarts and MacDonalds. Each company Roll was drawn up with scrupulous care every quarter, as ordered by the Muster Master in Edinburgh, and against each man's name was written his trade and his place of origin. Though some were listed as drovers, masons, or smiths, most were described as having "no trade".

Their pride, and their fierce fighting tradition were not enough to make them regular soldiers. In May, 1689, the Privy Council transferred "the best sixteen men in Bargany's Regiment" to Argyll's, therein to serve as sergeants, corporals or senior drummers. They were Lowlanders, with Lowland names like Hendrie, Dalyell, Purdie, Mitchell and Barber. They were rough, experienced men, determined to transform savages into foot-soldiers by the unrelenting use of blasphemy and threat, drill-book and halberd. But before any of the Campbells could be taught how to poise their muskets or advance their pikes, to tie their breeches below the knee and keep their hair in a poke, they had to swear a soldier's oath of loyalty. This they did upon the Bible or upon the dirk, upon whatever moved them to greatest reverence.

I do sincerely promise and swear that I will be faithful and bear true allegiance to their Majesties King William and Queen Mary, and to be obedient in all things to their Majesties, or to the Commander-in-chief appointed by their Majesties for the time being; and will behave myself obediently to my superior officers in all that they shall command me for their Majesties' service. And I do further swear that I will be a true, faithful and obedient soldier, in every way performing my best endeavours for their Majesties' service, obeying all orders and submitting to all such rules and articles of war as are, or shall be established by their Majesties. So help me God.

By this oath all officers and men were inextricably bound to do what they were told, when and where they were told. There was no qualification, and no appeal against it on grounds of conscience or conviction. So that they might know, without any doubt, what those articles were that they swore to obey without question, the sixty-nine *Laws and Ordinances Touching Military Discipline* were read aloud at the head of each company once a month, and were presumably translated into the Gaelic for those who had no English. By Article Nine, the giving of advice, intelligence or warning to the enemy was punishable by death. Article Sixteen authorised death for refusal to obey an order. Article Nineteen authorised death for murder and wilful killing. Article Twenty authorised death for theft and robbery. And the irony of Article Thirty-seven may have been remembered by

Glenlyon's men and Drummond's, when they fell-to in a snow-storm one February dawn in Glencoe.

If any shall presume to beat or abuse his host, or the wife, child, or servant of his host where he is quartered, he shall be put in irons for it. And if he does it a second time he shall be further punished, and the party wronged shall have amends made him. And whoever shall force a woman to abuse her, whether she belong to the enemy or not, shall suffer death for it.

Due to the reluctance of the Privy Council to advance sufficient money (the regiment's pay alone was more than £16,000 Sterling a year) it was two years before the Campbells were fully equipped and uniformed. For nearly twelve months the Earl of Argyll bore the cost out of his own purse, and complained bitterly about it. But by the end of 1691 all thirteen companies were better clothed than Hill's wretched men would ever be. The badges on their rough blue bonnets, an earl's coronet and the boar's head of Argyll, had been embroidered in London by William de Remon, an Huguenot exile. Geranium-red coats, faced with yellow, had replaced the tartan in which they had been hurriedly dressed when they were first mustered. Their loose breeches were grey, and tied with ribbons below the knee. Their stockings were yellow, and their black shoes were high-fronted and buckled with steel. Beneath their coats they wore long waistcoats of tartan, and in the first winter of their service some of them were issued with plaids instead of greatcoats. With the exception of this tartan cloth, which was made in Glasgow, most of their clothing was sent from London. That is to say, it was sent when Quartermaster John MacUre could bully the clothiers into making it, and the ship-masters into carrying it to Leith.

The old Highland weapons, broadsword, dirk and target, were set aside with the clansmen's saffron shirts and belted plaids. The Argylls were armed like any Lowland or English regiment. Of the sixty Private Sentinels in each company, twenty were pikemen and the rest were musketeers. The pike, a defensive weapon and obsolescent, was from thirteen to eighteen feet long, and tipped with a flat spear-head. The muskets, barrels burnished and the stocks a cherry-brown, were eventually all flintlocks, for the Highlanders despised the cumbersome and inefficient matchlock. Each man carried a hanger on his left side, a short, cross-hilted sword in a black leather scabbard. On the right of his belt was his patrontash, a stiff cartridge-box containing twelve rounds of powder and ball wrapped in cylinders of paper. On his left buttock hung a bayonet, not the old plug weapon which was rammed into the muzzle, and with which Mackay's men had been desperately struggling when Dundee's swordsmen came down upon them at Killiecrankie. This was the new dagger-blade, with a hilt that could be locked on the barrel, leaving the musket free for firing. Finally, each soldier had a grey knapsack for his ammunition bread, his spare shoes and coarse linen shirt. He slung it over his shoulder, or hung it from his musket when on the march.

Argyll was childishly pleased with his regiment when he saw it drawn up on parade at Perth or Stirling, blue, scarlet and yellow, the crimson sashes and golden gorgets of the officers, the foam of lace at their throats, the sun on the points of the pikes and the curved blades of the sergeants' halberts. In three ranks, the grenadier company stood alone by honour and by privilege. The rest of the battalion was formed in line, with Argyll's own company on the right wing, then his lieutenant-colonel's, then the major's, and so on to Glenlyon's, the most junior company, on the left. When the drums beat a ruffle, the pikemen marched from their companies to the centre of the line and the colours were broken at their head. Officers and sergeants swept off their hats in salute, and the drums beat again.

"I can assure your lordship," Argyll told Melville, "scarce any new regiment can be in better order than mine." In the beginning he did his best to make it so, and it was at his expense that the Surgeon was supplied with vitriol, camomile and liquorice, camphor, sassafras and jallop, basil, lemon, and oil of rhubarb, all sent from Glasgow in stout wooden boxes. Now he wanted his men to be put to work, with himself at their head. "I am concerned that I should not be with my regiment where His Majesty is to expose himself."

But in the months that followed Major Duncanson and Quartermaster MacUre were less sanguine. There was a limit to the Earl's generosity, and to the extent to which he thought he should support the King's soldiers. They were short of pay and without food. Some time in the summer of 1691 they threw down their arms and refused to serve any longer, unless they were given bread immediately. John MacUre saved the honour of Clan Campbell and the dignity of the Earl of Argyll. On his own credit, he borrowed £735 5s. 9d. Sterling from Edinburgh money-lenders, and bought the soldiers enough to eat. He borrowed another £100 when that was gone, and when he could borrow no more, and could not repay what he had already borrowed, the money-lenders had him thrown into the Canongate Tolbooth. He was still in prison a year later, writing unhappy letters to the Privy Council, complaining of "my great ruin by the loss of my employment and the disorder of my affairs". The Earl, who was then in Flanders or sweet Peggy's arms, did little to help his loyal servant. He had spent £12,000 Sterling of his own money on the regiment's pay, clothing and weapons, and the King had yet to repay him. Compared with this, John MacUre's misfortune may have seemed slight.

The Argyll men were in action before the first ten companies had been fully mustered, though they were too late to join Mackay at Killiecrankie. Under Campbell of Auchinbreck, they were sent to sea as marines, and off Kintyre they captured an Irish ship that was attempting to carry men and horses to Thomas Buchan. To his great satisfaction, John Campbell of Airds was ordered away with his company to retake Castle Stalker, but the Appin men were out in force between Loch Creran and Glen Duror. Airds had to wait nine months until Stewart of Ardshiel surrendered the castle to the Earl of Argyll and all his regiment. In the King's name, and in Clan Diarmaid's cause, the regiment then harried the Macleans who had repossessed lands lost to the Camp-bells fifteen years before. Transported by the *Lamb* and the

Dartmouth, Captain Pottinger's men-of-war, the soldiers went ashore on Mull and the Isles of Treshnish, and although they wore red coats and fought beneath the King's colours, they shouted their old clan slogan "*Cruachan!*" as they repaid the Macleans for the Atholl Raid. Tarbat was uneasy about the use of Royal troops in the settlement of private quarrels, but John Hill thought that the Earl of Argyll had acted "generously and self-denyingly, minding none of his own concerns, but the King's only".

In December, 1691, when Stair's orders mobilised the Army, Argyll's was the only reliable regiment in the Western Highlands. Since the departure of the Cameronians for Flanders, it was also one of the best in Scotland. In its first year it had lost forty men by desertion, but its morale was now high. It was fully clothed and fully armed, though here and there a man may still have needed a poke for his hair, cording for his bonnet, or a scabbard for his hanger. It was adequately and regularly fed, it had recently been paid. It was also in its own country, and turned toward Clan Donald.

On December 29, as a result of express orders sent to the Earl by the King two weeks before, seven companies marched for Dunstaffnage under the command of Major Duncanson. There, on the coast of Lorn, boats were waiting to take them up Loch Linnhe to Fort William.

4

MURDER UNDER TRUST

"I will ask Ardkinglas to receive you as a lost sheep"

THE CAPTAIN of the night brought John Hill the news. A Highland
gentleman had been passed over the moat and through the Main
Guard, and was now outside the Governor's door, asking for him.
Twenty-four hours from the end of the year, MacIain had come at
last to Inverlochy.

It was snowing heavily. For more than a week the weather had
been unusually bad and this night was the worst yet, bitterly cold,
with a rising wind and the snow driven into great banks against
the walls. The calls of the night-watch were muffled, and each
man kept to the shelter of the embrasures. A huge fire cracked
and hissed by the main gate, and there was another by the sally-
port. Across the parade, snow was quickly filling the hoof-
prints of MacIain's garron and the marks of his gillies' feet leading
to the south-east ravelin. In the Governor's room candles were lit
and a peat-fire burned. Alasdair MacDonald appeared in the doorway like a giant from the Feinn, snow on his bonnet, his plaid and
his hair, his eyes proud above the fierce curl of his moustache. He
wore trews and boots, his famous buff coat and a wide belt with
broadsword and hanging pistols. He and Hill had not met for
thirty years, and the Governor must have searched the old brown
face for some warming memory of the young man he had once
known. MacIain greeted him courteously but briefly, and before
he would take a chair or a glass of wine he explained why he was
there.

"I have come," he said, "to swear the oath. Will you administer
it, that I may have King William's indemnity?"

Hill was astonished, and then he was angry, as much with his own helplessness as with the MacDonald's obstinate pride. He knew that MacIain was no fool, and understood as well as any man that he had no power to administer the oath. He said so, sharply, as if he were talking to a child. I am a soldier, he said. You are a soldier, agreed MacIain, implying that there would be no shame in submitting to him, you are the Governor of Lochaber. Hill shook his head. The words of the Proclamation had been plain enough for a boy to understand. The oath must be taken *in the presence of the Sheriffs, or their deputies, of the respective shires where any of the said persons shall live.*

"I cannot administer the oath to you!" said Hill impatiently, "You must go before Campbell of Ardkinglas at Inveraray."

MacIain said nothing, but his silence and the bitterness in his face spoke for him. He could not take the oath before a Campbell sheriff in a Campbell town, where he had been imprisoned and men of his name had been hanged. Suddenly Hill could no longer be angry with him, understanding the obstinate man's pride, and forgiving him the childish attempt to avoid the full humiliation of submission. Ardkinglas was a good man, the Governor pleaded gently, there would be no shame in submitting before him, did MacIain not understand that? Did he not understand the dangers he risked, for his people as well as himself, by coming to Fort William and not Inveraray, with little more than twenty-four hours before the time ran out? The Proclamation of August had made that risk brutally clear: *Such as shall continue obstinate and incorrigible after this gracious offer of mercy, shall be punished as traitors and rebels to the utmost extremity of the Law.* There was more that Hill could have said, had his duty and his honour permitted, of the soldiers marching on Inverness and Inverlochy, of Stair's savage and unequivocal threats. "The MacDonalds will fall in this net . . . this is the proper season to maul them . . . the Highlanders cannot escape us, nor carry their wives, bairns and cattle to the mountains. . . ."

MacIain was about to fall into that net, and although Hill could say nothing of it, the tone of his voice was enough to make the chief uneasy. His expression softened, and behind it Hill may have seen the fear that had been there all the time. The Governor sat down at his desk, pulling paper, quill and ink-horn before him. He looked up at the stiff buff coat, the bonnet held in a tight fist, the melted snow beading on tartan and leather. The time was short, said Hill, the weather bad, and he doubted that MacIain would reach Inveraray before the first hour of the New Year. "But," he smiled kindly, "I will ask Ardkinglas to receive you as a lost sheep." And he began to write.

When the letter was finished, folded and sealed, MacIain thrust it inside his coat and tugged down his bonnet. Hill took his arm. "Now I must hasten you away." Throwing a cloak over his shoulders, he walked with the chief to the Main Guard, and there shook his hand and wished him God speed. He watched by the fire as the old MacDonald rode off, legs out-thrust from the tiny pony, the gillies running softly. In a few seconds they were lost in the darkness and the snow. Hill could not even see the lights and the cottages of Maryburgh across the moat. He went back to his room, with a prayer for God's mercy on this lost ram of an erring flock.

MacIain and his gillies travelled slowly over the drove-road to Ballachulish, eight miles through a wild, white darkness. It was still not dawn when they came down by Callart. Across the leaden water of Loch Leven, MacIain could see a prick of light from his house at Carnoch half a mile away. He turned from it, westward to the ferry. Ashore at Ballachulish he sent one of the gillies to Glencoe with word for his wife and sons, telling them where he was going and why, urging them to keep in good heart, for he carried John Hill's letter in his coat and there was time yet before the old year ended.

The way he had chosen to reach Inveraray was not the shortest. In summer he would have gone southward from Laroch, up Gleann an Fiodh where the Norsemen had built their great camp, and then over a thin ridge to Glen Creran and Benderloch. But even a stag would not pass that way in winter. He went by Appin along the shore of Loch Linnhe. Before noon on Wednesday,

December 31, he came to the narrows of Loch Creran where there
was a ferry between two points of land, each called Rubha Garbh,
the rugged cape. To his right across the loch, on the white aird of
Benderloch, MacIain could see the black pencil of Barcaldine
Castle, one of seven defensive keeps built long before by the
Campbells in Appin. To his left, and also across the water, was the
narrow pass of Gleann Saloch, full of wind and snow. This would
take him down to Loch Etive where, if their old promise of
mutual succour meant anything now, he might get a cup of wine
and the warmth of a fire from Archibald Campbell of Inverawe.
He was an old man, he had been twenty-four hours and more
without sleep, most of which he had spent in the open in bitter
weather, and he was still far from Inveraray.

Roused from his bothy, the Appin boatman took the Mac-
Donalds over Loch Creran. They were stumbling ashore through
the frozen mud and snow when a patrol of red-coats ran toward
them from the aird, their muskets unslung. They were Thomas
Drummond's grenadiers, from the advance company of the four
hundred Argylls whom Duncanson was taking to Inverlochy.
Hostile, suspicious of men with heather in their bonnets, and
nervous as all recruits on their first campaign, they would not
listen to MacIain's protests, and shook their heads at the letter he
pulled from his coat. They took him two miles down the aird to
Barcaldine Castle where Drummond was at breakfast. The Lowlander was equally indifferent to Hill's letter, though he read it.
He told his men to put MacIain's gillies in a hole beneath the
castle. The chief was locked in a narrow *garde-robe*, where he
stayed for twenty-four hours in what must have been cruel
agony for a man of his size and age. Drummond had no authority
to ignore Hill's letter entirely, for the Governor would soon be his
commanding officer, but a day was long enough to satisfy his
spite and self-importance. The old year was gone when he finally
released the MacDonalds.

It was perhaps noon of January 1 when MacIain passed through
Gleann Saloch to the Bonawe Ferry, and another snowstorm was
thickening in the Pass of Brander, three miles to the south-west.

Now and then the unrelenting wind lifted the clouds trom the white scalp of Ben Cruachan. MacIain may have stopped at Inverawe House, but he was probably unwilling to trust any wayside Campbell now, and had fading hopes in Ardkinglas's clemency. He and his men took what rest they could afford in empty shielings, and paused at isolated cottages for bread and a dram. If they saw any more of Duncanson's companies they kept out of sight themselves. They went through the Pass of Brander and its snowstorm, following a narrow track above the furious river. In this weather the garron and the patient gillies could travel no more than a mile or two in an hour, and their strength was weakened by each. At nightfall they skirted the head of Loch Awe and the scattered lights of Campbell townships. Out on the water, Breadalbane's castle of Kilchurn was a snow-headed rock. Moving more and more slowly, they kept on throughout the night, down the shore of Loch Awe for five miles, and then southward across the high hills to Loch Fyne. Here the land was like a white, wrinkled blanket, each fold smoking with snow, and no clear division between earth and sky. At dawn on the second of January, three days after they had left Glencoe for Inverlochy, they came down through the bare timber planatations of Glen Aray to the Campbell capital.

To the exhausted gillies, following the heels of MacIain's pony, the sight of Inveraray must have been unnerving, the tall castle with round turrets, the streets of huddled houses, the merchants' shops, the Tolbooth and Court House, the herring-boats riding snow and wind on the loch water. Here was Campbell wealth and Campbell power, and here was Doom Hill where more than one Lochaber man's life had been choked from his throat. Beyond the castle were great parks of snow, avenues of trees and splendid gardens awaiting spring. This was the town their fathers had twice looted, and they walked softly and cautiously by the step-gabled houses.

MacIain took lodgings at a discreet change-house. The townsfolk in their Lowland breeches had not finished their New Year drinking, and he wanted no quarrels, no dirking between them and his gillies. He sent word to Ardkinglas and waited. A Town Officer came to him eventually, an old man in a scarlet coat, pacing out his steps with the haft of his Lochaber axe. He had numbing news.

Ardkinglas was away from Inveraray. He was across Loch Fyne, seeing in the New Year with his family, and no reasonable man could expect him back before the weather improved.

For three days the MacDonalds kept to the change-house. This was no time for a man with Clan Donald's badge in his bonnet to be abroad in the heart of Argyll. They waited, and they chewed bitterly on their pride. On Monday, January 5, Sir Colin Campbell of Ardkinglas returned from his New Year's holiday and summoned MacIain to the Court House. Although he was not an ungenerous man, he was sharp-tongued and irritable when put out of temper. He scolded MacIain for being late, would not accept the delay caused by either the weather or Drummond's men, and refused to administer the oath. MacIain gave him Hill's letter, and Ardkinglas hesitated as he read the Governor's appeal *... he has been with me, yet slipped some days out of ignorance, but it is good to bring in a lost sheep at any time, and will be an advantage to render the King's government easy.* The hesitation was brief, again the Campbell shook his head. The law was the law. The Proclamation had been issued five months ago, time enough for MacIain to have come before this.

And then he stared with astonished disbelief. MacDonald of Glencoe was weeping.

He wept without shame, tears on his leathered face and defiant moustache. His head was erect and his eyes were staring at the Sheriff, yet suddenly he was an old and broken man. Though Ardkinglas was close to the south and its colder emotions, he was as much Highland as MacIain, and he was moved by the nakedness of the MacDonald's fear. He said nothing. He waited kindly.

"Administer the oath to me," said MacIain at last, "and upon my honour I promise you that I shall order all my people to do the same. Those who refuse you may imprison, or send to Flanders as soldiers."

It was a terrible submission, and Arkinglas had no will or strength to resist it. "Come to me tomorrow," he said, "and it will be done."

The next morning MacIain walked from his tavern to the Court House, his gillies behind him, his bonnet cocked and his head up. Before the Sheriff and the clerks, before the Town Officers in scarlet and the townsfolk at the windows, he swore and signed the oath of allegiance to King William and Queen Mary, asking their pardon and craving their protection and indemnity. A night's thought had chilled some of the Sheriff's sympathy, and perhaps he remembered that here was a man whose insolent tribe had grievously abused both the Law and Clan Campbell. Once more he lectured MacIain for coming late, and warned him that there could be no assurance that the Privy Council would accept his oath. Then, softening again, he said that he would send Hill's letter to the Sheriff-Clerk of Argyll, who was then in Edinburgh, and also his own recommendation, asking the Sheriff-Clerk to place them before the Privy Council.

And so, lighter in heart, MacIain went home to Glencoe. The weather had lifted, the sun shone, melting much of the snow. He ordered a great fire to be lit on top of the rock in the elbow of the River Coe, summoning the men and women of his clan to Carnoch. He told them that he had taken the oath in their name as well as his own, and he ordered them to live peaceably under King William's government. If the oath were kept, there was nothing to fear.

A few days later John Hill got word from Ardkinglas. "I endeavoured to receive the great lost sheep Glencoe," said the Sheriff, "and he has undertaken to bring in all his friends and followers as the Privy Council shall order. I am sending to Edinburgh that Glencoe, though he was mistaken in coming to you to take the oath of allegiance, might yet be welcome. Take care that he and his friends and followers do not suffer till the King and Council's pleasure be known."* With happy relief John Hill

---

* Ardkinglas's letter has not survived. This extract appears in paraphrase in the Report of the Commission of Enquiry.

wrote to MacIain, telling him this good news and assuring him that he and his people were now under the protection of the garrison at Inverlochy.

In Edinburgh about the middle of January, Colin Campbell of Dressalch, Writer to the Signet and Sheriff-Clerk of Argyll, received a packet of papers from Ardkinglas. The first was a certified list of all those who had taken the oath at Inveraray, including the name of Alasdair MacDonald of Glencoe. The second was Hill's letter begging that the lost sheep might be received. The third was in Ardkinglas's own hand and addressed to his Sheriff-Clerk. He asked Dressalch to place these papers before the Council, and to let him know as soon as possible whether MacIain's oath had been accepted or not.

It may be that Dressalch felt no pleasure at seeing Glencoe's name on the certificate. He had lost a dozen fine cows to MacIain's men during the Atholl Raid, and he was still petitioning for £240 in compensation. He was also a man with a literal mind and a great respect for the letter of the Law, and he was reluctant to place the certificate before the Council without first taking advice from members of his own profession. They were also members of his own clan, for the Campbells counted many heads at the Bar. He went first to another Writer, John Campbell, who could give him no firm guidance, and together they approached a third Campbell lawyer, Lord Aberuchill, a member of the Privy Council. Dressalch asked him if he would canvass the private opinion of some Council members on the legality of leaving MacDonald's name on the list. Aberuchill willingly did so, and reported a day or so later that "it was their opinion that the certificate could not be received without a warrant from the King". One of those whom he has asked was the Viscount Stair, father of the Master.

This was not at all what the generous Sheriff of Argyll had wished. He had asked Dressalch to place the certificate and letters plainly and openly before the Council board. But even now the three Campbells were not finished. They went to Sir Gilbert Elliott and David Moncrieff, Clerks to the Council, both of whom said that MacIain's oath could not be accepted after the expiry of the time set.

Thus Alasdair MacDonald's name was scored from the certificate by several strokes of a pen, though not heavily enough to become illegible. It was done in the office of the Clerks to the Council and in the presence of John Campbell, David Moncrieff, Lord Aberuchill and Colin Campbell of Dressalch. Which one of them struck out the name was never determined. Three years later Colin Campbell of Dressalch, who had lost twelve fine cows to the Glencoe men, said on oath that he may have done it, and then again it may have been done by his servant.

"I entreat that Glencoe may be rooted out in earnest"

MAJOR DUNCAN MENZIES, now recovered from his journey and aware of an ugly danger, wrote anxiously to Sir Thomas Livingstone. He said that he had been unable to reach the Highlands before the time for taking the oath had expired, and therefore could not use his influence with those chiefs who might still be obstinate, "some persons having put them in a bad temper". If the time were extended, he was sure he could still persuade them. On January 5 Livingstone read this brave letter to the Privy Council, which refused to answer it, advising the handsome Commander-in-Chief to send it to Kensington Palace without comment. All great men in Scotland were looking over their shoulders to England, and those who had some suspicion of what was in the Master of Stair's mind were not inclined to prejudice their interests by idle compassion.

It was a time of uncertainty, a time of no news. No one yet knew how many chiefs had taken the oath, or indeed if any had done so. Breadalbane's law-agent in Edinburgh, Campbell of Carwhin, sent his master what information he could, and passed on to the Highlands what news he received of Grey John's affairs in London. Nothing must be done by the Earl's servants to hazard his delicate position at Court. "You did not tell me," Carwhin wrote to Barcaldine at Balloch, "what Keppoch and Glencoe has done or resolves to do. It is not safe now to correspond with any who are not come in, without allowance from the Government, wherefore take notice of what you do." When news of the troop movements north reached Edinburgh, Carwhin was delighted that the ingrates who had rejected the Earl's unselfish intercession would now regret it. "Those people are fallen into a strange delusion and they will certainly find the evil of it. How are all the fair promises they had from others now performed when the forces are marching toward them? Where are all the other great performances when . . ." And here, as always, Carwhin was the true echo of his master's voice. ". . . when nothing but ruin and desperation is said to be determined for some of them?"

In London, however, the Earl of Breadalbane was less happy than his agents. He was to be found every day in the corridors of Kensington, but was told little. There was bleak comfort in the Palace this winter. Wren's handsome red building, half-finished and with £60,000 already spent upon it, had been badly damaged by fire eight months before, and on damp days it still smelt abominably of charred wood.* Although Breadalbane lodged elsewhere, he spent as much time as he was allowed in Stair's ante-room. He had an audience with William and Mary, kissed their hands, and was granted "several conferences". But there was, he sensed, a growing lack of confidence in him, or at best an irritating indifference, and he complained of this pettishly. He was desperately anxious for news from Scotland, finding this useful in holding the attention of Stair. His vanity, ambition and fears were inextricably mixed this January, and he cherished a smile from the Queen, even a spattering cough in his direction from the King. But certain truths were evident, or he pretended they were. "Now my commission is extinct," he wrote to Carwhin on January 5, "and so is my meddling. All methods have been ordered before I came here, for that which will shortly be put in execution. I have not meddled in it, measures were agreed on before I came."

It is not easy to see what he meant, or what he wished Carwhin to believe. That he knew what was being planned, and was in no way responsible? That he was responsible, but wished Carwhin

---

* To the bloodthirsty regret of Iain Lom, William and Mary escaped from this fire in their night-clothes. The Bard of Keppoch said that it was a pity that only a few of William's supporters had been roasted alive.

to declare his innocence in the Highlands? Perhaps the strongest feeling he had was resentment at being shouldered from the centre of events, from the confidence of a man who had once written so flatteringly of "your Lordship's scheme". What was to happen now, said Breadalbane, would be "the work of the Government and Army wherein I am no member".

The seventh day of January dispelled some of his rancour. The Master of Stair came to dine with him at his lodgings, although his delight may have been soured by the fact that his nephew, the Earl of Argyll, came too. Nothing is known of the conversation across this intriguing dinner-table, but it is unlikely that Stair came for the pleasure alone. It was the eve of great decisions. That morning the Master had written to Livingstone. "To-morrow," he said, "we fall upon the Highland business." And now he sat with the greatest chiefs in the Highlands, both with a family and personal hatred of the Lochaber clans, both ambitious, both anxious. And both, too, had a detailed military knowledge of the glens, of how, and when, and where troops might be moved in winter. There would have been no reason for keeping from them what Stair had already told Livingstone. "You know in general that these troops posted at Inverness and Inverlochy will be ordered to take in the house of Invergarry, and to destroy entirely the country of Lochaber, Lochiel's lands, Keppoch's, Glengarry's, Appin and Glencoe." A Lowlander who, so far as is known, had never been in the Highlands, Stair would want to know what difficulties there might be, which glen offered the best approach, and which would be impassable. His later letters show a knowledge of the district about Glencoe which he could have got from these Campbells only.

He was still thinking of a punitive assault on all the Lochaber clans, Camerons, Stewarts and MacDonalds, if they had not taken the oath. Perhaps he watched Breadalbane above his glass, blandly waiting for the Earl to defend his "doited cousin" Lochiel. Too concerned with self-protection, Breadalbane would not have risked his own interests so foolishly, but he or Argyll would have argued against the practicability of such a proposal, particularly since Stair intended the punishment to be bloody and merciless. "I hope the soldiers will not trouble the Government with prisoners," he had told Livingstone, "slighting the offered mercy will justify all the severity used."

But, if a lesson must be taught. . . . After this evening Stair wrote and spoke of the Glencoe MacDonalds with venomous hatred and contempt. They were Papists, murderers and thieves, a damnable sept whose extirpation would be regretted by none. And if none would grieve their total destruction, all would see in it the strength and anger of the King. These were thoughts which an Argyll or Breadalbane chief, long victims of the Gallows Herd, could put into a Dalrymple's mind.

Four days later, Breadalbane received news of Lochiel's submission from the Cameron himself. He wrote a testy and immediate reply, advising Lochiel to post for London as early as he could. "You may expect the greatest flyting* ever you got in your life." Lochiel meekly did as he was told. He came to Kensington Palace at the end of the month, knelt, and humbly kissed the hands of William and Mary.

On Friday, January 9, dispatches sent from Edinburgh by flying pacquet told Stair that the chiefs of Appin, MacNaughten, Keppoch and Glencoe had also sworn within the time set. The report was half truth and half rumour. John MacNaughten of Dunderave, a merry man with the bottle and an ardent Jacobite despite the fact that he lived in the shadow of Inveraray Castle, had certainly taken the oath before Ardkinglas, and Coll of Keppoch had gone to Inverness. But Robert Stewart of Appin and his Tutor Ardshiel had not left their homes, and MacIain was still struggling down Glen Aray when the pacquet sailed from Leith. Stair accepted the report. He was sorry Keppoch and Glencoe were safe, he wrote to Livingstone that night, but nothing was changed. There were those who still held out, he was thinking of Glengarry again, and for them there could be no mercy. "I would be as tender of blood or severities as any man, if I did not see the reputation of the Government in question, and the security of the nation in danger."

* Scolding.

He advised Livingstone to be ready. He had been with the King this day, and His Majesty's instructions would be sent by the next pacquet on Monday.

On Sunday he worked alone with his clerk upon those instructions, and upon other letters to Scotland. The cold, half-built Palace was quiet, the workmen resting on the Sabbath. Beyond the tall windows there was frost on the trees, the deserted scaffolding and columns of bricks, the gardens and the clearing where the King wished Sir Christopher Wren to build an orangery. The only sounds in the world were the scratching of a clerk's pen, the whispering of the fire, and the Master's smooth voice dictating.

There were two sets of instructions to be ready for the King's signature that evening. The first was brief and to the Privy Council of Scotland, in which the King declared: "We do consider it indispensable for the well of that our kingdom to apply the necessary severities of law." To that end, he was sending orders to the Commander-in-chief for the employment of troops "to cut off these obstinate rebels by all manner of hostility". He required the Council to give all the assistance it could to Livingstone, to make known the extreme penalties men would risk in assisting the rebels, and to take special care that no harm came to those who had taken the oath.

Livingstone's orders were more detailed and set out in seven clauses, and the first was plain and unequivocal:

'You are hereby ordered and authorised to march our troops which are now posted at Inverlochy and Inverness, and to act against these Highland rebels who have not taken the benefit of our indemnity, by fire and sword and all manner of hostility; to burn their houses, seize or destroy their goods or cattle, plenishings or clothes, and to cut off the men.

The castle at Invergarry was to be taken and garrisoned. The Argyll companies at Fort William could be used against the MacDonalds of Skye and Clanranald. Governor Hill at Inverlochy and Baillie Duff at Inverness would supply subsistence, transport and all other necessaries for these expeditions. Where the intransigent Macleans were concerned, Livingstone was to take the advice and orders of the Earl of Argyll's agents, for the Earl had a legal right to Sir John Maclean's estate. The Commander-in-chief was also to use discretion and mercy where both seemed advisable, "that the rebels may not think themselves absolutely desperate".

By that evening the King had slashed his oblique signature above and below both letters of instructions, and the Master was alone in the candle-light, writing covering letters. He wrote to the Earl of Tweeddale. "There is a necessity," he said, "that the world may see the Government, being ill-used, will turn severe, and the obstinacy of those deluded rebels will justify all the rigour that can be done to them." He was amused by the irony of the situation. "It's a jest to think how they have been forced at last to do what might have got them money if timeously done."

He folded the letter, sealed it, and took another sheet of paper. *Dear Sir Thomas, I send you the King's instructions, super and subscribed by himself. . . .* He was confident that Livingstone would see thereby that he was given full powers in very plain terms. Since the rebels had madly rejected the King's clemency, there could be no just complaint against their punishment. Stair admitted he was much concerned for those he called "the poor commonalty", but if nothing were done to disable them too, they would continue in absolute obedience to their rebellious chiefs. He thought of Keppoch and Glencoe with angry frustration. He had no kind thoughts for them or their people, he said, and they were fortunate to have accepted the King's mercy. He paused, looking at the letter. A good servant deserved the promise of favour to encourage him in his further duties. He wrote on. "I did remember the King to-day that you are now a twelve-month a brigadier, and longer Commander-in-chief of his forces there, which must occasion you to be at greater expense, and yet you have no more but the colonel's pay." The King had promised to mend the matter. It could not be done by this post, of course, but Stair would not forget.

There was a scratch at the door and he looked up. A servant bowing, and behind him the tall figure of Argyll, his face flushed beneath his great wig. He had come at once, from dinner or Peggy Alison's bed, to tell Stair the news which Ardkinglas had sent at the turn of the year. He stayed a brief while only, the Master was obviously busy. He said that the clansmen of his regiment, sent to Inverlochy under Duncanson, had taken rations for a fortnight only, and they would have hard living if further arrangements were not made. When his visitor was gone, Stair turned back to his letter. He was elated.

Just now, my Lord Argyll tells me that Glencoe hath not taken the oaths, at which I rejoice. It's a great work of charity to be exact in rooting out that damnable sept, the worst in all the Highlands.

He scribbled a hasty conclusion to the letter, asking Livingstone to care for Argyll's Regiment, and then sealed it. Fresh instructions would have to be drawn up for the King's approval, now that MacIain had set himself beyond mercy, but these already before him on the table could not wait, and must be away on the morning tide from Wapping. The great work of charity would yet be ordered.

Five hundred miles away at Inverlochy the New Year had brought joy to John Hill, joy in Lochiel's submission and in MacIain's, albeit late. The season was cold, he reported to Edinburgh, there being great snows, and the people about the fort were miserably poor. Duncanson's men were now with him, quartered inside the walls or in the houses of Maryburgh, and some detachments were stationed down the shore of Loch Linnhe. "All is peaceabie," he said, "as the streets of Edinburgh." MacDonald of Moidart had sent word by the Laird of Morar that their chief, the boy Clanranald, was storm-bound on South Uist, but he would undoubtedly take the oath as soon as he could, and if he were then given a pass for France. From Skye came news that young MacDonald of Sleat, in his dying father's name, would also submit, and Coll of Keppoch was asking for commissions in William's army for himself and his brother (swearing that they were Protestants and no Papists). The best news of all was that MacDonald of Glengarry had changed his mind. He had heard of the troop movements against him, and had decided that the walls of Invergarry would not long stand against the cannon, petards and grenades that were being gathered at Inverness. He told Hill that if some of his gentry were given passes, to go abroad for service under King Louis, he and the rest would lay down their arms and surrender the castle to Livingstone's officers.

Governor Hill chided them all, telling them that since they were late with their submission, the King might well think of punishing them. But he did not believe this himself. So much had been done without bloodshed. Clan Donald was bending its knee at last.

In London, Stair knew nothing yet of the meek surrender of the detestable MacDonalds. It would not have altered his decision, his eyes were clouded with blood. On January 16, he placed before the King those additional instructions he thought necessary for the great work of charity. In the four days since Stair's last letter to Livingstone there had been a change of intent, and this may have been at William's wish. He needed Scots regiments for his spring campaign in Flanders, and it would have been foolish to provoke a war in the Highlands that once again kept them at home. Livingstone was now told that, upon his own discretion, he could "give Glengarry the assurance of entire indemnity for life and fortune, upon the delivering of his house and arms, and taking the oath of allegiance". There was no suggestion of punishing the obstinate MacDonald for not taking the oath within the time. His surrender was all that was required. But to encourage him, and all others who had been or would be tardy, the violent lesson had still to be read and learned. It was stated bluntly in the last clause of these new instructions.

If M'Kean of Glencoe, and that tribe, can be well separated from the rest, it will be a proper vindication of the public justice to extirpate that sept of thieves.

The great plan for punishment, upon which Stair had been working since the middle of December, had now contracted into one small, bloody proposal of massacre.

King and Minister faced each other across the sheet of paper.
Neither man believed in showing his emotions, the King cold
and withdrawn, the Master bland and deferential. Though they
may not have heard it, there was an echo in the little privy chamber, the voice of a Prince of Orange refusing to take an oath that
bound him to persecute his new people, and a Dalrymple assuring
him that no law of the nation put that obligation upon him.
William was no stranger to profit by murder. In Holland in his
youth, he had secured the office of Stadholder (which he believed
to be his by birth) after his supporters had brutally slaughtered
the Republican brothers De Witt. And they had been civilised
men. The MacDonalds of Glencoe were thieves and murderers
and savages whose continued resistance to his authority made him
a joke among European princes. Upon the Master's word, their
removal would bring relief and satisfaction to all the people of
Scotland.

He picked up a pen and signed the new instructions. He signed
them at the head and the foot, and therefore no one can reasonably
claim that he did not read and fully understand what was written.

The Master of Stair returned to his own room. There was a
night's work ahead before the pacquet left. A double of the instructions had to be sent to Colonel Hill with a covering letter. There
were letters to Livingstone, to Tweeddale and others. His pen
scratched busily in the candle-light. "I am extremely glad," he
told Tweeddale, "that the murderer MacIain of Glencoe did not
accept the benefit of the indemnity. I hope care will be taken to
root out that thieving tribe." His pen, in pale fingers thrust from
a cuff of lace, was the servant of his hatred, a living thing almost,
hysterically repeating the same words, the same phrases in each
letter. "For a just example of vengeance," it told Livingstone, "I
entreat that the thieving tribe in Glencoe may be rooted out in
earnest." It wrote again with equal venom to John Hill. "I shall
entreat you, that for a just vengeance and a public example, the
thieving tribe of Glencoe may be rooted out to purpose."

Hill was assured that when this work of charity was begun, his
garrison would have assistance. And here, perhaps, the Master

betrayed something of the conversation that had passed across Breadalbane's dinner-table.

The Earls of Argyll and Breadalbane have promised that they shall have no retreat in their bounds. The passes to Rannoch would be secured, and the hazard certified to the Laird of Weem to reset them. In that case, Argyll's detachment, with a party that may be posted in Island Stalker, must cut them off; and the people of Appin are none of the best.

And now, in London, there was little to do but wait. How much Breadalbane knew, cannot be said with any certainty. But he was uneasy again, and Stair's visit to his lodgings had led to no further confidences. "I am ill-requite on all hands," was his melancholy complaint to Carwhin, "for I am here ill-treat for these persons not ending timeously, and am again ill-treat for my good nature in dealing with them after such usage." His own good nature was a great comfort to him as he suffered nobly under the spite and jealousy of others. There was little else to comfort him. He had been told that the Government did not intend to pay the money he had promised the chiefs, and the sombre gravity of his expression became heavier with self-pity. But if all others mistrusted him, he still had the solace of his own virtues. "I thank God I do not repine for all the trouble and charges and danger I have been at for them and the nation, which is my duty and interest to endeavour it to be in peace and prosperity." But, as he stepped out of his carriage at Kensington Palace, as he waited anxiously in Stair's ante-room, as he bowed to the passing shadow of the King in the corridors, he was desperate for news from the Highlands.

That month the storms were so great in the north that they kept the Post from the roads and most ships in port. In Edinburgh there was published a list of all those who had taken the oath, and it included MacIain's name, with the qualification that he had been six days late at Inveraray. To Breadalbane's chagrin, he heard this news at Court rather than by letter from Carwhin, and he wrote sourly to say that he was pleased to hear that Glencoe had changed his mind. He may well have meant it. At this moment, for all his denial of involvement, he was a frightened, unhappy man.

Stair's mind was unchanged by the news of MacIain's submission, and he informed Livingstone of this by letter on January 30. There must be no half-measures.

I am glad that Glencoe did not come in within the time prescribed. I hope what's done there may be in earnest, since the rest are not in the condition to draw together to help. I think to harry their cattle or burn their houses is but to render them desperate, lawless men, to rob their neighbours; but I believe you will be satisfied it were of great advantage to the nation that thieving tribe were rooted out and cut off. It must be quietly done, otherwise they will make shift for both men and their cattle. Argyll's detachment lies in Letrick* well to assist the garrison to do all on a sudden.

It must be quietly done. . . . When he had finished this letter to Livingstone, Stair drew another sheet of paper before him and wrote to John Hill. He had received the Governor's letter of January 14, explaining that the Highlands were now at peace and that the chiefs were disposed to take the oath. He told Hill to make the best of this situation, "by any means settle all one way or the other". But he was to expect no more instructions than those he

---

* In the printed Report of the Commission of Enquiry into the Massacre of Glencoe (published in London by Thomas Bragg, 1703) this place-name appears as *Letrickweel*. In an abstract of this letter from the Stair Collection, published in The Highland Papers (Glasgow, 1844), it is given as *Keppoch Well*. But a study of the manuscript of the Report in the Public Record Office (from which Bragg took his version), makes it clear that the place is meant to be *Letrick* only, and that *well* is an abverb used elliptically for "well-placed". Where Letrick was is not easy to determine. It has been assumed that Keppanach was meant, since this was and is a township on the north side of Ballachulish ferry. But there is no evidence of any troops there at the time Stair wrote this. I am indebted to Sir William Arbuckle for a more likely explanation. On a 17th-century map of the area *Letre Rouaga* is a point on the south side of the Loch Creran ferry, where MacIain was taken by Argyll's men on his way to Inveraray. Thus "Argyll's detachment" may be Drummond's grenadiers. However, perhaps the point is academic only.

must already have received under the King's hand of January 16.
The orders for exterminating the Gallows Herd were not changed.

Pray, when anything concerning Glencoe is resolved, let it be secret
and sudden, otherwise the men will shift you, and better not meddle
with them than not do it to purpose; to cut off that nest of robbers who
have fallen in the mercy of the law now, when there is force and
opportunity, whereby the King's justice will be as conspicuous and
useful as his clemency to others. I apprehend the storm is so great that
for some time you can do little, but so soon as possible I know you will
be at work... Deal with them as you find their consternation and the
circumstances allows you, but by all means be quick. . . .

A calm man at work by candle-light in a small room, each
movement precise, delicate, as though rehearsed. The regular dip
of the quill into the ink-horn, the flourish as the paper was
sanded, and now and then a sweep of the hand to clear the curls
of his wig from his face. Yet there was a madness in the man.
What he was ordering, though it had arisen out of the situation,
was no longer relevant to it. The tardy chiefs would be allowed,
and were ready, to take the oath under William's mercy, and
therefore this deliberate act of terrorism was neither necessary nor
defensible. It seemed to come from Stair alone, like a reflex of
heart or muscle. But if he were not the King's minister at this
point, neither was he his own. He was the instrument of *Mi-run
mor nan Gall*, the Lowlander's great hatred of the Highlandman,
exacting vengeance for past fears and humiliations, preparing for
the future, the future Union of Parliaments when Englishmen
would accept Scots as their equals.

The night was almost gone when he rose from his desk. The
events he had set in motion from it, by a feathered quill and a well
of ink, were now inexorable.

The pacquet carrying the King's instructions of January 16, with
their order for the extirpation of the Glencoe men, had arrived at
Leith four days later. Major Forbes collected the letters for Hill,
opened them, read them, and sent them on to Fort William. With
them in the same bag, perhaps, went a letter from Livingstone to

Hamilton, whom both the Master and the Commander-in-chief now regarded as the only reliable officer at Inverlochy.

Since my last I understand that the Laird of Glencoe, coming after the prefixed time, was not admitted to take the oath, which is very good news here, being that at Court it's wished he had not taken it, so that thieving nest might be entirely rooted out; for the Secretary in three of his last letters hath made mention of him, and it is known at Court he has not taken it. So, Sir, here is a fair occasion for you to show that your garrison serves for some use; and seeing that the orders are so positive from Court to me not to spare any of them that have not timely come in, as you may by the orders I sent to your Colonel, I desire you would begin with Glencoe, and spare nothing which belongs to him, but do not trouble the Government with prisoners.

The letters reached Fort William at the end of January. John Hill was struck by the paralysis that came over him when faced with a distasteful duty that challenged his common sense, his conscience, and his simple Christianity. But for the moment he was not required to do anything. Lieutenant-Colonel James Hamilton had been put there for this purpose, and he acted immediately.

It was upon his orders that two companies of the Earl of Argyll's Regiment marched for Glencoe under the command of Captain Robert Campbell of Glenlyon.

"He is an object of compassion when I see him"

HE WAS sixty years of age. He was a gambler and a heavy drinker. He was improvident and bankrupt. He was so much in debt to his kinsmen, his friends and his enemies that he could not live long enough to repay them. Like all Breadalbane Campbells he had bred a large family, six sons and five daughters, and he shame-lessly accepted the charity of the survivors as if this had been the purpose of their conception. The only land he now owned in Glen Lyon was the estate at Chesthill, and even that was held in his wife's name to prevent him from throwing it away on the turn of a dice-cup. At the age of fifty-nine he had taken a captain's commission in the Earl of Argyll's Regiment, and this must be recognised as an act of courage.

Robert Campbell, fifth Laird of Glenlyon in Breadalbane, never lacked courage, although toward the end of his life he was more desperate than brave. He had splendid, florid good looks, which are done less than justice in the only surviving portrait of him. It was painted when he was a young man, to celebrate his first experience of war, perhaps, and his long head is curiously femi-nine, and seems to have no blood and tissue connection with the lobster-shell of black armour upon which it is conventionally mounted. His hair is the fine reddish-yellow of the Campbells, his mouth thin and petulant and too small for his heavy jaw. It is the face of a weak and self-indulgent man, and it would excite no passion now, but in his youth women thought he was an Adonis. His tall, well-articulated body moved with an affecting grace, his manners were polished and charming. With men he could be robustly jovial, and he had the disarming Highland way of calling them by affectionate diminutives of their Christian names, as if he wished all the world to be his friends. Indeed, since he was soon in debt to most of it, he could afford no enemies.

The valley his family had occupied for nearly two hundred years is the longest in the Highlands, twenty-five wandering miles from Loch Tay to Loch Lyon and the passes to Rannoch Moor. It is beautiful, and has been given many names—the Glen of the Black Water, the Desert Glen, the Crooked Glen of the Stones. "Fionn MacCumhail had twelve castles in the Crooked Glen of the Stones," said the old legends. On the northern hills that protected it from Rannoch, the warriors of the Feinn were sleeping, and in his boyhood Robert Campbell went with other children to find the long, green mounds that were their beds. They were high on the braes, beyond the dark-headed, scarlet-stemmed plantations of fir, the orange cloudberry, and the open peat as black as pitch after rain. The valley was also called the Glen of the Chapels, as much a part of Christian history as Glencoe. Saint Adamnan, abbot of Iona and biographer of Columba, converted the early people, built them a school and a corn-mill, and instructed them in the civilised arts. He and his monks quarrelled quietly over the ritual of Easter and the exact purpose of the tonsure, celebrated mass and baptised the new-born, but they never convinced the people that there were not other supernatural beings besides choirs of angels. The *sitheachan*, for example, cunning fairies who lived by the River Lyon, stealing children from the cradles if they were not first propitiated by pagan ceremonies.

The Campbells came late, from the east with the first Glenorchy lairds. Many clans fought for the valley, or lived together there in uneasy neighbourhood. The MacDiarmids are believed to have been the first, in the trail of Saint Adamnan's robe, and after them were MacArthurs, MacCallums and MacGregors. For a while in the 14th century a MacDougall of Lorn, Black John of the Spears, held the glen on a grant from King David Bruce, and defended it bitterly against the Chisholms who came down on him from

Strathglass, far beyond the Great Glen. At the end of the 15th century Black Colin Campbell, first Laird of Glenorchy, claimed the valley from the Stewarts of Garth, using sword, axe, bow and fire as his most persuasive arguments. More circumspectly, the second Laird of Glenorchy got a Crown Charter for the barony and gave it in fee to his younger son Grey Archibald, the progenitor of all the Glenlyon lairds. For four generations the Campbells of Glenlyon held this property against their MacGregor tenants, their Menzies neighbours, their Glenorchy cousins, and the marauding forays of the Lochaber Men. Grey Archibald was a wise and peaceful man. He hanged no one unless they deserved it, took nothing to which he had no right, and was therefore given little space in recorded history. His son, however, was more in character, a fine, robust fellow known as *Dhonnachaidh Ruadh na Feileachd*, Red Duncan of the Hospitality. He built almost as many castles as Fionn Mac-Cumhail, and most of them on the same ground, guarding the narrows of the glen, the bends of the river. Their doors were always open to wandering bands of harpers from Ireland, to smiths, wrights and artisans from the Lowlands. His title was an irony, however, and one Highland visitor put the general thought into verse.

> If thou art Red Duncan the Hospitable
> far will I bear thy fame.
> As we turn our backs on each other,
> it is I whom am shirtless, not thou.

For what was put upon the backs of the Campbells of Glenlyon had usually been taken from the shoulders of a MacGregor, a Stewart, or a Menzies.

The third laird was Mad Colin, whose wits never recovered from a blow on the head in his youth. He was a violent man, malevolent and arrogant. His life was a furious storm of ill-temper, relieved only by the letting of blood. It was he who hanged thirty-six raiders from Keppoch and Glencoe on the braes of Meggernie, after first pistolling their leader. For a hundred years the Lochaber Men spoke of Glen Lyon as if Mad Colin were still there, leering from the walls of Meggernie Castle at the bodies of three dozen MacDonalds. He quarrelled with everyone, the King and his Glenorchy cousins, his wife and his children. He would shelter the MacGregors one day to spite his Campbell kin, and hang them the next to amuse himself. From his violent loins came a surprisingly gentle successor, another Red Duncan who preferred avenues of sycamores to hanging-trees. He did not molest the MacGregors of Roro who lived in Glen Lyon, protected them from Glenorchy's harrying, and was not too angry when his daughter eloped with one. But he did more damage to his family than Mad Colin's temper could ever have done. He was a passionate and unlucky gambler, creating a labyrinth of debt and mortgage from which his son escaped only by dying before he inherited it.

Robert Campbell, the fifth Laird, succeeded his tree-loving and amiable grandfather at the age of eight, and he was fourteen when the Gallows Herd went home from Montrose's wars by way of Glen Lyon. He was well grounded in French, Latin, mathematics and the story of his family's vengeful hatred of the MacDonalds. Among the earliest sounds he heard was the cry of Clan Donald's slogan and the rattle of his grandfather's dice, and both were to have the strongest influence over his life. His redoubtable mother was Jean Campbell, a sister of the tenth Laird of Glenorchy and the aunt of Grey John of Breadalbane. She made marriage and childbirth her vocation, having three husbands and sixteen children. After the death of Archibald Campbell, Robert's father, she married Patrick Roy MacGregor. He was a vigorous and mettlesome gentleman, but no match for her, and when he went the way of his predecessor she married Duncan Stewart the Third of Appin by whom, understandably perhaps, she had one child only. This girl married a Campbell of Lochnell, and their daughter Sarah became the wife of Alasdair Og, the younger son of MacIain the Twelfth of Glencoe.

When Jean Campbell died, the Stewarts of Appin, the MacGregors of Roro, and the Campbells of Glenlyon held a wake that was remembered in Breadalbane for two hundred years. The days

between the death of the valiant old woman and her interment
were filled with riotous drinking, feasting and games, as was the
custom. All three clans competed against each other in wrestling,
fencing, throwing the stone and tossing the caber. The Campbells
outmatched their opponents, until a MacGregor threw a stone
between the fork of a high tree and could not be beaten. Believing
that Glenlyon should be the first at his mother's funeral as it had
been in her marriage bed, Robert Campbell sent for one of his
herdsmen, a MacArthur who lived fifteen miles up the glen. This
sturdy fellow arrived the next morning on the run, and without
removing plaid or bonnet he threw the stone between the same
tree-fork and far beyond the MacGregor's mark. The delighted
Robert Campbell broached more whisky and postponed his
mother's burial for another twenty-four hours of games and
drinking.

Glenlyon's apologists, and they grew fewer as his creditors
increased, said that since he had grown up under the restrictive
rule of the Commonwealth there had been little to occupy him
but gambling and drinking. The Restoration, however, increased
his taste for both. Once he was free from the guardianship of his
uncle, and the full inheritor of a debt-burdened estate, he borrowed money from the kin of his first step-father, which says
much for his power of persuasion and their magnanimity, since
the MacGregors claimed Glen Lyon as theirs by right. He
borrowed from all the Campbells of Breadalbane, and from any
Perthshire laird who was foolish enough to listen to him, and to
repay one debt he saddled himself with three more. He signed
bonds and mortgages with a recklessness that would have
terrified his grandfather. He was so busy with dice, drinking and
debts that he was thirty-eight before he thought of marrying. His
wife was Helen Lindsay from Angus, a loyal woman who bore his
improvidence and his children with patient stoicism. To put her
in a setting that fitted his station, he signed more bonds, borrowed
more money, and enlarged Meggernie Castle.

His infuriated creditors took him to law, where he was compelled to raise some of the money owing them by leasing the

fir-woods of Glen Lyon to John Crawford and a company of Lowland merchants. For three years Glenlyon watched in sullen resentment as Crawford built a sawmill, dammed the River Lyon, and began to fell the splendid red trees. The people of Glen Lyon were resentful too. They did not like the Lowlanders, and they accused Crawford of building his mill on the site of Saint Adamnan's corn-mill. They put the Evil Eye on his water-wheel and roasted his oxen over the timber he had cut. Crawford complained, but Robert Campbell had now remembered that he was the great-grandson of Mad Colin who had hanged a King's Messenger and put his foot upon the King's order. On the real or imagined excuse that the Lowlanders had gone beyond the terms of their lease, he called out his people in arms. According to a complaint made to the Privy Council, they "came on 26th July, 1677, armed with swords, guns, dirks, pistols and other weapons, and fell upon the wrights and workmen at the mill and stole their tools and worklooms, and threatened to hang them if they worked any longer". Three times Glenlyon and his brother Colin raided the mill, and when Crawford died "the said Robert Campbell and others came to the said John Crawford's house where his corpse was lying, and violently seized the chest wherein were his whole papers, particularly some discharges and receipts granted him by Glenlyon, and carried it off to his own house at Chesthill".

Crawford's successor was a Stewart and a Highlander, and he knew how to deal with a situation like this. He came back the next year "with others of his name, armed with swords, pistols, hagbuts and dirks". Thus protected, he cut down eight thousand trees, built more dams, and burned the houses and crops that stood in the way of his ox-wagons. Glenlyon complained to the Privy Council this time, saying that the woodmen had ruined the salmon-fishing from which he drew most of his rents, and asking for £34,333 Scots in compensation. It was a brave try, but the unsympathetic Council told him to behave himself, and put him under oath not to molest Patrick Stewart of Ballechan lest he have Letters of Fire and Sword issued against him.

The people of Glen Lyon relished the affair, and their Bard

composed a song in honour of it—"How we burned the wide-horned oxen on the boards of Crawford's saw-mill."

The only man in Scotland now willing to lend Robert Campbell a shilling was his cousin Grey John, who advanced him £5,000 against his bond. There were so many charter-chests filled with so many bonds signed by Robert Campbell of Glenlyon, that the Earl cannot have hoped to see his money again. But he had a clannish concern for the feckless man, and he believed that credit cemented the loyalty of his vassals as well as kinship. Two years later Glenlyon repaid some of this debt, or at least an interest on it, by leading Grey John's army into Caithness against the Sinclairs.

He was fifty when his debts, his drinking, his gambling, and the destitution they had brought upon his family, at last became a matter of honour to Clan Campbell. He was ordered to accept the *comhairl'-taigh*, the guidance of his house as given by its chief, the ninth Earl of Argyll. He took it like a frightened child, willingly signing all papers put before him by Campbell lawyers in the presence of the Provosts of Perth and Edinburgh. He confessed that his way of life had brought his estates and family into ruin, and that he could not alone save them.

And likewise understand how easy I may be circumvented and deceived in the management of my affairs by subtle and crafty persons who have designs on me, and may entice me to the dilapidation of my lands, goods and gear, to my great hurt and prejudice. And I being fully persuaded and having good proof and experience of the love and kindness of my noble and real friends, Archibald, Earl of Argyll, and John, Earl of Caithness whose counsel and advice I now resolve to use and by whom I am hereafter to be governed in all my affairs and business.

He promised to sell no more of his lands or rents, to make no further bonds or obligations without the joint consent of Argyll and Grey John. If he did so they would be "null and void, as if the same had never been made".

Five years later he broke this promise. Argyll had died under the Maiden, but the terms of the bond still made Glenlyon subject to Breadalbane's consent. Grey John was tired of his cousin Robin, and refused to lend him any more money. Glenlyon was filled with rage as violent as any that had ever convulsed Mad Colin, and he swore that if he could get no help from his own kinsmen he would sell all he owned in the glen, that not one blade of grass would thenceforward belong to a Campbell. Breadalbane threatened him with the bond, and he ignored it. His people offered him half of their cattle to pay his debts, but he refused it. On a deer-hunt some days before the sale, a ball from another gun narrowly missed him, passing between his legs. "Would it have been your loins," said his gillie, "then Glen Lyon would not be sold."

It was sold, to the Murrays of Atholl. All that was left to Glenlyon was the house and estate of Chesthill, the dower-land of his wife, and this too was to go to the Murrays when she died. When it was raped by the Glencoe men after Killiecrankie, Glenlyon was poorer than he had ever been. He drank more and gambled more, his fair skin flushed and his voice loud and quarrelsome. In 1690 he raised a ragged force of men from Argyll and went raiding in Strathfillan, hoping to lift enough cattle to pay some of his debts. Breadalbane was sure that he was now mad. "He ought to be sent to Bedlam," the Earl told Carwhin, "I wish we had chambered him years ago," Yet the man's pathetic dignity, even in drink, was disarming, the call of clanship was always strong, and Grey John could sometimes feel sorry for him. "He is an object of compassion when I see him, but when he is out of sight I could wish he had never been born."

Glenlyon may well have wished this himself now. Since the savage raid by the Glencoe men there had been no rents collected on Chesthill. His family almost starved in the winter of 1690, and to buy them meal he borrowed a little money on a short term from one of the Murrays. When he failed to repay it, the Murray had him outlawed, and he would have been hunted in the hills had his son-in-law not honoured the debt for him. He now bitterly regretted the sale of Glen Lyon to Lord Murray, which

Breadalbane had been disputing for years. In his drunken rages, his mornings of maudlin self-pity, he complained that he had been tricked by the "subtle and crafty persons" whom he had once before blamed for his misfortunes. Impatient with Breadalbane's failure to get the sale reversed, he asked Argyll for assistance. He took a commission in the Earl's regiment at this time, and this may have been as much an attempt to help his petition as it was a desperate and last effort to support his family.

Argyll persuaded him to accept a decision reached by himself and the Earl of Arran as arbitrators. Glenlyon agreed, and the two Earls decided in favour of the Murray claim. Lord Murray's support for King William, against the Jacobite sympathies of his father and clan, needed some generous acknowledgment, and Glenlyon's support was of value to nobody. Breadalbane was enraged, though not so much on his cousin's behalf. "It has been done of purpose against me," he said, and the next time he saw Lord Murray at Holyroodhouse he set about him with his fists.

Which did not, of course, help Robert Campbell of Glenlyon who was now a captain of Foot at eight shillings a day.

"There put in due execution the orders you have received"

BEYOND THE mouth of Gleann an Fiodh, the Valley of Wood less than a mile from Invercoe, Glenlyon halted his command. On this narrow, lochside track he had formed his companies in close order and by half-files, a column of scarlet, black, yellow and grey, fifty yards long with an advance file and an after-guard. The soldiers' breath hung above their bonnets in a white roll, their sergeants' cries echoed across the water. *"Order your muskets . . . order your pikes . . . rest on your arms!"* The brass heels of the muskets struck the frosted earth, the pikes slanted and were still. The musketeers blew on their naked fingers and envied the leather gauntlets of the pikemen.

Only the leading files could see the reason for the halt. Across their path, from the brae to the edge of the loch, were twenty Highlanders, still and suspicious, like a deer-herd nervously scenting danger. Before them stood a gentleman in plaid and trews, his head up in question. Glenlyon could see no weapons, no point of sword or swing of dirk beneath the tartan, and the gentleman himself was plainly unarmed. He called up a lieutenant, his wife's kinsman John Lindsay, and sent him forward with the quartering-papers. He waited, leaning on his half-pike, listening to the sound of Lindsay's feet, the hawking and coughing of his men.

As soon as the first boat had been seen on the ferry the news had run from Ballachulish to Invercoe, from the big house at Carnoch to Inverrigan, Achnacone and Achtriachtan. Although he had John Hill's promise of protection, and expected no danger, MacIain told his people to hide their arms in their peat-stacks, or on the brae beneath heaps of stones. If the soldiers were coming to disarm Glencoe, let them be given no more than rusty, useless weapons. He sent his son John, whose calm judgement he could trust, to meet the soldiers with some of his clan, to ask them their business and to make them welcome if they came in peace. Now John MacDonald looked beyond Lieutenant Lindsay to the tall figure at the head of the soldiers. If he recognised the flushed face, the fair hair and staring eyes, he cannot have been easy in spirit. Lindsay was holding out the papers in a gauntleted hand, but MacDonald did not take them. "Do you come as friends," he asked, "or as enemies?"

"As friends," said the lieutenant, pushing forward the papers again. On his parole of honour, no harm was intended MacIain or his people. But here were orders, as Mr. MacDonald would see if he read them, signed by his commanding officer and demanding quarters in Glencoe for two companies of the King's Foot. MacIain's son took the papers, and now Glenlyon came forward, his plaid thrown back from his red coat, his hand out, and the light cold on the gilt gorget at his throat. He greeted the Mac-Donald boisterously, asking for news of his niece Sarah and his nephew Sandy, making a family gathering of the meeting by introducing the lieutenant as one of his kin too. He was probably nervous, remembering that less than three years before this quiet man, and others of the clan, had brought him and his family close to starvation. And John MacDonald must have thought that of all the officers who could bring troops to Glencoe, in peace or hostility, the one least welcome would be he who had most reason to hate MacIain. And to come with Argyll men at his back, forbye. . . .

Glenlyon's husky, shouting voice beat down their mutual doubts. Here were bad times, when men must impose themselves upon others' hospitality in such weather. But the fort was full, did MacDonald know that? A great gathering of soldiers to punish Glengarry when the weather lifted, and until then, until they were called, he and his men would be grateful for what quarters

Glencoe could find them. It was in order, MacDonald would see that from the papers, but it was also the Highland way to ask for bed and comfort as a gentleman and a friend, and this he did willingly. Would MacIain refuse him?

"You and your men are welcome in Glencoe," said John Mac-Donald, and he held out his hand. Behind him, his scowling clansmen moved and broke, running back to Invercoe with news that the soldiers were coming. The drums beat, the companies marched, and John MacDonald walked beside Glenlyon to his father's house.

The Argyll men were halted again on the flat, frosted meadow by Carnoch, and the people of the glen gathered to stare at them uneasily. Among the grenadiers, MacIain's gillies may have recognised the soldiers who took them and their chief prisoner at Loch Creran ferry a month before, and this would have deepened their uncertainty. MacIain came from his door with his wife at his side, and once more Glenlyon asked for quarters and hospitality, promising that the burden he put upon them would soon be lifted when orders set him and his men against Glengarry. "You are welcome," said MacIain kindly, and perhaps his greeting was all the warmer because he was relieved to hear that no more than this was expected of him. John Hill and Ardkinglas had promised him the protection of the garrison at Inverlochy, and he could, if he wished, see these soldiers as evidence of it. Nothing was said on either side of Glen Lyon cattle steaming in Glencoe byres, of a red stallion that had been taken from the stables at Chesthill, of a copper kettle once belonging to Helen Campbell and now in Lady Glencoe's kitchen, or that Robert Campbell would not have become a King's officer in a red coat had it not been for the raiding of MacIain and his MacDonalds. Glenlyon asked again for his niece Sarah and her husband Sandy, his voice growing softer as his confidence grew. He introduced his officers punctiliously, and each gentleman removed his hat in salute, bowing over the crimson sash at his waist.

The records of this day, and of the thirteen that followed in Glencoe, mention three officers and one non-commissioned officer only—Glenlyon, Lieutenant John Lindsay, Ensign John Lundie and Sergeant Robert Barber. But there is no reason to believe that there were not more. The names of Lindsay and Lundie do not appear on the last surviving Muster Roll* of Glenlyon's company. They could have replaced officers who were on leave, or they could have been recent and specially selected appointments. Although Captain Thomas Drummond was not yet present to command his grenadiers, his junior officers, Lieutenants John Kilpatrick and Robert Campbell may well have been. Certainly both companies would have had their full establishment of sergeants, two to the battalion company and three to the grenadiers. Barber was the senior sergeant of Glenlyon's, with James Hendrie as his junior. Walter Purdie, Walter Buchanan and Walter Bruss were sergeants of the grenadiers. All were Lowlanders who had been transferred to Argyll's Regiment from Bargany's or other units. In addition, there were two drummers and three corporals to each company, and most of them were also from the Lowlands. More than two-thirds of the private sentinels were recognisably Highland by name, from the clan lands of Argyll and his vassals. The majority of those with Lowland names were in the grenadier company.

The soldiers were quartered three or five to a cottage, from Carnoch eastward to the loch below Aonach Eagach, where Sergeant Barber took the largest single party and lodged himself upon MacDonald of Achnacone, the senior tacksman of Glencoe. Glenlyon refused the offer of MacIain's house, saying that he would stay with MacDonald of Inverrigan at the bend of the glen. But John Lindsay was quartered in or about the chief's house, and Lundie close by. The others were placed at Brecklet, Laroch or Achtriachtan. In almost every house or cottage in the glen there were red coats and boar's-head bonnets. Glenlyon's choice of quarters is curious. His love of good living, and his vanity, would perhaps have persuaded him to take the best the glen could offer, and MacIain was well known for his liberal hospitality. But

---

* For October, 1691. At that time Glenlyon's junior officers were Lieutenant John Millan and Ensign John Campbell. See Appendix.

in that first hour the Campbell may have felt in no mood to stay in a house that was well stocked with domestic goods that had once been his and his wife's. He may have been uncertain, too, of how easy might be their relationship if he lived too close to the chief. It may even be that he did not trust the old man.

The days that followed were unusually mild for February, melting the snow on the floor of the valley and filling it with the music of singing water. Early in the mornings, the first paradiddle of Reveille beaten by a grenadier drummer rolled against the Cliff of the Feinn opposite Inverrigan, answered by another at Carnoch and a third at Achtriachtan, and the hurry-hurry call of the sergeants brought the soldiers out on to the flat ground by each township. They drilled until noon, scarlet and yellow on the black earth, the skirts of their coats swinging, and the butts of their muskets slapping against their thighs. The people of the glen grew accustomed to the crying of English voices. *"Pikemen take heed . . . advance your pikes . . . to the front, charge your pikes!"* And the solemn, slow ritual of the musketeers. *"Poise your firelocks . . . shoulder your firelocks . . . Rest!"* And perhaps they smiled, and pitied the Campbells for poor kye who knew no better than to dress in red coats and to do what they were told by the English-speakers.

But some saw no humour in it. A hundred of them went one morning to Invercoe and asked MacIain to drive the strangers from the glen. He was angry with them. He said that the soldiers were the guests of Glencoe. They were Highland and they had broken bread with Clan Iain Abrach, therefore no harm would be done by them, and no offence should be given them. Some of the people still could not feel easy with Campbells in red coats for lodgers, but most of them accepted MacIain's reassurance. The soldiers had come under trust, and under trust they had been accepted by Alasdair MacDonald. Though a Highlander might shoot a man from the fork of a tree, or dirk him in the dark, hospitality given and taken was inviolable. When the strangeness of their presence had passed, the Argyll men were made welcome as friends. Although there were men among them who had lost a cow or a goat, a plaid or a pair of brogues, a cottage burned in the

Atholl Raid, and others who had seen their kinsmen hanged or shipped to the plantations, equally there were MacDonalds whose kin had died by a Campbell rope on Doom Hill. There was blood between them, but in those twilight days they bridged it by a handclasp and by their mutual respect for the traditions of their race. Only the Lowland men, though they were treated with respect, were left outside the unnatural warmth of this friendship.

During the short afternoons the Campbells joined the Mac-Donalds in their games, wrestling, throwing the stone and tossing the caber. There was *camanachd*, the fierce game of shinty which was so called, said Martin Martin, because the players' legs were frequently broken by blows from the hooked sticks. Whichever team won, both got drunk on the whisky which customarily celebrated the victory. There was archery, for the Glencoe men were vainly proud of their skill with the bow. There were sword-dances in the bright cold air, and the notes of the pipes like thin wires strumming. At night, when the sergeants had mounted the watch, Campbells and MacDonalds gathered by the peat-fires in the cottages, dark tartan and red broadcloth lit by the flames of the resinous pine-knots which the Highlanders called fir-candles, or by smoking lamps of mutton-fat. They sang the songs of the glens, carefully chosen airs that would give no offence to a host or a guest. They told tales of Fingal, of the love which Fionn MacCumhail had for Grania, and the wisdom he got from the magic salmon he caught and cooked. They talked of hunting and the white hind of Rannoch, of wild boar and the last wolf to be killed. They got drunk and they bragged, and they stared at each other through the peat-smoke, their eyes red-rimmed and smiling. And so to another morning, another day, and another night of the same.

Every morning Glenlyon walked from Inverrigan's house to the home of his niece Sarah, and there took a cup of spirits with her husband Alasdair Og. His voice was bright, his tongue loose, and although Alasdair's nerves were on edge with distrust, he obeyed his father and made the Campbell welcome. Every night Glenlyon gambled. He played cards and backgammon with his host Inverrigan. He played with his officers and with MacIain's sons. He played until the last man left the table or fell unconscious beneath it. He returned to Inverrigan at dawn, when the sun was already pink on the snow-line, and the orderly drummer stood at the door, blowing on his fingers to make them supple.

Alasdair MacDonald tolerated the Campbell drunkard, and may even have felt sorry for him. He was relieved and grateful that Glenlyon made no issue of the old grievances between them, and he invited him to dine frequently at Carnoch in "the hospitable house of wine-cups and panelled walls". Together they matched drink for drink, and listened to the piping of Big Henderson of the Chanters. MacIain had another guest, Murdoch Matheson,★ a young bard of honourable descent, the admired composer of stirring songs and witty lampoons. He had been to Inveraray with a message from his master, the Mackenzie Earl of Seaforth, and he had stopped in Glencoe on his way home. In the glen of poets he was welcomed with respect by the old chief whom he later mourned as "a hero without flaw, without fear, unsurpassed in beauty or in eloquence."

Miracle-working King of the Sun, who sits on the mercy seat, make peace with the children of that splendid and generous man. When he raised his banner, slender shafts, bright heather and pipes, sweet women beat their hands in lament for the keen-weaponed warriors in battle.

Owing them nothing but contempt, Matheson was less flattering to the Argyll officers whom he had joined at MacIain's table.

★ The authority for Matheson's presence in Glencoe at this time is a story preserved in the Dornie Manuscripts. He was known as the *Bhard Mhathanach*, the Matheson Bard. The most famous Gaelic poem on the Massacre of Glencoe has been credited to the *Bhard Mhucanach*, the Muck Bard, who is believed to have been a Glencoe poet living, for no known reason, on the Isle of Muck. This poem was first printed in 1776 from an original manuscript now lost. In a paper delivered to the Gaelic Society of Inverness in 1952 (see Bibliography) the late Professor Angus Matheson suggested that *Mhucanach* may in fact have been a misrepresentation of the Irish script for *Mhathanach*, and that Murdoch Matheson was the author. The poem itself seems to support this, and in the absence of any information to prove the existence of a MacDonald Muck Bard, I have accepted Professor Matheson's suggestion.

He called them "uncouth savages . . . mulish louts . . . folk who puff out their cheeks as they sit on stools".

On February 4, three days after the Campbell soldiers arrived in Glencoe, John Hill reported that MacDonald of Glengarry had sworn the oath of allegiance, and had promised to surrender his castle by the twelfth of the month. There is no evidence that this news was sent to Glenlyon. Nor is there any reason to believe that he yet knew the real purpose of his presence in Glencoe. That he had been deliberately chosen by Hamilton and Duncanson there can be no doubt. Other company officers of Argyll's Regiment had strong reasons for hating MacIain and his people, any one of the Barbreck Campbells for example, or young MacAulay of Ardincaple. None, however, had suffered so bitterly at the hands of the Gallows Herd as Robert Campbell of Glenlyon, and none, presumably, could be so eager for revenge. But he was a loose-tongued, quarrelsome man, unmanageable in drink, and without caution or discretion. He could not be trusted with any plan for long, particularly one which Stair had insisted should be secret and sudden. It was still secret, and perhaps even Robert Duncanson knew no more of it at this moment than what the Deputy-Governor thought necessary to tell him. A special duty . . . and more of it later . . . an officer of your command . . . one with no love for that thieving tribe. . . .

Hamilton probably intended that the bloody extirpation of Clan Iain Abrach should take place within two or three days of Glenlyon's arrival in Glencoe. The bad weather which had stopped all troop movements had now lifted, and there was nothing to prevent the speedy march of other companies to Glenlyon's assistance. Duncanson would take the rest of his command eastward from Ballachulish, and Hamilton would block the pass to Rannoch with four hundred of Hill's Regiment. To delay meant risking the worst of February's blizzards. But there was a delay, it lasted for seven days and then for five more. John Hill was responsible. Although, as he bitterly admitted to Major Forbes, he had left the management of the affair to Hamilton and Duncanson, his signature was necessary on the final order. He could not write it. His mind was in a cataleptic state, he was immobilised by shock and revulsion. Day by day he waited for a reply to the letter he had written to Stair on January 14. He could not believe that there would still be a demand for blood, now that the chiefs were taking the oath and Lochaber was as quiet as the streets of Edinburgh. The tortured old man turned his back on the impatient Hamilton, and waited.

Stair's reply, written at Kensington Palace on January 30, reached Fort William some time toward the end of the second week in February. Hill read it with sickening despair. "*You cannot receive further directions . . . be as earnest in the matter as you can . . . be secret and sudden . . . be quick. . . .*"

He sat alone with the latter, and rationalised the doubts of his conscience. There was no escape from his duty except by the dishonour of refusal. He was old and he was poor. The Government was grievously in debt to him, and would be denied at his own expense. His daughters had none but him to support them. When his service was over he might reasonably hope for a customary knighthood, even a small pension in addition to his half-pay. The order would not be his, he was the instrument of Their Majesties and he had sworn upon his honour to serve them. "I will be a true, faithful and obedient soldier, in every way performing my best endeavours for Their Majesties' service, obeying all orders and submitting to all such rules and articles of war as are, or shall be established by Their Majesties. So help me God!" He was a human man, however, and his unhappy indecision was not due to conflict of conscience alone. He was a human man, with vanity and self-respect. Twice in recent months both had been bitterly offended, once by Breadalbane, and then again by James Hamilton's insulting appointment. He knew that his Deputy-Governor would eventually order the slaughter of the MacDonalds, without his agreement if necessary, confident of the protection of the Master of Stair. After so many empty years, so brief a time of authority, Hill could not endure that indignity. Three years later he told the King's Commissioners of Enquiry that he had signed the order because "I was jealous of my own

5. *"Cunning as a Fox, Wise as a Serpent"*
Sir John Campbell of Glenorchy, Earl of Breadalbane and *MacCailein 'ic Dhonnachaid*.

6. "I'd Dirk AnyMan, If the King Gave Me Orders!"
Robert Campbell of Glenlyon, captain of the Earl of Argyll's Regiment of
Foot and commander of the soldiers quartered in Glencoe.

authority and concerned in honour that the orders should have been sent immediately to my lieutenant-colonel, and in order that nothing might be done without me". Unable to resolve the great problem of personal responsibility, he fretted instead over a small vanity, understandable yet terrible in its paradox. Unable to prevent a dishonouring act, he persuaded himself that his honour would be preserved by becoming a party to it.

Yet he had not entirely convinced himself. The wording of the order he wrote, on the afternoon of Friday, February 12, was a weak and sad evasion. He relied too much on the Scriptures for the thought of Pilate not to have passed through his mind.

To Lieut. Col. Ja. Hamilton,
Sir,
You are with four hundred of my regiment, and the four hundred of my Lord Argyll's regiment, under the command of Major Duncanson, to march straight to Glencoe, and there put in due execution the orders you have received from the Commander-in-Chief. Given under my hand at Fort William, the 12th February, 1692.

Jo. Hill

Hamilton was ready. Seven companies of Hill's Regiment were put under orders for a forced march before midnight, and their grenadier drums were beating as he wrote a hasty letter to Duncanson. The Argyll man was now quartered on the north side of the Ballachulish ferry, with the remaining five companies of the command he had brought up from Inveraray. It is plain from Hamilton's letter that Duncanson had been taken into the Deputy-Governor's full confidence some days before, and knew all that was planned. Fourteen companies of Foot, more than nine hundred officers, non-commissioned officers and men, were to destroy the MacDonalds at dawn.

For Their Majesties' Service. For Major Robert Duncanson of the Earl of Argyll's Regiment.

Fort William, 12 February 1692
Sir,
Pursuant to the Commander-in-Chief and my Colonel's orders to me for putting in execution the service against the rebels of Glencoe,

wherein you with that party of the Earl of Argyll's Regiment now under your command are to be concerned. You are therefore to order your affairs so that you be at the several posts assigned to you by seven of the clock to-morrow morning, being Saturday, and fall in action with them, at which time I will endeavour to be with the party from this place at the post appointed them. It will be necessary the avenues minded by Lieutenant Campbell,* on the south side, be secured, that the old fox and none of his cubs get away. The orders are that none be spared, nor the government troubled with prisoners, which is all I have to say to you till then. Sir, your humble servant,

JAMES HAMILTON

Please to order a guard to secure the ferry and the boats there; and the boats must be all on this side of the ferry after your men are over.

Toward dusk this order reached Duncanson's camp at Balla-chulish. It had now become very cold, and all afternoon the sky had been heavy and black with the threat of snow. A wind was rising, and the waters of Loch Leven moved restlessly. Duncanson gave orders for a boat-party to make ready. Ferrying three hundred men across to the Appin side would be a long and dangerous business, and the tide-race at the narrows of Balla-chulish was treacherous enough in daylight. He wrote an order to Robert Campbell of Glenlyon. The man who carried it was probably Thomas Drummond, for he was at Inverrigan when the work began some hours later, and it is natural that he would wish to be with his grenadiers. Like Hamilton, he is a shadowy figure, and appears twice only in the story—at Barcaldine Castle in the New Year, and at dawn in Glencoe on Saturday, February 13. On each occasion he is seen to be a hard man and without compassion. As a captain of the grenadier company he was senior to Glenlyon, but there was no suggestion that he take command when he arrived at Inverrigan. Undoubtedly he knew the contents of the order he carried from Ballachulish.

* From the text of Duncanson's order it is evident that Hamilton meant *Captain* Campbell, and there seems to be no reason, other than haste perhaps, why he should have made this mistake in rank. The "avenues" he spoke of are Gleann an Fiodh behind Laroch, Gleann Leac na Muidhe, and possibly Lairig Gartain.

For His Majesty's Service, to Captain Robert
Campbell of Glenlyon.

Sir,

You are hereby ordered to fall upon the rebels, the MacDonalds of
Glencoe, and to put all to the sword under seventy. You are to have a
special care that the old fox and his sons do upon no account escape
your hands. You are to secure all the avenues that no man escape. This
you are to put in execution at five of the clock precisely; and by that
time, or very shortly after it, I'll strive to be at you with a stronger
party. If I do not come to you at five, you are not to tarry for me, but
to fall on. This is by the King's special command, for the good and
safety of the country, that these miscreants be cut off root and branch.
See that this be put in execution without feud or favour, else you may
expect to be dealt with as one not true to King nor Government, nor
a man fit to carry Commission in the King's service. Expecting you
will not fail in the fulfilling hereof, as you love yourself, I subscribe
these with my hand at Ballachulish, Feb 12, 1692.

ROBERT DUNCANSON.

It is not an order that would have been written to a man who
had been given some prior warning of what he was to do, and
who had declared himself in agreement. It is heavy with threat,
of the loss of his commission, of extreme punishment under the
articles of war. *Expecting you will not fail . . . as you love yourself.*
The pitiable affairs of this pathetic bankrupt were no secret, and
Duncanson could be certain that he would not sacrifice himself on
a point of honour, and that for a people who were principally
responsible for the ruin of himself and his family. The order and
the threat are plain, but there is something in the letter which is
not, and which betrays Duncanson's own instinct for self-
preservation.

This you are to put in execution at five of the clock precisely. . . .
Five o'clock? Hamilton's letter, which Duncanson had before
him as he wrote, ordered him to march his companies to the posts
assigned them by seven o'clock, and this included Glenlyon's
move to close the passes to the south. Yet Duncanson told Robert
Campbell that he would be in Glencoe at five, "or very shortly
after it". It was not a mistake, unlikely though that would have

been, for he repeated it. *If I do not come to you at five, you are not to*
tarry for me, but to fall on. Why should he think he might not get
there by five, if that were his intention? Ballachulish is only three
miles from Invercoe, and he had all night to prepare against the
bad weather coming. It must be concluded that he did not intend
to be there at five, or even "very shortly after". His orders from
Hamilton plainly told him to march his men to Glencoe and to
"fall in action with the rebels", and there was no suggestion that
the work should be done by Glenlyon's command alone. But on
his own authority,* Duncanson ordered Glenlyon to begin the
killing two hours before the twelve companies of Argyll's and
Hill's Regiments were due to arrive in the glen. By seven o'clock
the slaughter should be over.

Duncanson was an obedient and brave soldier, but he was also
shrewd enough to realise that much might be made of this affair
later, and little to the good of those concerned in it. Though the
order had originated in London, great men are inclined to
sacrifice their servants when their plans go amiss, and he was
determined to minimise the risk to himself. Beyond his concern
for his career, there was also the thought of his lands and property
in Stirlingshire, close to the Highland Line and open to the
vengeance of MacIain's outraged friends. He did not refuse the
order, he translated it in such a way that the worst excesses of it
would become the responsibility of Robert Campbell of Glenlyon.

* Unless it were with Hamilton's knowledge and consent. In this context
it is interesting to consider the Deputy-Governor's uncertainty about his own
punctuality: "By seven o'clock . . . I will *endeavour* to be with the party from
this place." Was Hamilton also hoping that the slaughter would be over before
he arrived? In fairness, however, it must be said that he had more than
twenty miles to march, against Duncanson's three, and in increasingly bad
weather.

"All blame be on such as gave the orders, we are free"

WHEN IT was over, men remembered the strange and terrible
warnings that had been given. It was said that *An Duine Mor*, the
Great Man who appeared only when gentlefolk were in danger,
was seen by the loch at Ballachulish on Friday. That afternoon
some of the cows at Carnoch broke from the byre and ran up the
brae, crying pitifully, though there had been nothing to startle
them. For some days the *Bean Nighe* had been seen by the water-
falls of the Coe, a supernatural washing-woman who cleansed a
shroud again and again, and none who saw her had the courage to
ask whose it might be. For several nights the *Caoineag* had been
heard, the keening woman who could be neither approached nor
addressed, but who always foretold death. In a cottage by
Achnacone some of the people consulted the shoulder-blade of a
sheep they had killed for their Campbell guests, and one of them
looked at it and cried, "There is a shedding of blood in the glen!"
Another said, "There is only the stream at the end of this house
between us and the blood". And they fled over the hills to Appin
with their wives and children.

Truth and legend were now to be inextricably mixed.

It was said afterwards that MacIain had grown more and more
uneasy about his guests, and that he left his house at Carnoch for
Gleann Leac na Muidhe, although this offered little comfort in
winter. It was said again that he took some of the women of his
house to the comparative safety of Gleann Leac because they had
been molested by the soldiers, and that he and his wife returned
to Carnoch on Friday. In the evidence later given by his sons and

others there is nothing to support these stories, and they could
have been told by men who did not wish their chief to be
remembered as a credulous and trusting fool. There is no proof
that the old man was ever uneasy. On Friday morning he met
Glenlyon in a change-house kept by one of his clan at Invercoe.
They drank together in good spirits, and MacIain invited Robert
Campbell to dine with him the next day, with Lieutenant Lindsay and Ensign Lundie. He was proud of the reputation his people
had for hospitality, and glad to demonstrate it to the Campbells.
"Well could you drain flagons and empty ankers of wine," sang
Murdoch Matheson, remembering those days among the Mac-
Donalds, "Well did you carry yourselves when you met over the
cup, playing backgammon and other games. At the board your
actions were never contemptible. . . ."

Toward evening, the wind blew more bitterly from the north-
east, and the ominous ceiling of snow-clouds stretched from Ardgour to Rannoch. What remained of daylight was flat and colour-
less, the unnerving pallor that precedes a storm. It was a time to
be by the fire, and few men were abroad after noon. MacIain's
sons, however, came to Inverrigan's house to play cards with
Glenlyon, as they had done many times these past two weeks.
Robert Campbell was in his usual good humour, his face flushed
by wine, his voice husky and his eyes bright. He welcomed them
noisily, and told them that he was to dine with their father the
next evening. By supper time, or soon after, their gambling was
interrupted by the arrival of Thomas Drummond, shaking snow
from his cloak and pulling Duncanson's order from the cuff of his
gauntlet. His eyes passed briefly over the MacDonalds and back to
Glenlyon in warning. The brothers saw nothing in the Campbell's
face to alarm them as he read the order, but the gaming ended
then. His orders had come, said Glenlyon, and there was much he
had to do, but their burden was now to be lifted. He pressed his
thanks upon them for their kindness and hospitality, and if his
gratitude seemed extravagant, his voice too loud, they were not
suspicious. They went home, leaving him with the order for their
murder.

Robert Campbell of Glenlyon knew what was being asked of his honour. He was Highland, and he knew the solemn and binding obligations of hospitality given and taken. He had broken bread with the MacDonalds for two weeks, as their guest and under trust. Now, with the advantage of that trust, he was ordered to kill them. Nothing in his known past foreshadows the eventual assassin, except a weak self-indulgence, an obstinate despair that can compel a man to sin against others for his own preservation. His moral problem at this moment was the same as Hill's, and he resolved it more quickly. He folded Duncanson's order and put it in his coat, pinched out the candle and walked from Inverrigan's house to find his officer of the watch.

It was colder still, the wind stronger and the snow thickening. Orders had to be sent to all the commanders of his scattered detachments, westward a mile to Carnoch and Invercoe, and eastward for five to Achtriachtan. They could not be given inside a cottage, or close by its listening walls. They were given in the darkness in the wind, the whispering lips of a lieutenant put close to the ear of a sergeant, and the darkness was a merciful mask on the horror or indifference with which the news was received.

The private soldiers were told nothing until the hour they were needed. James Campbell, who served in Glenlyon's company, later swore on oath "I knew nothing of the design of killing the Glencoe men till the morning that the slaughter was committed, at which time the companies were drawn out and got orders from Glenlyon and our other officers to shoot and kill all the countrymen we met with." The stories which the Glencoe people told, generation by generation, suggest that the soldiers knew much earlier, even twenty-four hours before, which is absurd. On Friday afternoon, it was said, when the Argyll men and the MacDonalds were playing shinty, a Campbell and a child watched the game together, their backs against a boulder that was known as MacHenry's Stone. The soldier looked hard at the child to hold its attention, and then struck the rock with his hand. "Great stone of the glen!" he said, "Great is your right to be here. But if you knew what will happen this night you would be up and away." In a cottage at Achtriachtan, it was said, a soldier sat by the fire with a family who had treated him kindly and as a son. He was from Glen Lyon, from his captain's country, and that evening he said nothing, nor could he be persuaded to speak. Then he looked at a dog, curled by the fire. "Grey dog," he said, and looked up from it to his hosts. "If I were you, grey dog, my bed tonight would be the heather." When he slept, or pretended to sleep, the MacDonalds went quietly from the cottage and escaped into the hills.

At Brecklet, in Gleann an Fiodh, three soldiers were quartered on a family called Robertson. That Friday at supper one of the Campbells plucked at the corner of his host's plaid. "This is a good plaid," he said, "Were this good plaid mine, I would put it on and go out into the night to look after my cattle." He lifted his eyes and stared boldly at the Robertsons. "Were this good plaid mine, I would put it on my shoulders and I would take my family out to drive my cattle to a safe place." And this is what the Robertsons did, while the soldiers were sleeping.

And it was said that Glenlyon's piper, Hugh Mackenzie, went that evening to MacHenry's Stone and stood upon it. He played the lament called *Women of the Glen*, knowing that any Mac-Donald who heard it would recognise it as a warning.

Great Stone . . . grey dog . . . good plaid . . . women of the glen. . . . All the stories could be one story only, out of which the inventiveness of the tellers created several. But in that one story there could also be a truth, of a soldier keener in intelligence than the rest, or hearing that whispered order to his sergeant in the darkness, and having long enough to decide that because he could not kill his hosts he must warn them.

It was reported in a London pamphlet,* within weeks of the massacre, that MacIain's younger son, Alasdair Og, could not sleep that night, nor keep to his house while his thoughts were uneasy. He hid by the bothy which the soldiers used as their Main Guard, and did not like what he saw. He went to his brother John's house, and told him that there were too many soldiers

---

* Published by Charles Leslie, a non-jurant Jacobite minister. See page 259.

abroad this night, far more than there had been during the past twelve days. John MacDonald was not alarmed. It was a wild night, he said, and cruel. Glenlyon was showing good sense, and a correct concern for his men's comfort, by doubling the watch and relieving the sentinels often. But Alasdair insisted that they should tell their father what was happening, and at last John agreed. MacIain, no doubt annoyed at being called from bed, told Alasdair that his suspicions were foolish and unjust, but if the brothers wished to satisfy themselves they had his permission to look further into the matter. And he went back to bed.

They, well knowing all the skulking places, went and hid themselves near to a sentinel's post, where instead of one they discovered eight or ten men. This made them more inquisitive, so they crept as near as they could without being discovered, so near that they could hear one say to his fellows that "he liked not this work, and that had he known of it he would have been very unwilling to have come there, but that none, except their commanders knew of it till within a quarter of an hour". The soldier added that "he was willing to fight against the men of Glencoe, but it was base to murder them". But to all this was answered "All the blame be on such as gave the orders, we are free, being bound to obey our officers".

Before the brothers could warn their father, said the pamphlet, the massacre had begun.

In the depositions made by John and Alasdair Og, three years later, neither said that they had hidden and watched the sentinels. After their game of cards with Glenlyon they went home and to bed. Before dawn, John MacDonald was awoken by voices outside his house, a shouting from the night. He went to the window and saw the flames of pine-knots, red coats and dark bonnets, the barrels of muskets shining. The soldiers called to him again when they saw his face, but before he could understand what they cried, a taunt or a warning, they were gone. He was alarmed, but he softly reassured his wife, and when she slept again he wrapped a plaid about him and went out, stumbling against the wind and the drifts to Inverrigan. Here there were more lights, torches staining the snow by the little burn, and lamps lit at the windows. Soldiers stood at rest, their empty faces staring at him above their bayonets as he went by them and in at the house. The room was full. He did not see Inverrigan, but Glenlyon was there with some of his officers and sergeants, and they were priming muskets and pistols. Robert Campbell turned to John MacDonald, quickly covering his surprise with a smile. Before he could speak the MacDonald asked him for an explanation. Why were the soldiers abroad so early, why were they preparing their arms?

Glenlyon interrupted him briskly, a soldier expressing cheerful disgust with the sudden demands of a soldier's life. Orders had come, John MacDonald knew that, orders to be up and away before dawn against some of Glengarry's men. And then, as if he had suddenly understood MacDonald's suspicions, and was hurt by them, "You think we intend Glencoe some ill? Is that it? Man, if that were my orders do you think I'd have given no warning to my niece and your brother Sandy?"

He could have said many things. He could have angrily resented the suggestion that he was ready to abuse MacIain's hospitality, to kill those who trusted him. He could have spoken of his honour, and the offence given it. Already alarmed by the naked bayonets outside, by the acrid smell of priming-powder in this room, by the hard eyes of Drummond and the smirking stares of the Lowland sergeants, John MacDonald would not have believed him. Consciously or not, Glenlyon said the one thing MacIain's son would believe. No Highlandman could murder a woman of his family. The MacDonald was content. He took Glenlyon's hand again, wished him well on his march at dawn, and went home to sleep.

Robert Campbell could also have shot him as he stood there unarmed, but it was not yet five, and five was the hour. In the byre beyond the smoky room, hidden by a cow-hide curtain, MacDonald of Inverrigan and eight members of his household lay bound and gagged, awaiting slaughter.*

---

* That Inverrigan and members of his household were bound hand and foot was later sworn by witnesses. This must have happened long before five o'clock. The house was Glenlyon's headquarters and if he had not immobilised his host and the servants they would have given a warning to the rest of the glen.

When the hour came there was movement in the valley, scarlet men forming line outside the cottages, and perhaps the same soft reassurances were given to the sleepy voices of their hosts. It was said that a great fire was lit upon Signal Rock, so that the soldiers might know when to begin the killing. Such a fire may have been lit on Glenlyon's orders, but few would have seen it. By five o'clock the snowstorm was now a blizzard, a swirling white darkness.

"Why is he still alive? What of our orders? Kill him!"

THE FIRST of the clan to be killed was Duncan Rankin who lived by the chief's house. He ran from the soldiers to the river, and was shot down as he floundered across it three hundred yards from the mouth. The current carried his body into Loch Leven.

When they had killed Duncan Rankin, and wounded another man who escaped them by a miraculous leap across the river, Lieutenant John Lindsay marched his men to MacIain's door. He struck it several times with the butt of his half-pike, calling out in a friendly voice. A servant awoke Alasdair MacDonald, saying that the Campbell soldiers were leaving for Glengarry's country and wished to thank him for his kindness. MacIain slipped his legs from the blanket and shouted for a dram to be taken to the young officer. He told his wife to dress, the hour was early but their guests should be seen on their way with proper courtesy. He was standing by his bed with his back to the door, pulling on his trews, when Lindsay came in with a pistol in one hand and his half-pike in the other. He yelled, and the room was full of soldiers, melted snow black on their red coats, their bayonets cold in the flame of the night-light.

The servants of the house heard two shots, their lady's scream, Lindsay's maddened voice, and the vengeful cry of Clan Campbell's slogan. They ran from a darkness suddenly stabbed by musket-fire. They ran into the snow and more soldiers, more guns and two of them were killed at the door of the house. A third man called Duncan Don, who was not a Glencoe man but who came occasionally from the Brae of Mar with letters for MacIain, was wounded as he stumbled half-naked in the night. He fell, and the soldiers believed him dead.

Old Glencoe was dead, comically and ignobly, with his trews untied and his nightshirt on his back. There was one bullet in his body and another, from Lindsay's pistol perhaps, through the back of his head. He lay across his bed, his proud face blown open by the breaking exit of the ball. His lady had thrown herself upon him, but the soldiers pulled her aside. Some of them took the old man's body by the heels and dragged it out of the house. Others tore the clothes from his wife until she was naked, and they drew the rings from her fingers with their teeth. But they did not kill her, and this may have been their mercy.

A servant shook John MacDonald from his sleep. MacIain's son did not have to ask the reason, he saw it in the man's face and he heard it in the sounds outside. He went to the door. A hundred yards away, plunging in the drifts, twenty soldiers were slowly approaching the house, and long after he could still remember the bayonets on their muskets. Before they arrived, he got his wife* and his household away up the brae to the cover of the trees on Meall Mor. There he found Archibald MacDonald, one of his father's servants, and also Murdoch Matheson the bard, and both of them told him what had happened in the chief's house.

A servant also awoke Alasdair Og, shouting in his ear, "It's no time for you to be sleeping when they're killing your brother at his door!" Alasdair gathered his family and his people quickly, and they too went up Meall Mor and came by accident upon his brother's little party. Bitterly cold and numb from shock and fear, the MacDonalds crouched in a corrie, listening for sounds from below. Sometimes they heard shots, and cries, and for long moments there was nothing to be heard but the keening wind.

---

* She is believed to have been Eiblin MacDonald, daughter of the tacksman of Achtriachtan. She and John had a young son of two, Alasdair, who later led the clan in the Rebellion of 1745. He was carried by a nurse this night, wrapped in a plaid. A story long remembered said she took the boy to Glenmoriston, but this is hard to believe. Glenmoriston is fifty miles to the north, up the Great Glen, and the nurse would have had to pass the garrison and the patrols of Fort William.

Now and then, when the snow swirled and parted, they saw a flower of flame at Carnoch or Invercoe, and smelt the sweet scent of their burning homes. At last the brothers sent the women and young children higher into the hills, over the western shoulder of Meall Mor, and southward to the upper braes of Gleann an Fiodh or Gleann Leac na Muidhe. There would be little shelter there from the snow, and less mercy from the wind, but dawn was now an hour away, and when it came there would be no safety where they were. When they were gone, quickly lost in the blizzard, the brothers went up the glen with Matheson and Archibald Mac-Donald. They passed over the frozen burn and narrow valley that led to Inverrigan below, and they climbed to the high ground above Achnacone. Here they found more frightened women and children, and they urged them on up Gleann Leac.

Night had gone and the light was grey, but the floor of the glen was still hidden by driving snow. The MacDonalds listened to the heavy thud of shots, the muffled shouts of Campbell soldiers. To keep his thoughts from the bitter cold, his heart from breaking, Murdoch Matheson began to compose the great lament he was to finish later that day. *Dear to me are the white bodies of those who were generous, manly, delightful men. . . . Had we been under arms, before the hunt gathered against this land, there are Redcoats who would never have returned!*

At Inverrigan, said James Campbell of Glenlyon's company, "I saw eight persons killed and several houses burnt, and women flying to the hills to save their lives." At five o'clock, Glenlyon had closed his watch and put it in his pocket. MacDonald of Inverrigan, and the eight men of his household, were carried beyond the door, still bound hand and foot. They were thrown upon the dung-hill, and there Glenlyon shot Inverrigan. One by one the others were also killed, a slow, methodical slaughter with musket and bayonet. A soldier who rifled Inverrigan's coat brought his captain a paper he had found, and Glenlyon called for a torch to be held closer so that he might read it. It was a letter from John Hill, giving the MacDonald protection, and assuring him that he and his family, his land and his stock, were free from molestation. It may have been the bloody irony of this letter, or it may have been a sudden and sick revulsion that made Glenlyon stand between his soldiers and a young man of twenty, the last of the nine victims still living. He cried *"Hold!"*, and the soldiers stared at him from faces of clay. Then Thomas Drummond came, his eyes going from the bound and frightened man to the waiting soldiers, and on to Glenlyon's white face. He said "Why is he still alive? What of our orders? Kill him!" When no one moved, Drummond raised his pistol and shot the young man through the head.

A child ran out of the darkness, a boy of twelve or thirteen, and he clawed at Glenlyon's legs, crying that he would go anywhere with the Campbell if his life were spared. Glenlyon could say nothing, and the boy was shot on Captain Drummond's order.

In the township of Inverrigan the soldiers also killed a woman and a boy of four or five. They bayoneted men in their beds, or dragged them outside and shot them on the dungheaps. They drove cattle, sheep and goats from the byres, looted the houses and burned the thatch and timber. They were shrieking shadows against the smoke, the snow and the flame. "I saw my two brothers killed," said a man who escaped them, "and three men more, and a woman, who were all buried before I came back."

At Achnacone, by the mouth of Gleann Leac and a mile and a half eastward from Inverrigan, Sergeant Robert Barber had drawn out his men before five o'clock and told them what they were to do. They marched off by sections to all the houses of the township, and Barber took eighteen of them to the home of MacDonald of Achnacone who had been his kindly host for thirteen days. The soldiers' early rising had awoken the people of the house, and nine of them were now gathered drowsily about the fire, taking a morning's dram against the cold. John Mac-Donald of Achtriachtan was there, having spent the night with his brother of Achnacone, and they were seated together when Barber's men burst in the door and thrust their muskets through the windows. Achtriachtan's servant, a man called Kennedy, threw himself between his master and the soldiers. Eighteen shots were fired, almost at once, filling the small room with terrible noise and a fog of white smoke. Achtriachtan and Kennedy were killed instantly with three others, the remaining four were wounded and pretended to be dead. His anger raised, Barber groped in the smoke for Achnacone's shoulder, turning the tacksman on his back. "Are you still alive then?"

"I am alive," said Achnacone, "and if I am to be killed by you I would rather it were not beneath my own roof."

"I've eaten your meat," said Barber, enjoying the jest against a Highland custom, "So I'll do you the favour and kill you without."

Achnacone was carried outside, where the Argyll men were biting open fresh cartridges and ramming powder and ball into their muskets. He was placed against the wall of his house, and the black-lipped soldiers moved close to him, their pieces almost touching his body. He flung his plaid over their heads and ran. Inside the house the other wounded men broke through a back wall and escaped, and none of them could be followed in the snow and the dark. The body of John MacDonald of Achtriachtan, who had also been given Colonel Hill's protection, was thrown on a midden with Kennedy and the other dead. Barber urged on his men with fury. They stabbed, hacked and shot as the frightened MacDonalds ran from their doors, and it was said that when the soldiers were too weary to lift their arms they burned fourteen people alive in one cottage. They killed an old man of eighty. They killed a small child, and nothing was found of the boy but a bloody hand on the snow.

On the side of Meall Mor, fifteen hundred feet above the Field of the Dogs, Murdoch Matheson listened to the shooting and the cries. . . . *How pure was the blood that was poured on the earth! King of Angels, Creator of the elements, have pity on these poor souls!*

There was more killing at Achtriachtan, the village of poets. Here in the smooth hollow between Aonach Eagach and Bidean nam Bian the snow was sometimes so thick that a man could not see his extended hand, and sometimes the wind sucked it upwards, leaving the air empty and strangely still. Among the soldiers quartered there, under Sergeant Hendrie or Sergeant Purdie, was a Breadalbane man from Glen Lyon who was said to have been maddened by the memory of the Glencoe raids on his own country. With each shot, each thrust of his bayonet he shouted "There's for Catherine's blanket!" and "That's for Colin's cows!" If Ranald of the Shield were still alive, and a very old man, he was killed by the Campbells that morning in Achtriachtan, though his sons escaped. Another respected bard, Iain Mac-Raonuill Og, was carried away on the back of his son, and a third poet who escaped was Aonghus MacAlasdair Ruaidh, a member of the tacksman's family who had fought at Killiecrankie and glorified it in a long epic poem.

The people who ran from the soldiers at Achtriachtan had nowhere to go but eastward up the glen. To the west was the loch, the firing of guns and the dull blot of flames. North and above them was the sheer escarpment of Aonach Eagach, three thousand feet high, and to the south was another wall of mountains, swirling with snow. Even in the east the glen narrowed to a great fall of rock, cased in ice, and to cross this would have been almost impossible for half-naked women and children. Some of the young men went that way, perhaps, and down Lairig Gartain to Dalness and Appin, but the rest can only have gone to Coire Gabhail, the Hollow of Capture, a mile and a half from Achtriachtan, climbing three hundred feet to its narrow entrance and blocking it with a tree.

At dawn the snowstorm was gone from the floor of the glen. By the chief's house, now in flames, Lieutenant John Lindsay heard the approach of Duncanson's companies. He saw them on the lochside, a column of red and yellow swinging to a drum-beat, the Major mounted and wrapped in his cloak. The killing was over, and it is said that Glenlyon's piper, Hugh Mackenzie, was playing a Breadalbane rant in triumph.

> Listen, then, to my pibroch,
> it tells the news and tells it well
> of slaughtered men
> and forayed glen,
> Campbell's banners and the victor's joy!

For three of the Argyll men, it was said, there was no joy and no victory. As they stumbled after some fugitives, below the trenches Fionn MacCumhail had dug on the Cliff of the Feinn, the Mac-Donalds turned on them, dirk in hand. The Campbells were buried where they died, beneath cairns of stones and a stunted blackthorn tree.

Duncanson looked down from his saddle at MacIain's corpse and asked for news of the old fox's cubs. No one had seen their bodies, and he rode on to Inverrigan in an ill temper. Between Achnacone and Loch Leven the valley was a sluggish river of smoke, and the air was filled by the melancholy lowing of cattle waiting to be fed. Blood on their coats, their faces blackened by powder, some of Glenlyon's pikemen were prodding sheep and cows to a meadow in an ox-bow of the river. They waved their bonnets and shouted to the fresh companies marching by. At Inverrigan, before the tacksman's burning house and by the bodies on the dung-hills, Duncanson asked again for news of MacIain's sons. They had not been killed, they had not been seen. He told Glenlyon and Drummond to drive all the MacDonalds' stock to Invercoe, and he looked anxiously eastward for a sign of the companies from Fort William.

James Hamilton had left Inverlochy shortly after writing his order to Duncanson. His four hundred men had twenty miles or more to march, seven of them southward from the fort on the high drove-road to the shoulder of Meall a' Chaoruinn, then eastward for another seven to the head of Loch Leven. This Hamilton reached some time during the night when the blizzard was blowing its worst. His staggering, shivering, cursing men were exhausted, in no condition to go over the Devil's Staircase even had the weather made it possible. They took what shelter they could, in the open or in the cottages of a little township by the loch, and they waited for the storm to drop. It is hard to believe that Hamilton ever thought he could finish the march, at night, in that weather, and over some of the cruellest country in the Highlands. He too, perhaps, was as uncertain of the future as Duncanson. John Forbes, his second-in-command, welcomed the delay with relief. This was not the work he had meant when he told his brother that for all his pains he asked no more than an opportunity to serve his King and country. Two lieutenants of the battalion companies broke their swords when they heard what they were to do in Glencoe. They were put under arrest, and Hamilton sent them to Glasgow within the week. They may have been Francis Farquhar and Gilbert Kennedy, for both these officers of Hill's Regiment later gave evidence against their lieutenant-colonel.

The command left Kinlochleven when the blizzard dropped at dawn. Its march south over the Staircase was slow and difficult. A fog of snow and cloud was low on the hills, the wind still blowing, and the track hidden by great drifts. At eleven o'clock the struggling companies climbed over the gorge at the Meeting of the Waters and came down to Achtriachtan. Westward, the pass between the Cliff of the Feinn and the spur of Bidean nam Bian was closed with smoke. They marched towards it, watched by the MacDonalds from Coire Gabhail. They marched without hindrance. At Achtriachtan they burned the cottages still standing, and they shot an old man who started from the ruins and ran to the river. They drove in the cattle and sheep they found, and at the bend of the glen they made contact with Duncanson's wandering patrols. Except for that stumbling, frightened old man, and the bodies on the midden at Achtriachtan, the companies from Fort William saw none of the people of Glencoe.

And Hamilton was as angry with Glenlyon as Duncanson had been, when he discovered that MacIain's sons were not dead.

By late afternoon that Saturday the soldiers were gone. The cottages still burned, and the trampled snow about them was red. At Achnacone and Inverrigan, Carnoch and Brecklet, the Argyll men had killed a steer or a sheep for their breakfast, and what they had left of the carcasses lay by the bodies of the men they had also killed. There was a smell of death, and the sweet hospitable smell of burning peat. There were no voices, and there was no lowing of cattle. The soldiers had taken with them nine hundred cows, two hundred horses, and a great many sheep and goats. They also took what they could carry from the houses: plaids and shoes, pans and kettles, brooches, buckles, belts and women's combs. They took plates and cups, spits and girdles, meal and whisky, herring and salmon from the roof-beams, hides, fleece and blankets from the beds. They took such things as the Glencoe men had once taken from Breadalbane and Argyll, from Glen Lyon and Kilbride, from Cowal, Lorn and Rosneath. In the opinion of many of them, an outstanding debt had at last been paid. And Robert Campbell may have recovered his fine red stallion from the stable at Carnoch, his wife's copper kettle from the kitchen.

"For a just vengeance and a public example," the Master had told John Hill, "the thieving tribe of Glencoe may be rooted out to a purpose." Duncanson had repeated this, ordering Glenlyon to "cut off root and branch". Glenlyon failed. When he reported to Hamilton outside Inverrigan at noon on Saturday, he said that his command had killed MacIain and thirty-six of his men, although it cannot be known whether he included in this number the women and children who had been shot. With the old man killed on Hamilton's march, the final figure accepted was thus thirty-eight, a tenth or less of MacIain's people.

One reason for Robert Campbell's failure to do as he was ordered lay in his own character, in a mind fuddled by drink and self-indulgence, in his indecision, in a professional incompetence that put no proper guards on the southern passes. But the principal reason was the weather, the blinding snowstorm that made pursuit and hunt impossible, that hid a wounded man like Achnacone, or women crouching like hares beside the dry-stone walls.

One more reason must be considered. Had other men been sent to Glencoe at the beginning of February, two of Hill's ruffianly companies for example, the clan-hating Cameronians or other Lowlandmen from Stirling, it is probable that more of the MacDonalds would have been killed, despite the weather. Fifty years later, after Culloden, Lowland regiments would be thorough and merciless in the killing of Highland men and women for whom they felt no respect and no kinship of race. The Campbells of Argyll's Regiment were Highland, and the inviolability of hospitality was as sacred to them as to any other clan, murder under trust was as great a sin. This is remembered in the stories which the Glencoe people told for another hundred and fifty years. Confused and contradictory though the legends became, they do record the truth that some of the Argyll men were revolted by the orders given them, and that within the oath of obedience they had taken they attempted to warn the people. In this, perhaps, they showed more humanity than John Hill. And for each warning remembered by the MacDonalds, there may have been another forgotten. When the order was given two hours before dawn on Saturday, there were soldiers who killed no one, who turned their backs on running shadows, who heard no frightened breathing in the dark.

A woman of Inverrigan, it was said, took shelter with her child and a dog beneath the bridge that crossed the burn of Allt-na-Muidhe. The crying of the child was heard, and a soldier was sent to kill it. He came to the bridge, and saw the woman holding her plaid over the child's mouth to stifle its cries. He bayoneted the dog and went back, holding up the wet steel. "That's not human blood," said the officer, though the story does not explain how he knew, "Kill the child, or I'll kill you." So the soldier went back to the bridge. He drew his hanger and he cut the little finger from the child's hand, smearing its blood on his sword.*

Before nightfall, some of the MacDonald men came down from the corries to bury the dead, or to hide them beneath cairns of stones against the day when they could be properly interred on Eilean Munde. At Invercoe, Archibald MacDonald came cautiously to the black ruin of the chief's house, and he saw the

---

* The story has a sequel, of course. Many years later the soldier was travelling homeward through Appin, and he stopped at a cottage for the night. About the fire he talked of his soldiering, and when he was asked to name the most terrible thing he had seen he said it was the Massacre of Glencoe. As he slept, his host said, "I'll make an end to him in the morning". At breakfast the soldier was again asked to tell of Glencoe, and he told the story of the child, at which his host held up a hand from which the little finger was missing. They parted as friends.

old man's body lying on its face by the door. Close by were two of his servants, and Duncan Don from the Brae of Mar, who still lived. Archibald MacDonald sat by him, and spoke to him.

Ronald MacDonald came back to his own house by Carnoch. That morning he and his father had been awoken by the sound of firing and the cries of their neighbours. Although Ronald Mac-Donald escaped, the old man was dragged from his bed to the door and there clubbed with musket-butts. When the soldiers were gone, he crawled to another house, and in this he was burnt to death. Now, at dusk, Ronald MacDonald gathered his father's bones from the smouldering wood and buried them. He walked on to Achnacone where, he said later, "I saw the body of Achtri-achtan, and three more, cast out and covered with dung".

Murdoch Matheson climbed to the top of Signal Rock, and there he composed his lament. He saw the cowl of smoke above the little loch in the east, the black embers of the snow, and the thought of treachery, he said, was like a cry of distress. *Oh, God I am filled with gloom as I see these hills!* The foray had come upon his friends as a rock comes down the hill. *Given equal odds between them and the Lowland band, the feathered birds of the mountains would have screamed from their enemies' corpses.* He thought with sorrow of the young hunters who were dead, who had killed the stag in the high forests and now were dead. *They were not cowards, these men who will sleep on the Isle of Munda. . . .*

Somewhere at this time, MacIain's sons must have found their mother, for it was from her, they said, that they learnt how the chief had been killed. They bandaged the fingers the soldiers had gnawed, they wrapped her in a plaid and took her away with them to the hills. No one knows what happened to the body of Alasdair MacDonald, twelfth Chief of Glencoe, though it is said to lie beneath the weeds and the corroded stones of Saint Munda's roofless chapel.

Because they believed that the soldiers would return, the MacDonalds did not remain in the glen. John MacDonald, who was now MacIain and the thirteenth of the name, gathered those he could and took them over into Appin, by way of Gleann Leac or Gleann an Fiodh. Some young men hid in the caves and the corries below the Pap of Glencoe, or went beyond Kinlochleven to Keppoch's people on Loch Treig. Some, from Achtriachtan, came down from Coire Gabhail and went out to Rannoch and their cold shielings on the Black Mount. Clan Iain was scattered, and would live or die like the cat, the eagle and the deer until summer. Many of the fugitives, the very young and the very old, did not survive the first night, for at dusk the wind rose again and there was more snow. It was said that old MacIain's wife died then. The suffering of the rest was told to their friends in Appin, who told it to others, who sent news of it to Edinburgh, from whence it went to London where the pamphleteer Charles Leslie put it into print.

How dismal may you imagine the case of the poor women and children was then! It was lamentable, past expression. Their husbands and fathers, and near relations, were forced to flee for their lives. They themselves almost stripped, and nothing left them, and their houses being burnt, and not one house nearer than six miles. And to get thither they were to pass over mountains, and wreaths of snow in a vehement storm, wherein the greatest part of them perished through hunger and cold. It fills me with horror to think of the poor stripped children and women, some with child, and some giving suck, wrestling against a storm in mountains and heaps of show, and at length to be overcome, and give over, and fall down, and die miserably.

Some days after the massacre, a man came to Appin from Loch Tay. When those he spoke to were satisfied that he could be trusted, he was taken to where John MacDonald was in hiding. He said that he had been sent by Alexander Campbell of Barcaldine, chamberlain to the Earl of Breadalbane. He said that if John MacDonald of Glencoe, and Alasdair Og MacDonald his brother, would swear and write under their hands that the Earl was innocent of the slaughter, then Breadalbane would use his influence to secure them full pardon and restitution.

5

UNDER THE BROAD SEAL

"For there was much blood on these people's hands"

BY THE end of March, Argyll's officers were in Edinburgh. Their
regiment was quartered on Leith, awaiting tents and transports
for Flanders. Any day Glenlyon could be seen in the Royal
Coffee-house by Parliament Close, his back against a wall, his
red coat open, and his dark eyes burning in his white face. Men
came to stare at him above a dish of chocolate, and their macabre
curiosity was dramatically satisfied. "I would do it again!" he
shouted, "I would dirk any man in Scotland or England, without
asking cause, if the King gave me orders!" And then, challenging
their hostile faces, "So should every good subject of His Majesty!"
There was another side to his vain-glory, which may have been
more sincere. He told some men privately that he had liked none
of the business. He had killed Inverrigan with regret. He would
have refused the order, but he feared a council of war, and what
man could honestly say he would have done otherwise? He
showed Duncanson's order to those who asked, and the Jacobites in the city made good use of the wretched man's indiscretion.
They left copies of the letter in all the coffee-houses, and they
spread a rumour that Glenlyon had petitioned the Privy Council
for a reward.

Six weeks earlier at Inverlochy, John Hill had frankly acknowledged his responsibility under the order he had given Hamilton.
On the evening of the massacre, his men and Duncanson's returned to Fort William, driving Glencoe's cattle before them,
their weapons bloody, their loot hanging from pike and musket.
Hill listened to reports from Hamilton and the Argyll officers,

and he spent all Sunday alone at his desk. He wrote to Livingstone and to the Earl of Tweeddale. "I have ruined Glencoe," he said, "their goods are a prey to the soldiers, and their houses to the fire." He sent the letters south the next morning by the hand of Captain James Cunningham, an officer of his regiment who had marched with Hamilton, instructing him to give by word of mouth any information the dispatches lacked.

For a week he kept his soldiers and the Campbells strictly within the limits of the garrison and Maryburgh. The MacDonalds' cattle, sheep and goats were herded on the recreation field by the burial-yard, until he could decide how many should be slaughtered for the soldiers' food, and how many might be sold to Lowland graziers for prize-money. For a week, too, he was afraid of savage reprisals. He sent out scouts from the Independent Companies of Atholl men, and they brought him confused news. The Camerons were in a rage, threatening to attack any redcoat patrol seen north of the River Spean. In Appin, John and Alasdair MacDonald had obtained arms for their men, and had scattered them across the hills between Dalness and Glen Duror. They were cold, starving and desperate, and the bitter suffering of the women and children had put the Stewarts in an obstinate temper.

And then, after days of uncertainty, a miracle happened. Terrible though the massacre had been in its violation of trust, it had been successful in its effect on the laggardly clans. Within eight days young Robert Stewart of Appin came to Fort William by boat, and was carried ashore on a stretcher. He wished to submit, he said, and would have come before had he not been too ill to leave his bed. He was the first of many. "They come from all parts to submit to the King's mercy," Hill reported with delight, "and to take the oath of allegiance and (according to my orders) save their lives. I hope this example of justice and severity will be enough." Clanranald, whom Hill thought was one of the most handsome young men he had ever seen, brought in his chiefs, kinsmen and friends from Moidart and the Isles, and all of them "took the oath with the greatest frankness imaginable". The boy Clanranald did more than take the oath. He asked leave to visit his uncle, the Laird of Macleod, from whom he wished to borrow money, and he also wanted a pass for London. There, he said, he would ask King William to find service for him in Flanders. Every day, long-oared birlinns came to the quay-side at Maryburgh, and proud men in tartan, with eagle or black-cock feathers in their bonnets, stepped ashore to submit, masking their fear behind the arrogant calm of their faces. MacNeill of Barra, the tall man whom James Philip had seen at Dalcomera with axe in hand and a rainbow plaid on his shoulder, was ready to come over from his blue isle when the weather permitted. And on Skye the Mac-Donalds of Sleat were said to be anxious to take the oath before they, too, were Glencoed. The noun had become a verb.

Now Hill could give some attention to his honest concern for the desperate and starving survivors of the massacre. Beyond the cautious aid and shelter given them by the Appin men, they had received little help. The great chiefs of Clan Donald cannily ignored them, but on the tiny isles of Monach, six miles into the Atlantic from North Uist, Archibald MacDonald of Grimmish loaded a boat with meal and steered it through a storm to Loch Linnhe, leaving the cargo on the shores of Appin. It was an isolated and brave act of compassion. The Glencoe men were rarely seen by the patrols which Hill sent to Appin or to the black and empty valley, but he received sound intelligence of their mood and temper, and he was afraid that unless something were soon done to help them they would "lie in every bush and glen in small parties to shoot men and rob up and down the country". At the end of February, he appealed to the indolent and indifferent Earl of Portland, using parenthesis like a prodding finger.

Those men of Glencoe that (by the help of the storm) escaped, would submit to mercy if their lives may be granted them, upon giving security to live peaceably under the Government, and not to rob, steal, or receive stolen goods hereafter, and I humbly conceive (since there are enough killed for an example, and to vindicate public justice) it were advisable to receive them, since it will be troublesome to take them, the Highlanders being generally allied one to another, and they may join with other broken men and be hurtful to the country. At the present they [the men of Glencoe] lie dormant in caves and remote places.

This sensible and generous suggestion was ignored. In March, Hill was hurt and angered by the news he received of the rumours then current in Edinburgh. It was said that he and his officers had exceeded their orders, that the savage slaughter had been without sanction. Remembering the long days he had spent, struggling with his conscience, before he could write that order to Hamilton, he sent an injured protest to Tweeddale.

I understand that there are some severe reflections made upon the action in Glencoe (and that perhaps by many good men too). Therefore I think it my duty to give your lordship a more particular account thereof. . . . I had several orders from London, and also several orders from the Commander-in-Chief, and all extraordinary strict, to destroy these people and take no prisoners, and (lest I should prove remiss) another of the same orders was directed to my Lieutenant-Colonel to do the same, and after all that another order under the King's hand to root out that sept of thieves.

He was saying that the responsibility for the act was not his. He had obeyed the ultimate authority of the Throne, and that in honour and good conscience he could not have refused. It was a defence more readily accepted in his day than it would be two and a half centuries later at Nuremberg, but even so the principle of his argument had already been challenged by the two young officers who broke their swords at Kinlochleven, by the unknown Campbell soldiers who warned or spared their hosts. Inwardly, Hill was desperately confused and unhappy. To keep his peace of mind, perhaps, he said that by their own incorrigible behaviour the MacDonalds had brought disaster upon themselves. It was a solacing argument, and would be used again by other men in his position after Culloden. In its easy contempt for the Highland people it would be used to justify their eviction and their dispersal across the world a century later. "If any censure the severity of man's justice," Hill told Tweeddale, "yet the justice of God is to be reverenced. For there was much blood on these people's hands. . . ."

The news of the massacre had reached London on February 27. As yet it was known to a few only, but one of them was Grey John, who had been told by letters from Barcaldine and Carwhin. He was astonished and angry, or at least he said he was. After weeks of uncertainty, he was beginning to feel more sure of his welcome at Court. Three days before, he had come back to his lodgings from Kensington Palace to find Coll MacDonald of Keppoch sitting comfortably in his dining-room. The leader of the Lochaber Men, having taken the oath within the time set, now wanted Breadalbane's help in securing a commission in the King's army. Breadalbane was glad to take this tamed eagle to Court, as evidence of his influence over the rebel clans, but the news from the north took the pleasure from the little success, and he was not sure what mental reservations the dark young Mac-Donald might now make as he bent to kiss the Dutchman's hand. Anxiously, Breadalbane went from one great man to another, boring them with his worried disapproval of the massacre, declaring it was neither legal nor honourable. Those who were English could not see why there should be so much concern over a handful of savages, and those who were Scots were disgusted by what they thought was the Earl's hypocrisy. The suave, unruffled Argyll smiled and shrugged his shoulders, and his indifference angered Breadalbane. What if the Glencoe MacDonalds and other broken men came down upon honest Campbells in reprisal? Argyll smiled and shrugged again. "I hope the King will protect them."

"The King's in London," said Breadalbane ironically, "and it's a far cry to Loch Awe!" It was an old saying, and once it had meant that Campbells were safe in their own country.

He was less worried about men of his name, however, than he was about himself and his own property. He was leasing some timber rights in Glen Orchy to two Londoners, who were now understandably reluctant to sign the papers. He urged them to go, and to take tobacco "to be in friendship with the Glencoe men".

Despite his protests, those he spoke to at Court held him responsible for the massacre, principally because it had been carried out
by his cousin and clansman. He was in a hysterical fury with the
drunken and loose-tongued Glenlyon, and was now convinced
that the man was insane. Who else but a madman would have
accepted the duty, when it could be said that he was exacting his
own and his chief's vengeance? Who else but a madman would
have exposed his wife and family to reprisals by the MacDonalds?
Breadalbane was glad to hear that Argyll's Regiment was under
orders for the Continent. "An ill and miraculous fate follows the
unfortunate Glenlyon in the whole tract of his life," he told
Carwhin. "He is not to be mended. I hope he will go to Flanders.
I wish his relations and children pay not for it." His anger against
Glenlyon was mixed with a maudlin pity for himself. "It's
villainy to accuse me for Glenlyon's madness, and it's the height
of malice if these people chase the poor woman and people out of
the country."

With subtle spite, Argyll enjoyed sticking pins into Grey
John's sensitive skin at this moment, telling him that Breadalbane
men were buying Glencoe cows from Inverlochy at a dollar a
head. "If it be true," said Breadalbane angrily, "I'll make them
restore them to the widows and fatherless!" He probably meant
it, for he sent those instructions to his agents in the Highlands. It is
difficult to dismiss as lies all his protestations of innocence, or his
argument that he had too much to lose by the massacre to have
"so contrived it when a profound peace was best and intended".
Though he was a hypocrite and a trimmer, he had hoped to
succeed as a peace-maker. He would have been a fool to risk this,
and the goodwill he expected from the Jacobites under the
Private Articles of Achallader, and though he was frequently a
rogue, he was never a fool. Had he been a full party to the scheme,
he would not have urged his innocence so vehemently upon men
like Argyll, who would have known him to be guilty. It is probable that he put the idea of bloody coercion into Stair's mind, in
Flanders or across the dinner-table in London, but he drew back
from it later, in disapproval or self-preservation, and he re-

You are hereby ordered to fall upon the Rebells, the
McDonalds of Glenco, and putt all to the sword under
seventy. you are to have a speciall care that the old
Fox and his sones doe upon no account escape your
hands, you are to secure all the avenues that no
man escape. This you are to putt in execution
att fyve of the clock precisely; and by that time,
or very shortly after it, I'le strive to be att you
with a stronger party: if I doe not come to you
att fyve, you are not to tarry for me, butt to fall on.
This is by the Kings speciall command, for the good &
safty of the Country, that these miscreants be cutt
off root and branch. See that this be putt in execu-
tione without feud or favour, else you may expect to be
dealt with as one not true to King nor Government,
nor a man fitt to carry Commissione in the Kings
service. Expecting you will not faill in the full-
filling hereof, as you love your selfe, I subscribe
these with my hand att Balicholis Feb: 12, 1692

For their Majesties service.
To Capt
Robert Campbell
of Glenlyon.

7. *"You Are To Put All To the Sword Under Seventy"*
Duncanson's dispatch, sent to Glenlyon on the evening of February 12 with
orders for the destruction of the MacDonalds.

8. *"I Am Filled With Gloom As I See These Hills"*
(OPPOSITE P. 257)
The centre of the glen beyond Achnacone, looking eastward with Aonach
Eagach on the left. Towards noon on February 13, Hamilton's men came
over the rise in the middle distance, beyond which is Loch Achtriachtan.

peatedly said that he had been excluded from the Master's confidence when the act was planned. He had agreed to bar any retreat into Breadalbane by the MacDonalds, and this was the extent of his involvement. Beyond this, "I am as free of accession," he said, "as the man in Spain". He asked Barcaldine to tell the people of Glencoe that he had had nothing to do with the affair, but with his cousin and debtor as chief executioner no one believed him. For this reason alone was he violently angry with Robert Campbell of Glenlyon.

Soon there was not an ear at Kensington ready to listen to him. He decided to go home, and he told Carwhin to find him lodgings for a few days in Edinburgh. Then he would go on to Loch Tay. He had a Highlander's longing to be in his own glen when his spirits were troubled. Less sentimentally, he wanted to be sure that the two Londoners could extract turpentine from his fir-woods without having their throats cut by MacDonalds. He left London on April 12, and on that day copies of the *Paris Gazette* arrived from France, making the massacre public knowledge.

The Laird of Glencoe was butchered several days ago in the most barbarous manner, although he was amenable to the present Government. The Laird of Glenlyon, a captain in Argyll's Regiment, following the explicit orders of Colonel Hill, Governor of Inverlochy, went at night to Glencoe with a body of soldiers; and the soldiers, having entered the houses, killed the Laird of Glencoe, two of his sons, thirty-six men or children, and four women. It had been resolved in this manner to wipe out the rest of the inhabitants, not withstanding the amnesty that had been granted them, but about two hundred escaped. It has been rumoured that the Laird was killed in an ambush with his weapons in his hands, in order to diminish the horror of so barbarous an action, which would have made all nations see what little trust can be placed on the words of those who rule.

Though the report was not wholly accurate, it was close enough to the truth. The information had been sent to France by the Jacobites of Edinburgh, who had not only obtained copies of Duncanson's order but also Hamilton's, both of which they circulated in taverns and coffee-houses. And they may have been

responsible for the sentimental ballads that were cried in the
streets.

> On that dark and fateful night
> They broke my bower and slew my knight,
> Just in my soft and longing arms
> Where I believed him free from harms,
> They pierced his tender gentle breast
> And left me with sad griefs oppressed.
> And was I not a weary wight,
> A maid, wife, widow all in a night?

The Jacobites were less horrified by the massacre than they were
determined to injure William and the Government by exploiting
it. In the busy stir they made, they were joined by many ardent
supporters of the Revolution who seized upon the affair as a spade
to turn the earth of the Master's political grave. Among them was
James Johnston of Warriston, soon to become Joint Secretary
with Stair. He was a shrewd, fair-skinned lawyer who had gone
into exile when his father was hanged after the Restoration,
returning twenty-five years later to prepare the ground for
William's invasion. Macky thought he was honest, virtuous and
incapable of a lie, but Swift said he was a knave, one of the greatest
in Scotland, a country notoriously full of rogues. Johnston was
disgusted by the Master's cynical and luke-warm Presbyterianism,
and was as anxious to unseat him as the Dalrymples had been to
remove Melville. At the end of March he began to drip poison
into the ear of Tweeddale, who was then in London. "This
business of Glencoe makes a scurvy noise. Major Duncanson's
Christian order is in the coffee-houses. It's said that Glencoe had
been admitted to take the oath and that the troops were quartered
upon them and so against all the laws of hospitality and in cold
blood killed their hosts, that women and children were not
spared." Knowing that Tweeddale would show his letters to the
King, Johnston was careful to make it plain that he believed
William to be innocent of any charge. The King's clemency had
been abused, his orders had been made the instrument of private

murder and robbery. MacIain and his tacksmen should have been seized and brought before proper justice, not slaughtered. "If any of the inferior officers to whom the execution was committed have been guilty of irregularity in the manner of doing it, they rather than the reputation of the Government ought to suffer by it." There would be a time when Johnston, and others, would feel bold enough to say that a King's minister, too, ought to suffer by it, but as yet no one knew how Stair could be brought down without shaking the Throne itself.

The Master was unmoved by scurrilous rumour and malicious gossip. Before leaving London to join William in Flanders, he wrote to Hill, acknowledging the reports he had received from the Governor and from Hamilton. There was much talk of the Glencoe affair in the city, and that MacIain had been murdered in his bed after taking the oath of allegiance. "For the last," said Stair, lying blandly, "I know nothing of it. I am sure neither you nor anybody empowered to treat or give indemnity did give him the oath, and to take it from anybody else after the diet elapsed did import nothing. All I regret is, that any of the sept got away...."

In Edinburgh, Livingstone was of the same intractable mind. Four days after the massacre, Hamilton reported that he had taken "some Lochaber men" prisoners. They were probably Mac-Donalds whom the garrison patrols had surprised among the embers of Glencoe, or on the braes of Appin. "I must say it was a mistake," said Livingstone irritably, "that these villains were not shot in the place where they were found . . . let no prisoners be brought in, but let them be dispatched in the place where they are found, for such robbers and thieves are not to be treated as regular enemies".

When the *Paris Gazette* reached London it was eagerly read by an emotional and wordy Irishman called Charles Leslie. A son of the Bishop of Raphoe and Clogher, he had been both barrister and minister, but when he refused to take the oath to William and Mary he had been deprived of the curacy of Donagh. He went to England where he became one of the most readable of the anonymous Jacobite polemicists. After he read the *Gazette*, he

wrote to Scotland for details, and he gave London its first full
account of the massacre in a letter which he said he had received
from a friend in Edinburgh. He had some difficulty in finding a
printer bold enough to set it in type, but he finally published it as
an irrelevant appendix to a now unimportant pamphlet on the
Protestant Church in Ireland.* His "Gentleman in Scotland" was
undoubtedly an invention, a single voice for all the information he
got from Edinburgh, from the same Jacobites who had sent the
news to the *Paris Gazette*. Four thousand words in length, the
letter contained copies of the orders from Hamilton and Duncanson, and it compares well with evidence later given under oath by
witnesses of the massacre. It invited its readers to test the truth of
the story.

To put you out of all doubt, you will e'er long have my Lord Argyll's
Regiment with you in London, and there you may speak with Glenlyon and Drummond and the rest of the actors in that dismal tragedy;
and on my life there is never a one of them will deny it to you; for they
know it is known all over Scotland, and it is an admiration to us that
there should be any one in England who makes the least doubt of it.

On a Thursday morning late in June, Leslie himself took a hack
into Middlesex where Argyll's thirteen companies were now
quartered on the citizens of Brentford, ready to sail for Flanders
when the King had further need of their bayonets. He spoke to
many of the soldiers, though not, it would seem, to either Glenlyon or Drummond. Some of them, he said, were ashamed of
what they had done. They told him to look at Robert Campbell,
and in that wild, ageing man he would see the guilt they all felt.
"MacIain hangs about Glenlyon night and day," they said, "You
may see Glencoe in his face."
Now that the story was public knowledge many men were
ashamed and uneasy, and many more were unctuously pleased
that they had had no part in the bloody business. The members of

* *An Answer to a Book intituled The State of the Protestants in Ireland under the
late King James's Governments.* The book in question had been written by
William King, an ardent Whig and the Bishop of Derry.

the Privy Council were relieved that it had been ordered without their official approval, and Johnston delighted in informing his colleague Stair that there was no word about Glencoe on the Council's records. "So either the Registers are defective," he wrote sarcastically, "or someone in Scotland forges orders." In the Highlands there was fear of more bloodshed and betrayal. Hill's position was delicate and difficult. He was still under orders to kill the Glencoe men wherever they were found (Livingstone's irritable letter to Hamilton had made that plain), but he could not believe that the King now wished him to hunt them down and slaughter them like animals. He worked tirelessly at his desk throughout the candle-hours, pleading on their behalf, assuring the Council that under his protection the MacDonalds would be willing to come down from their mountain caves and live in peace. "They are very quiet," he said, "only in small parties, desire a little meal to keep them from starving, and are punctual in observing such directions as I give them, and await the King's pleasure as to their settlement." Quiet they may have been for the moment, but there was a growing suspicion that they might not long remain so. Since the spring thaws and the opening of the passes from the east, loose and broken men from all over the central Highlands had been joining John MacDonald's scattered bands below Bidean nam Bian, hungry for revenge, for plunder and the fat cattle of the Lowlands. This, as much as John Hill's sensible advice, forced the Council to a decision. At the beginning of May it placed the MacDonalds under the Governor's protection ordering him "to take what security he shall think meet for their living peaceably until His Majesty signify his pleasure therein".

Before the Council issued this order, news of William's cold pleasure was already on its way from The Hague. It came in letters from Stair, addressed to the Earl of Tweeddale and to John Hill. The Master was clearly unmoved by all the fuss about the massacre, as indifferent to public opinion as ever. "It's true," he said, "that affair of Glencoe was very ill executed, but 'tis strange to me that means so much regret for such a sept of thieves". For all the outcry, the indignation, the talk of treachery and murder, he and his royal Master were still determined to destroy Clan Iain Abrach. Though the sword had not succeeded, there was still another way.

The King has ordered me to write to your Lordship and to Colonel Hill that he is willing to pardon them they going abroad to the plantations, Ireland, or any place else, but he will not allow them to settle in their old quarter which is so commodious for their thieving trade. I fancy they will be glad of what's allowed, having their lives safe, and more can not in the will of the country be asked.

There is no evidence that John Hill told the MacDonalds that the only mercy they could expect was to be transported as bonded servants, to become slaves on the plantations of America. Yet he must have done, for he was a conscientious officer. For three months, throughout most of the summer, the MacDonalds remained on the high braes like frightened deer. They were without spirit and without songs, and they had no will to fight except in desperate defence of their liberty. The thought of transportation was a greater horror than the memory of the massacre, and in their fear they did what they could to prove to the Government that they were ready to live in peace, if only they might return to their glen. John MacDonald sent away the broken men who had come to him in the spring. Two more, who had robbed and wounded a traveller by Inverlochy and who had sought shelter on Bidean nam Bian, were bound hand and foot and delivered to one of John Hill's patrols.

Throughout the summer, too, Hill pleaded with the Council, and through it with the King. He asked for kindness, compassion and good sense. He supported his pleas with the news that all great men in the hills were now anxious to serve the King, and nothing should be done to sour their good humour. Lochiel, he said, had come to him most humbly, promising to behave as a dutiful subject. He forwarded a slavish letter from Sir John MacLean in which this chief offered to surrender his house and castle and wait upon the King in Flanders.* "I wish I could have an answer about

* Once there, however, MacLean changed his mind and joined King James at St. Germain.

the settlement of the Glencoe men," said Hill, when he sent such news to Tweeddale, "I beg your Lordship's assistance in it, since I know it will conduce more to His Majesty's favour and the peace of the country than any other matter."

In August he at last got his way. The inhuman proposal to transport the MacDonalds was at last abandoned, and Hill was told that the King was now willing to allow the Glencoe men to return to the Valley of the Dogs. The Governor wrote at once to John MacDonald, advising him to go to Inveraray as soon as possible and there submit and swear before Campbell of Ard-kinglas. It was a week before the courier could find MacIain in the mountains and return with his reply.

Right Honourable,—I am exceedingly sorry that your line came not to my hands till this day, to the end I might give you my most hearty thanks for your goodness in procuring the King his pardon and remission, the which I will most cordially embrace and will betake myself to live under His Majesty's royal protection in such a manner that the Government shall not repent or give you cause to blush for the favour you have done me and my people. I am this day to take my voyage to find security to your honour's contentment, and thereafter I will do myself the favour to come to your garrison and be honoured with a kiss of your hand and end my affairs, which with cordial thanks for your courtesy never to be forgot by him who is
Yours most assured to obey your commands,
JOHN MACDONALD

Were it within his power, said Iain Lom the Bard of Keppoch, he would give all the lands of Breadalbane to John MacDonald of Glencoe. He would give all the sheep of Cowal to Alexander MacDonald, the son of the murdered tacksman of Achtriachtan. He would put the curse of barrenness on the race of Diarmaid so that their glens might pass into the hands of his injured kinsman of Clan Donald. And he would flay the skin from the back of Grey John Campbell, the Laird of Glenorchy.

But John MacDonald was content with no more than an opportunity to take his people home to Glencoe, and to kiss Colonel Hill's hand in gratitude. His brother Alasdair Og was more obstinate, and it was October before he accepted the Governor's protection. On the spot where their father's body had been thrown by the soldiers, the brothers planted a tree. It was still in leaf when their descendants were gone from the valley.

Nothing came of the great stir that had been made in the spring. The enemies of Stair were as yet too weak to pull him down, and Parliament and Council were divided into squabbling, selfish factions. The Jacobites were silenced by the exposure of another of their clumsy plots, and by the terrible defeat of a French fleet off Cape La Hogue.

In August, ten days before John MacDonald took his people home, William fought a battle against the French at Steinkirk. It was a bloody, useless struggle across fence and ravine, and was remembered only by a cravat that took its name. The King wept as he watched the slaughter. Of his twenty British battalions eight were Scots, and their presence in Flanders had been made possible by the Massacre of Glencoe. Hugh Mackay died at the head of one of them, men of his own clan. He did not like the orders given him, but he said "The will of the Lord be done!" and marched forward. Ten battalions were sent from England to reinforce this shattered army, and among them was the Earl of Argyll's Regiment. William welcomed it. Having seen Scotsmen die for him, Highland and Lowland, he said that they had made good their motto, *Nemo me impune lacessit.*

No one attacks me with impunity.

"The laws of God and Nature are above those of men"

THE LETTER was signed by the Earl of Annandale on May 23, 1695, and the rider who carried it from Edinburgh reached Fort Wiliam within the week. John Hill read it with confused feelings. "Sir, It hath pleased His Majesty to give a Commission under the Broad Seal to the Marquis of Tweeddale, the Earl of Annandale and seven more, to take trial by what warrants and in what manner the Glencoe men were killed in February, 1692, and for that end to call for all persons, letters, and other writings that may give any light in it . . . to examine witnesses . . . that there may be a full discovery . . . require you to come to Edinburgh. . . ."

It was more than three years since Hill had sat at this same desk, in this same green room, and written his order to Hamilton. Sometimes he wished that men would forget all about Glencoe, and at others he longed for an opportunity to clear his name before the world. In the spring of 1693, the King had made the Duke of Hamilton his Commissioner to the Scots Parliament, with orders to hold an enquiry into the massacre, and in that year too John Hill had been told to make ready his papers and his defence. But the Duke was a lazy man and his instructions were inadequate. When he finally saved himself and all others considerable embarrassment by dying, the Enquiry came to nothing. Colonel Hill continued to do his duty in the Highlands, trusting in God and common justice, spending the candle-hours with his books of sermons. His garrison now consisted of his own regiment only, and this was as sad a burden as ever. Since it was first mustered he had lost seven hundred men, almost the whole regiment. Three hundred and seventy had died of sickness, in the fort or on patrol, and their bodies lay in the soggy burial-ground by Loch Linnhe, or were lost in the heather of the hills. As if this terrible erosion were not enough, three hundred and twenty-six more had been taken to make up the strength of those battalions William had wasted at Steinkirk and Landen.

This past winter had been the worst that Hill had spent at Inverlochy. Although he was never well, he refused to take to his bed. There were not enough coals to heat the barracks or the hospital, now staffed by two overworked young surgeons. There were no blankets, no replacements for worn clothing and shoes, and there was rarely enough food. Until he left in February, 1695, to become lieutenant-colonel of Lindsay's Regiment in Ireland, James Hamilton had been able to buy fish from Breadalbane's tenants on Loch Tay and Loch Awe. But this had been an occasional luxury only. John Forbes had taken £150 from his own pocket to buy meat and meal, and the Government had neither thanked nor repaid him. Hill was still waiting for the money he had spent in defence of Belfast six years before. It was hard to suppress the bitter feeling that his service and his sacrifices meant nothing to the King, that his regiment was no more than a holding battalion for others.

The hills were quiet and peaceful, and that at least was God's mercy. The Glencoe MacDonalds were abundantly civil, he reported, and obedient to his will. They had rebuilt their town-ships, and John MacDonald was planning a fine new house by the mouth of the Coe, with his initials carved on the stone pediment above the door.* For a while, in the summer of 1694, that "pretty boy" Robert Stewart of Appin had been troublesome, and Hill had been afraid that his clansmen might be drawn out on the heather. Though he had come to Inverlochy on a stretcher after the massacre, promising to take the oath, Appin had put off his submission for two years, and was at last called to Edinburgh to explain the delay. On his way there he insulted one of Hill's

---

* This pediment can still be seen in the wall of the MacDonald vault on Eilean Munde.

captains, and in Edinburgh he passionately assaulted two of the city's officers. The Privy Council locked him in the Tolbooth until his temper cooled, until he took the oath and promised to apologise to Hill and his captain. It was a small affair, but it showed how close to the skin of his docile submission was a Highland chief's arrogant independence.

And now Glencoe again. Hill was not surprised by the summons to Edinburgh. It had long been rumoured that Parliament was determined to debate the matter, whether or not the King set up an Enquiry. Public unease had been increasing. Sir John Lauder of Fountainhall was said to have refused to accept the Lord Advocate's office (when it was resigned by Stair) unless he were allowed to prosecute those responsible for the massacre. There was little sympathy for the MacDonalds in this agitation, only a jealous concern for private interest and public honour. "It's not that anybody thinks that the thieving tribe did not deserve to be destroyed," Livingstone had told Hamilton in 1693, "but that it should have been done by such as were quartered amongst them makes a great noise." Society is driven by political ambition more frequently than by humanity, and the Master's enemies were determined to ruin him in the name of common justice.

To bring him down, his servants were first to be discredited, and Hill knew that some men wished to put much of the blame upon him. One of them was Sir Ludovick Grant, the Laird of Grant and a Member of Parliament for Elgin and Inverness, who spread malicious gossip about Hill, which particularly hurt the old man. In the past he had done much to help the Grant family, and he asked his friend Duncan Forbes of Culloden to call "this bull-dog" from his heels. He hoped that Culloden would protect his reputation from the slanders then current in Edinburgh. He knew that he stood well in Secretary Johnston's favour, and in the opinion of honest men, but there were evil men throwing dirt, knowing that some must stick. He could not understand why he should be attacked, unless it were that he had never been one to dance to another's piper. "I pray that if you find mouths open in Parliament to our detriment you will, with the help of other friends,

endeavour to stop them." This reminded him of a passage he had
read in Mr. Joseph Caryll's *Exposition on Job*. . . . Caryll had been
Cromwell's chaplain, a great preacher in Lincoln's Inn Fields
during the Commonwealth, and the old soldier's youth was much
in his thoughts these days. . . . What Mr. Caryll had written
about the opening of mouths was very true. "It was on these
words, *Then Job opened his mouth and spake*, from which Mr.
Caryll observed that wise men open their mouths when they
speak, and fools speak with their mouths open."

There were many mouths open in Edinburgh and London,
both wise and foolish, and the Jacobite pack was again in cry.
James Johnston's intriguing against his colleague Stair had now
become an open campaign. He said that the Master's hatred
of the MacDonalds had been the cause of the Glencoe affair and
that it was "a foul business". He was still working to keep the
King free from any charge. He wanted an Enquiry, for by this
alone could William be exonerated and the Dalrymple ruined.
For three years he had been collecting information about the
massacre and sending it to John Tillotson, Archbishop of Canter-
bury. When Tillotson died in 1694, Johnston sent the same
information and more to his successor, Thomas Tenison, "that he
may tell his Churchmen how innocent the King is". And presumably that he might also tell William how guilty his Minister
was. Johnston enlisted the sympathy of the sentimental Queen,
telling her that the officers concerned in the slaughter should be
broken. The gentle woman was so horrified that she said they
ought to be hanged.

Since the Revolution the Scots Parliament, now stumbling
toward extinction, had had little real power, and that only in the
voting of supplies. Its Members had been increasingly angered by
William's indifference to Scottish affairs, except where the
country could furnish him with soldiers and money for his wars.
When they assembled in the spring of 1695 they were determined
to conduct their own Enquiry into Glencoe, and thus force the
King and his oligarchy of ministers to accept them as responsible
representatives of the country. At the end of April they crowded

into Parliament Hall, silk and black broad-cloth passing beneath the Royal Arms of Scotland and the figures of Justice and Mercy. They took their places beside the empty Throne or on the floor of the Hall, each Estate separated from the others so that there might be no consultation or collusion between them. The stone walls were warmed by tapestries, and sixty feet above the floor the excited hum of voices from the benches was lost among the hammer-beams. But there was an astonished silence when the Members were addressed by the Lord High Chancellor, the King's Commissioner to Parliament, John Hay, Marquis of Tweeddale. He told them that the King had anticipated their wishes. His Majesty had been "pondering what method will be the most effective for obtaining full information about the massacre of certain people surnamed MacDonald, and others of Glencoe, in the year 1692". He had now ordered a Commission of Enquiry, formed by eight of his most loyal and beloved kinsmen and counsellors. There was nothing the Members could do but wait until this Commission finished its work, and then press for its Report to be laid before them.

Were it possible to believe that any such Commission would find him guilty, it might be said that William's loyal and well-beloved kinsmen and counsellors had been well chosen to protect his reputation, for the most important of them had good reason to prove their somewhat tardy allegiance to the Throne and the Revolution.

The Marquis of Tweeddale had been an earl until recently, and his elevation demonstrated a considerable degree of Royal tolerance and trust. He had been involved in at least one Jacobite plot, and only a full and craven confession had got him out of prison. The second Commissioner was William Johnstone, Earl of Annandale, a handsome man not yet forty, with a dark and ironic face. Few men trusted him, for he did not let their affairs divert his own instinct for self-preservation. Though he had supported the Revolution in 1689, he later hoped for more from King James and joined The Club. A bungled, stupid plot took him to prison also, but he was soon released upon an apology and a promise of good behaviour. He was now a Lord of the Treasury. Sir James Stewart, the third Commissioner, was Lord Advocate, having been given the office when it was refused by Lauder of Fountainhall. He was an affable old man who made a virtue out of a lack of ceremony, and a career out of expediency. James II had outlawed him as one of the engineers of the Argyll Rebellion in 1685, but later recalled him and put him to work, a change of loyalties that put no great strain on Stewart's conscience. William knighted him, but was only slowly beginning to trust him. There was James Ogilvy, the Solicitor-General, a soft-tongued, beautiful young man of thirty-one, whose great strength was that he knew exactly what would please the King without ever having to think about it. The fifth Commissioner was Adam Cockburn of Ormiston, the Lord Justice Clerk, a bigoted and zealous Presbyterian who saw no virtue and no honesty in any man who was not. He was a fine gentleman in his person and manners, and believed that King William could do no wrong. John Lord Murray was the son of the Marquis of Atholl, and he had supported the Revolution when his father and most of his clan had declared for James. He was proud and passionate, with a violent temper that brought him to blows with Breadalbane over Glenlyon's lands, and he would serve the King so long as William kept his word. The two remaining Commissioners were Sir William Hamilton of Whitelaw, and Adam Drummond of Megginch, both of them lawyers.

It was before these men that John Hill was summoned at the end of May. "I shall give all ready obedience," he told them, "taking only two days to settle affairs and give the necessary orders here. I shall bring such of the officers as are upon the place, many of them being abroad getting up recruits." And perhaps he may have wondered if Hamilton, wherever he might be in Ireland, would be as willing to go to Edinburgh.

The Commission sat in Holyroodhouse during the last week of May and the first three of June, a bank of scarlet and white robes, nodding grey wigs, and the brittle flash of jewelled rings. Witnesses appeared before them under their protection, whatever charges might be against them. They heard John Hill and John Forbes, Francis Farquhar and Gilbert Kennedy. They heard depositions from Sir Colin Campbell of Ardkinglas and Colin Campbell of Dressalch, and they listened to James Campbell of Glenlyon's company, now a soldier in the garrison at Stirling. They examined Lord Aberuchil and Sir Gilbert Elliott, Clerk to the Privy Council. They called ten men of Glencoe before them, giving them protection against "all captions, arrests, or other diligences of that sort until the tenth of July next to come". The MacDonalds walked boldly into the great hall of the black palace, where their sons and grandsons would one day dance before a young Stuart prince. They stood below the Commissioners with their plaids thrown back and their bonnets in their hands, and they told what they remembered of that dawn when their Campbell guests had turned upon them. They were

> John MacDonald of Glencoe and his brother Alasdair
> Alexander MacDonald the son of Achtriachtan
> Alexander MacDonald the tacksman of Dalness
> Ronald MacDonald an indweller of Leacantium
> Ronald MacDonald in Inverrigan
> Duncan MacEanruig in Inverrigan
> Donald MacStarken in Laroch
> Alexander MacDonald in Brecklet, and
> Angus MacDonald in Strone.

But the Commissioners did not examine Major Robert Duncanson of the Earl of Argyll's Regiment. They did not hear Captain Robert Campbell of Glenlyon, Captain Thomas Drummond, Lieutenant Lindsay or Ensign Lundie. They did not question Sergeant Barber or Sergeant Purdie, or any of the sergeants, corporals, drummers and sentinels, excepting James Campbell from Stirling Castle. The Argyll men were in the trenches before Namur, and it would seem that none of the Commissioners thought it advisable to ask the King to send some of them home. They did call Lieutenant-Colonel James Hamilton from Ireland, but he ignored the summons.

John Hill gave his evidence to the Commission on Saturday, June 7, within a day of arriving by express from Fort William. He and the officers he brought from his garrison, Forbes, Farquhar and Kennedy, made a brave show of scarlet and gold in the dusky hall. He was plain and honest, and said what he knew and what he had done. He was content that judgement upon him would be guided by God's mercy. MacDonald of Glengarry was examined on the same day, and both he and Hill told the Commissioners about the Private Articles which Breadalbane had agreed with the chiefs at Achallader. Though these had been rumour and gossip for nearly four years, and though the King had been informed of them, the Commissioners now felt obliged to place them before Parliament. The Members scented blood. Breadalbane had no friends, and his enemies leapt baying from the kennels. They voted for his arrest, and ordered the Lord Advocate to prepare the charge of treason. The old man was lifted from his lodgings one morning, and taken up the cobbled street to the Castle. He was in sudden terror for his life, and believed that he would leave his prison only to die beneath the Maiden. Tweeddale was unhappy, and he asked the King what he should do to save Breadalbane from Parliament's vindictive fury. He got no immediate reply.

On June 20 the Commissioners signed their Report, and the next day it was sent to the King in his camp before Namur. Bad storms delayed the pacquet, and William did not receive the long and detailed account until late in the first week of July. By then its contents were known in Edinburgh, and had been hotly debated beneath the tapestries of Parliament Hall. To nobody's surprise perhaps, the King's loyal and beloved Commissioners decided that his orders had not authorised the slaughter, "even as to the thing itself, and far less as to the manner of it, seeing that all his instructions do plainly import that the most obstinate of the rebels might be received into mercy upon taking the oath". As for his additional instruction of January 16, 1692—that if the Glencoe men could be well separated from the rest it would be a proper vindication of the public justice to extirpate them—the Commissioners said this meant "they were only to be proceeded against in the way of public justice, and in no other way". This unique definition of the verb *to extirpate* will be found in no dictionary.

Having begun with an exoneration of their Royal Master, the

Commissioners continued by blaming his principal servant in Scotland. Stair's orders, they said, had exceeded the King's wishes, and had been "the only warrant and cause of the slaughter which, in effect, was a barbarous murder". They would not allow him the excuse that he had not known of MacIain's journey to take the oath at Inveraray. They quoted his letter to Livingstone of January 30, proving that he did know and that he was glad Glencoe had not come in within the time prescribed. Their condemnation of Glenlyon, Duncanson, Hamilton, and other soldiers, was implicit, and although they did not name Colin Campbell of Dressalch and Gilbert Elliott in their conclusions, the responsibility of these men was also made plain. The scoring of MacIain's name from Ardkinglas's certificate had been a great error, "and those who advised the not presenting thereof [to the Council] were in the wrong, and seem to have had a malicious design against Glencoe". Those who had advised the not presenting thereof were almost all Campbells.

When the Members of Parliament heard that the Report was away to the King in Flanders they insisted upon seeing a copy of it, and all relevant papers, "for their satisfaction and full information". Between two masters, Tweeddale surrendered to the most immediate and pressing, and gave the Members what they demanded. He told the King that they had been deliberately delaying the other business of Parliament until they got the Report, and he apologised for making it public, but it had seemed necessary "to vindicate the justice and honour of your government by laying the blame upon the instruments of so inhumane and barbarous a slaughter". His choice of words was rarely felicitous, an instrument is but a tool in a responsible hand. Since he had not been able to refuse Parliament, he asked William for permission to extend the time it was to sit, "that your service may be done with cheerfulness and alacrity". He was miserably aware that this would enrage the King, who was usually out of sympathy with the noisy self-importance of the Scots Parliament, and thought it could be of little service to him now that it had acknowledged him King of Scotland.

Parliament enjoyed itself. It had not had such power since the Convention of the Estates six years before when it had recreated itself. It was the responsible voice of Scotland, and it would not be heard again with authority for fifteen years, when it would then debate its own suicide. The Members listened to a reading of the Report and all the depositions of evidence, the cold voice of a clerk beating against the noise of the city beyond, telling the story of MacIain's death, of a child's bloody hand upon the snow, of the burning of houses and the lifting of cattle. There were several pleasant days of debate on whether Parliament should or should not send an Address to the King when it reached its conclusions. On June 26 it was at last in agreement, such an Address should indeed be sent. Wearily, and wondering what store of Royal resentment he was laying up against himself, Tweeddale again wrote to the King, asking for authority to extend the session for another fortnight. There was now another debate on a motion to send the Address immediately, without further discussion, and this was comfortably defeated, since the Address would mean nothing if it did not clearly determine responsibility. Was the Master of Stair to blame, or was . . . nobody mentioned the name. The old fox of Breadalbane was in the Castle, and now the Members fell upon the Dalrymples. In a long sitting of nine hours, well into candlelight and well past a civilised man's supper-time, one question was furiously argued. Did Stair's orders exceed the King's warrant? The motion was at last put, whereupon the Earl of Argyll, who had been silent until now, decided to speak upon it, and was ruled out of order. What he wished to say can only be guessed at, a defence of his friend Stair perhaps, a plea for the honour of his regiment and the men of his clan who had been the executioners. He was the only one of the Master's few friends in Parliament who opened his mouth at this moment. The rest cautiously abstained, and the vote was carried. Stair had indeed exceeded the King's instructions, and had urged the destruction of the Glencoe men "with a great deal of zeal as a thing acceptable, and of public use". In this way many Members repaid the Secretary for a wounding shaft of mockery or an ignored petition for preferment, for his lack of Presbyterian zeal, his cynical intelligence, and his brilliantly contrived success. He was not condemned for Glencoe so much as for what he had been all his life.

Parliament had not done with the matter, and was still in debate when July began. The sittings were sometimes rowdy, and sometimes charged with deep emotion and hatred. The dignity of the Members was outraged at the end of June by the publication of a pamphlet called *Information for the Master of Stair*, written by, or at the command of, the Secretary's younger brother Hew Dalrymple. It was a loyal attempt to defend him, arguing that he had given no direct orders, that he had merely used words like *hope*, and *think*, and *believe*. It laid the responsibility for the massacre upon Sir Thomas Livingstone, and condemned the officers and men of Argyll's Regiment for carrying it out. This latter charge was valid, and would still be so two and a half centuries later.

Though the command of superior officers be very absolute, yet no command against the laws of nature is binding; so that a soldier, retaining his commission, ought to refuse to execute any barbarity, as if a soldier should be commanded to shoot a man passing by, inoffensively, upon the street, no such command would exempt him from the punishment of murder.

The point had been debated by Parliament on June 28, and the arguments it heard were reported by the writer of a News Letter.

It being objected that a Secretary might explain and order what he pleased, to which it was answered that the thing required by the Secretary must be lawful in itself, as the killing of any of the Highlanders that had refused the indemnity was, had it been the King's mind; but that if the Secretary had written to do a thing in itself unlawful, as the killing of men under trust, his letters, no more than the instructions could justify any man that obeyed them, because the laws of God and nature are above those of men. And therefore, whoever made quarter upon the Glencoe men in order to kill them, if they had any orders to produce, they could not be justified by them.

Though they were of one mind with Hew Dalrymple on this matter, the Members thought his pamphlet was impertinent. They declared it "false and caluminious", and ordered it to be so marked. They summoned Hew Dalrymple before them, to explain why he had circulated such a vile paper when they were still in discussion. He apologised promptly, saying that it had been written and printed before Parliament began its debate, and that what was offensive in it was a mistake of judgement which he truly regretted.

On July 10, Parliament drew up its *Address to the King Touching the Murder of the Glencoe Men*, and dispatched to it William. It was a far more emotional and critical document than the Commission's Report, and it condemned the slaughter as "Murder under Trust". It exonerated the King, of course, since its declared objective was to vindicate the honour of Crown and Government. It also excused Thomas Livingstone on the ground that he had not known of MacIain's oath. This was special pleading, and a victory for Livingstone's friends in Parliament. The Commander-in-Chief certainly had not known of the tardy oath when he wrote to Hill and Hamilton on January 18, ordering them to fall upon the rebels who had not submitted. He may not have known when he received the King's Additional Instructions of January 16. But he did know on January 23, admitting it in a letter to Hamilton of that date, telling the Deputy-Governor that it was none the less the Court's wish that the thieving nest of Glencoe should be entirely rooted out. He had had an opportunity to refuse his orders, like Kennedy or Farquhar, and he had done nothing. Whatever Parliament decided, his guilt is plain.

"We proceeded to examine Colonel Hill's part of the business," said the Address, "and were unanimous that he was clear and free of the slaughter." Though orders had been sent to him, he had avoided them and had given no instructions to his officers "till such time as, knowing that his Lieutenant-Colonel had received orders, he, to save his honour and authority, gave a general order to Hamilton to take four hundred men and to put in due execution the orders which others had given him". This too was special pleading, perhaps, and did not relieve the old man of the moral responsibility which two of his lieutenants had met by breaking their swords. But at least he had been honest, more concerned

with duty and honour than self-preservation. He had remained in
Edinburgh to give evidence before Parliament, and now he must
have gone back to Fort William with a lighter heart.

Stair was the guilty man, and the Address bluntly stated its
opinion that he had been "the original cause of this unhappy
business". Guilty, too, was Robert Duncanson of Argyll's, and
Parliament regretted that it had not seen the original of his order
to Glenlyon. Other "actors in the slaughter of the Glencoe men
under trust" were Captain Campbell of Glenlyon, Captain
Drummond, Lieutenant Lindsay, Ensign Lundie, and Sergeant
Barber, and Parliament asked the King to send these men home
from Flanders for prosecution. But this was impossible, even had
William felt obliged to meet the request. The Argyll Regiment
was at that moment in the hands of the French, having been
shamefully surrendered by its general officer at Dixemude.

The Address concluded with a charitable and honourable appeal
to William.

We shall only add that the remains of the Glencoe men who escaped
the slaughter, being reduced to great poverty by the depredation and
devastation that was then committed upon them, and having ever
since lived peaceably under your Majesty's protection, have now
applied to us that we might intercede with your Majesty that some
reparation may be made them for their loss. We do humbly lay their
case before your Majesty as worthy of your Royal charity and compassion, that such orders may be given for supplying them in their
necessities as your Majesty shall think fit.

John MacDonald of Glencoe, and his kinsman Alexander
MacDonald, the son of Achtriachtan, had put a petition before
Tweeddale and Parliament. Their widows and orphans, they said,
were starving, and all were extremely poor. They had lost all
their clothes, money, houses and plenishings by plunder or fire.
They had been robbed of fourteen or fifteen hundred cows, five
hundred horses and many sheep and goats. This was a great deal
more than the Argyll men were reported to have taken from the
valley, but the difference in accounting is of no importance.
Clan Iain Abrach received no reparation.

Neither the Commission nor Parliament had been able to examine Lieutenant-Colonel James Hamilton. He had been summoned, and he had stayed where he was in Ireland. On July 5 he wrote to Annandale, explaining why he would not come. He had no doubt of the justice of the Commission, he said, but he was unwilling to expose himself to the spite and odium of others in Edinburgh. "I implore the Almighty God to judge my innocency. I beg your Lordship's and the Members' Christian charity, and shall hope for their judicious consideration of all. . . ."

Parliament's interpretation of God's judgement and Christian charity toward Hamilton had taken another form. Angered by the wilful absence of this man "who was not clear of the murder of the Glencoe men", it demanded his arrest. On July 4, in an order signed by Annandale, he was ordered to appear before Parliament within forty-eight hours, failing which he would be denounced as a rebel and put to the horn. All officers of the Crown were told to apprehend him wherever he would be found, and to "incarcerate him ay and while he find caution for his compearing in manner and to the effect foresaid".

Toward the end of July a Lieutenant-Colonel Hamilton did arrive in Edinburgh from Dublin, carrying letters to Tweeddale from Lord Capel, brother of the man who had once been John Hill's patron. He may have been the Hamilton so earnestly desired by Parliament, and now confident enough of powerful protection to risk a visit to Scotland. It is impossible to say, but this much is certain: on July 20, Lieutenant-Colonel James Hamilton of Lindsay's Regiment, late of Hill's, was given a pass to go to Holland. The warrant was dated from Whitehall. In August he was in the King's camp at Waterloo. Robert Pringle, the Under-Secretary of State for Scotland who was then in Flanders, told Tweeddale that Hamilton had come to throw himself upon William's mercy. "I understand not what he proposes to himself by that," said Pringle coldly. "I do believe the King can have not leisure to consider his case. I think the King will not think it very fit that any denounced by his Parliament should come and stay avowedly and openly in his Army." Hamilton can have got little encouragement from Stair, he was probably driven away as a dog is kicked aside when it embarrasses his master, and there was no sweet talk now of kissing the King's hand, of forgiveness for past omissions. With one brief appearance later, Hamilton drops from history as mysteriously as he had come.

The Jacobites seized upon the Report and the Address with delight, determined to use it to injure both Throne and Government. Charles Leslie republished his *Letter from a Gentleman in Scotland*, in one pamphlet with a derisive and sometimes obscene examination of the Report.

Gallienus Redivivus

or

MURDER WILL OUT, ETC.,

Being a True Account of the

DE-WITTING

of

GLENCO

By comparing William with the tyrant Gallienus, who ordered his soldiers to kill those who spoke against him, and by recalling the murder of the De Witt brothers in Holland twenty-three years before, Leslie's title promised the indictment of the King that appeared in the text, "Here is a precedent made, and that by Parliament, that the King may send his guards and cut any man's throat in the nation in cold blood. . . . What can you expect from him but to be Glencoed for your pains? He scorned to except the pitiful women, as Gallienus did. What need they be excepted? Why, he excepted nobody!" Leslie laughed at Johnston's efforts to clear the King by the Enquiry, and he accused the Secretary of starting a hare by arranging Hamilton's excape.

There is one noble stroke of Secretary Johnston's behind whereby he thinks he has wiped his master clean from all imputation of the massacre; and that is, he has persuaded Lieutenant-Colonel Hamilton to abscond for some time, and then to slip over to K.W. in Flanders, which he has done. This shows as if he were more guilty than the rest. He is made the scape goat, and all this sin laid upon his head. But if Hill gave his orders to Lieutenant-Colonel Hamilton, why was it more criminal in Hamilton to hand down his colonel's orders to the next subaltern?

Qui Glencoat, Glencoabitur! said Leslie hopefully. But the scurrilous pamphlets which the Jacobites published on the same subject at this time entertained Society more than they damaged the King. Pringle asked Tweeddale to send one of them, it may have been Leslie's, to the camp in Flanders, and when it reached there it was contemptuously dismissed as "very inaccurate, the work of some silly agent or serving-man".

The King was out of patience with Tweeddale and Parliament, with the latter for sitting beyond its time, and with the former for giving it leave. He was irritated by the stir the Enquiry had caused, and he resented Parliament's advice on whom he should or should not punish. This concern over a handful of savage thieves, whose deaths nobody really grieved, seemed strangely irrelevant. The war was going badly, and the war was William's principal concern. He told Pringle to keep the Glencoe affair from him until he asked for the papers. This was not easy. Stair came to Flanders that August, bland and calm, and as smooth-tongued as ever. Breadalbane's son, Lord Glenorchy, came too, asking William to release his father from prison. The King would scarcely speak to Stair (who soon left for England again), but he listened to Glenorchy, not so much out of concern for Breadalbane, whose duplicity he understood better than most men, but because he considered Parliament's impeachment of Grey John an insufferable impertinence. He smiled on the Campbell, and pretended to believe that Breadalbane had agreed to the Private Articles in order to ingratiate himself with the Jacobites and thereby discover their plots.

In October the Army went into winter quarters, and the King came back to London. Stair had resigned the Secretaryship and retired to the country, cannily aware that he could do himself little good by coming to Court like a supplicant pauper. He was a superb tactician still, and although he gained no ground he lost none by refusing to defend it. A man who will not answer charges against him can sometimes make a stronger declaration of innocence than one who protests. Stair also understood the King, and he knew that William would be impressed by this silent suggestion that his opinion and his favour were all that mattered to Stair. Glenorchy was still tugging at the Royal sleeve, however, and the King at last signed an order for Breadalbane's release. Grey John came out into the golden smoke of an Edinburgh autumn, and left for Loch Tay as soon as he could.

For nearly two months William refused to consider any State affairs, English or Scots. A widower now, he lived like an obstinate recluse in the cold rooms of Kensington, and his Court became "Glencoe desperate". And then, on December 2, he made his mind and his feelings plain. All those members of the Scots Privy Council who were in England were summoned to him, and they gathered like frightened or expectant schoolboys before a pedagogue. The winter mists that came up from the river at Chelsea choked the King's weak lungs, and he looked with sickly eyes on the worried faces, the fingers plucking nervously at lace cuffs, the silver-buckled shoes scraping on the floor of his chamber. He told the Scots that the massacre of the Glencoe men had filled him with horror, and that it "had lain very near his heart" for a long time, which must have surprised them all. He astonished them further by saying that he had known little of the matter until eighteen months after the slaughter, when the Duke of Hamilton asked him if he had been given a true account of the business. James Johnston, who was taking discreet notes of the audience, was particularly surprised to hear this, for he remembered that at the same time he had been told on good authority that William was fully informed. A King was a King, however, and entitled to his peculiar view of the truth. Thinking of the future, Johnston decided to "take the middle way, to say just no more than was necessary". And Stair may have smiled cynically, remembering how the King had known enough about the massacre to order the transportation of the survivors.

Now was the moment for the Master to speak in his own defence, since this display of royal innocence left him to bear all the guilt. He spoke with great passion and an advocate's skill, using all his talent for ridicule and supercilious contempt as he attacked his accusers, looking the while at Johnston. The Secretary was so stung by Stair's bitter tongue that he forgot to make any more notes, and the rest of this meeting was thereby lost to us. But he did remember afterwards that he told Stair that far from being the work of prejudiced enemies, the Commission of Enquiry had been proposed by Archbishop Tillotson and his successor Tenison, and that the Queen herself had also urged it. And he did not think it necessary to add that none of them might have been concerned had he not brought the matter before them.

This meeting, on a cold day in a December palace, was the end of the Glencoe affair. The King did nothing, he punished nobody, and it may be a charity to argue that he could not because he was aware of his own moral responsibility. Though he did not reinstate Stair, who had now succeeded to the viscountcy, or give him further office, he publicly exonerated him, and the wording he used may also have been an acknowledgement of his own responsibility, and an attempt to excuse it.

The Viscount of Stair, then Secretary of State, being at London, many hundred miles distant, he could have no knowledge nor accession to the method of that execution; and His Majesty being willing to pardon, forgive, and remit any excess of zeal, or going beyond his instructions by the said John Viscount of Stair, and that he had no hand in the barbarous manner of execution. . . .

The massacre, said this pardon, had been "contrary to the laws of humanity and hospitality", and those who should be blamed for it were the immediate actors, the soldiers and officers quartered upon Glencoe. None of these men was sent home for prosecution and punishment, as Parliament had desired. "If we had them again," wrote Charles Leslie bitterly, "how we would hang the rogues!" But no one was hanged, though this was what the compassionate Queen, now dead, had once thought necessary for the nation's honour.

6

GLENCOE IN HIS FACE

"I think you begin to forget me, or I live too long . . ."

FOR SEVEN years the new Viscount Stair lived quietly on his western estates, further enriched by a Royal gift of the bishop's rents and feu-duties of the barony of Glenluce. He did not embarrass the King by involving himself in public affairs, and he had too much contempt for the mob to give it the pleasure of throwing stones at his coach. And it was with the King's approval that he refrained from taking his seat in Parliament as a peer. For the moment he was content that the rewards of office would go to others of his family, to his loyal brother Hew, for example, who was appointed Lord President of the Court of Session in 1698. But he had not forgotten the great work yet undone.

In March, 1702, William died, his weak lungs unable to survive a hunting accident, and Jacobite hagiology now included the mole whose earth had brought down his horse. The raddled, once-handsome Earl of Portland held the King's hand, and by the death-bed stood another Dutch favourite, Arnold Joost van Keppel, a boy of twenty-three who was already an earl, a Knight of the Garter and a major-general.* Princess Anne, the second daughter of James II, became Queen, a dropsical sentimentalist, a compulsive eater and card-player with a bizarre and painful history of miscarriages. She felt none of the guilt that may have troubled her brother-in-law, and having little regard for the

* His son, the second Earl of Albemarle, became Commander-in-Chief in Scotland after the failure of the last Jacobite Rebellion in 1746, during a period of harsh repression unequalled in British history.

opinions of her late father's supporters she welcomed Stair back to public life, making him a Privy Councillor. A year later, she rewarded his shrewd counsel and support with an earldom.

England was now ready and eager for the Union of the Parliaments, and Stair was one of the Commissioners sent from Edinburgh to negotiate the Treaty. It was almost a Dalrymple Commission, for Hew went with it as Lord President, and so did another of the family, Sir David, the Solicitor-General for Scotland. The English and Scots delegates met in Whitehall for the first time on April 16, 1706. On that same day, forty years later, the warrior strength of the clans, and the independence of the Highland way of life, would be bloodily destroyed at Culloden.

"We are bought and sold for English gold!" sang the Jacobite ballads, but it was the more corrupting influence of an ideal that persuaded Stair to work for the surrender of his country's political identity. For nine months he put a merciless strain on his mind and body. The Union was strongly resisted in Scotland, and the most effective voice of opposition in Parliament belonged to John Hamilton, Lord Belhaven. In a florid declamation, later called "Belhaven's Vision", he pictured Scotland's ancient mother, Caledonia, expiring from the fatal blow of the Treaty and murmuring *Et tu quoque mi fili!* Stair used all his advocate's skill and eloquence to defeat this and other emotional appeals. On January 7, 1707, he went home late after a long day's debate on Article 22 of the Treaty, one of the last important clauses, determining the proportion of Scots representatives in the united Parliament. He died in his sleep. He was fifty-eight years of age, and the Union, not Glencoe, is perhaps his monument. His relatives and his supporters thought so. The memorial broadsheets they paid for, framed in black and decorated with ambiguous skulls, declared that *The Union shall perpetuate his name, as long as there's an ear or mouth in fame!*

His death stirred the bile of hatred in many Scots, and they were ready to believe that he had hanged himself in a fit of mad remorse, for the slaughter of Glencoe, for the murder of Scotland.

They recalled the dark and extravagant rumours about his mother, his sisters, the death of his sons, and they enjoyed the epitaph suggested by a lampoon.

> Stay, Passenger, but shed no tear,
> A Pontius Pilate lieth here,
> Got by Beelzebub on a witch . . .

Argyll was already dead, with ducal arms on his hatchment. One of William's last acts had been to raise MacCailein Mor to the highest rank in the country. He had made his family's titles and estates secure, he had received more from and given less to his country than either his father or his grandfather, and he never mounted the steps of the Maiden. He died in September, 1703, and his countrymen were not surprised to hear a story that he had been mortally wounded in a brothel, though it was probably false. His obituaries were less concerned with his political life than his sexual adventures, and his mordant wit would have appreciated one called *A Satire on the Duke of Argyll that died in his whore's arms in England.*

> Pluto did frown, but Proserpine did smile
> In Hell to hear the knocks of old Argyll.
> Pluto cried, Let no gates opened be!
> If he comes here he'll surely cockle me.
> To which the Queen replied with sighs and groans,
> No fear, my Liege, for he's got bruised stones.

The libelled whore was Peggy Alison, in whose arms the Duke did indeed die at Cherton in Northumberland. His last hope was that his Duchess would allow his "dearest, dear Peggy" to live there in peace with her cousins and brothers. But Argyll was no sooner in his grave than the Duchess was doing her best to get "that slut" out of a house she now considered hers. To be exact, she did not wait until Argyll was dead. Four days before he vomited sixteen ounces of blood and died, she asked her lawyers to take the necessary steps for Mistress Alison's removal. They did so, and an order to quit was nailed to the door within a few feet of Argyll's coffin. It was probably Peggy, certainly not the Duchess, who paid an obituarist to write *Let his memory to future ages be kept in record for zeal and piety*. And that, too, would have amused Archibald Campbell of Argyll.

Grey John of Glenorchy obstinately survived. His few months in Edinburgh Castle in 1695 did not deflate his unctuous self-esteem. "I resolve upon my release," he told Barcaldine, "immediately to go home and make a progress, so that the poor wives of Glen Orchy may once again see me." Rejected by the world, as it seemed, it was a comfort to remind himself that he was still a great Highland chief, confident of the loyalty and love of his people. Back on Loch Tay, there were other reassurances. Argyll sent him word that the King still approved of his work, and that the fact that the Glencoe business had been brought into Parliament had angered His Majesty. He was safe.

He lived another twenty-one years. The greatness he had always coveted, and the leadership of Clan Campbell, escaped him. As the house of Argyll rose, so Breadalbane sank. He could never reconcile himself to this, and his bitterness released the latent Jacobitism that was behind almost all his public actions. He sympathised with the Jacobite Rising of 1715, though he cannily pleaded illness as an excuse for not going in person to the great clan gathering at Braemar. He was eighty, and the illness was real enough, as a Tayside minister testified. Grey John was "much troubled with Coughs, Rheums, Defluctions and other Maladies and Infirmities". He allowed his people to go, and they fought with fury as a Breadalbane regiment at Sheriffmuir. After the collapse of the Rising, Hanoverian soldiers came to Finlarig and found him lying on his bed, a black-eyed, white-haired figure in a nightshirt, staring into the past. An officer touched his shoulder. "Sir, you are my prisoner!"

"Sir," said Breadalbane, "I am the prisoner of the Almighty, and eighty-one years of age." He turned to a servant. "Duncan, take this poor man away and out of the country, before my people hear of the insult he has offered me."

He was left in peace, and within the year he was dead. It was a MacDonald bard of Keppoch, of a clan that had often raided his rich lands, who sang a lament for him, wishing that it had been he who had led the Jacobite men at Sheriffmuir.

> Oh, for thy wisdom, Breadalbane old!
> Had age given up her withering claim
> and restored thee one day thy manhood's frame,
> thou would be the man
> to propose the right plan!

But in truth, he had never proposed the right plan in all his life.

Robert Campbell of Glenlyon died at Bruges on August 2, 1696, a pauper and a debtor still. Since the day he went to Flanders with his regiment, helped by money from Breadalbane's purse, he had not returned to Scotland. Even by dying he placed himself in debt to others. His friend, Archibald Campbell of Fonab, a captain of Argyll's, attended to his funeral and drew up a list of the expenses incurred by his long illness and by his interment in an unknown grave far from the glen of the twelve castles. They amounted to £402 14s. At Chesthill in Glen Lyon, his wretched family made an inventory of the little property that could be sold against this and other debts.

> . . . an old pair of virginals, twelve pound . . . a large looking-glass estimate to five pounds . . . two buttercans worth five shillings the piece . . . a pistol and a mortar of copper worth four pounds . . . a smoothing-iron worth twenty shillings. . . .

A handful of stock in the field and the byres, horses, cows, sheep and hogs. A few silver dishes and pewter plates, brass candle-sticks and kettles, washing-tubs, cogs and girdles. . . . They paid few debts. John Campbell, Glenlyon's first son and now the new Laird, was only twenty, and he wrote humbly to Breadalbane, asking for help which, he said, would "certainly preserve a family who have been upon all occasions serviceable to your Lordship's most noble predecessors, whose footsteps therein I resolve to follow and ever to continue". Breadalbane gave some assistance, £22 10s. Scots, and declared himself the young man's "affectionate cousin".

Glenlyon left his family and his descendants an obligation they found unredeemable, and which they called "the curse of Glencoe". It may have been this that made many of them devoted Jacobites, and others the zealous supporters of the Hanoverian kings, as if only by such selfless service could they repay or justify the greatest debt of Glenlyon's life.

John Campbell, his heir, took five hundred Breadalbane men to the Jacobite Army in 1715, and led them on a raid into Argyll. There he was opposed by Campbell levies under Fonab, his father's last friend. They decided that, whatever the cause, Campbell should not fight Campbell, and they shook hands and led their men away. At Sheriffmuir, John and his regiment were brigaded with the MacDonalds, and no man remarked upon this strange alliance except Black Alasdair of Glengarry who looked sourly at Glenlyon. "Your father deprived us of an arm," he said, with more spite than accuracy, for there were a hundred or more Glencoe men in his brigade. "Of that I'm guiltless," said John Campbell, "and the only rivalry I have with a MacDonald is to prove which of us will fight best today." Glengarry took his arm and asked to be accepted as a brother. MacDonald and Campbell charged together.

After the failure of the 'Fifteen, John Campbell went into exile, until the influence of the 2nd Duke of Argyll and the 2nd Earl of Breadalbane secured him a pardon. He worked hard to pay some of his father's debts, and to regain a little of the land his family had once held in Glen Lyon. In 1745, when he was seventy, he risked all he had by declaring once more for the Stuarts. His eldest son, John, was a captain of the Black Watch who had fought for King George at Fontenoy and would not turn against that allegiance. His youngest son, his "darling boy Archie" who was fifteen, took the Glen Lyon tenants to Charles Edward. After Culloden, the Laird hid in the woods behind Chesthill, and the exposure and the privation killed him. There had been nothing like his funeral since the wake given for his redoubtable grand-mother, Jean Campbell.

The next Laird, John of the Black Watch, was known as *An Coirneal Dubh*, the Black Colonel. He was a brave, dour man who rarely smiled, and who said he should have been killed in battle many times, "but the curse of Glencoe is a spell upon me, and I must dree my weird". Unmarried, he gave his life to the Army, and what prize money he won in the West Indies toward the re-purchase of land in Glen Lyon. Late in his life, it is said, when he was an officer of Marines, he was given the responsibility for carrying out a macabre sentence upon some deserters. They were to be led out for execution, and only at the last moment were they to be told that they had been reprieved. When Campbell pulled the reprieve from his pocket, his handkerchief fell to the ground. The firing-party took this as the customary signal and fired. John Campbell looked at the dead men and cried, "It is the curse of Glencoe!" He resigned his commission and died soon after in 1784. The story may be true, but in such Highland tales there is always a strong wish to put a proper end to capricious misadventure.

Colonel John Campbell and his childless brothers, Archie and David, were the last of their direct line, and with them died the Campbells of Glenlyon.

The Earl of Argyll's Regiment earned King William's admira-tion in the only possible way, by dying for him. In July, 1693, the men of Cowal, Lorn and Kilbride fought their first battle. They marched upon the French redoubts of Dottignies at the head of Ramsay's Scots Brigade, and in their van was Thomas Drum-mond's company of grenadiers. They marched firmly, and at a steady pace with muskets shouldered. The summer heat was bitter, and the cross-fire unceasing. When they reached the parapet of the Pont David redoubt only a few of the grenadiers were left, and the other companies of Argyll's, including Glen-lyon's, passed through them and took the position. They had fought, and beaten, thirty times their own number. That night they joined their English comrades in burning the houses of Dottignies, and they destroyed the near-by village of Evergnies.

They raped women and terrorised children. They robbed a church, and they burnt it while it was still full of frightened peasants. The doorway was choked with charred bodies.

So great had been the Regiment's losses on the grass slopes below the redoubts that it was not sent into action again for two years. It fought before Namur and then joined the garrison of Dixemude under Major-General Ellenberg, a Dane who had little taste for his orders, and he surrendered to the French as soon as he could. The officers of the Argyll Regiment broke their swords, and the soldiers tore their colours from the staffs and burned them. On the day that the Scots Parliament demanded the return of Duncanson, Glenlyon and others, they were marching out of Dixemude in angry submission. They were shortly released under truce, but for Duncanson, who was now the lieutenant-colonel, the surrender had been a disaster. Ten days before, he had redressed the regiment in new uniforms, and much of the clothing and equipment was taken by the French with the regimental treasury. More than £1,000 was owing to John Michaels, a clothier of Edinburgh, and when Duncanson returned to Scotland, Michaels had him committed to the Tolbooth for debt. He was still in prison in 1697, when the Argyll Regiment was disbanded, "in a miserable condition and petitioning the Privy Council for his release". He was finally bought out, by Argyll one would like to believe, and he went back to the Army. He was shot down at the siege of Valencia de Alcantara eight years later, a colonel of his own regiment.

Thomas Drummond survived the French fire that destroyed many of his grenadiers before the redoubts at Dottignies, and he left the Army when the regiment was disbanded. He joined the Company of Scotland Trading with Africa and the Indies (his brother, Robert, was one of its sea-captains) and he sailed with the first settlers the Company sent to Darien on the isthmus of Panama. A member of the Council there, he quarrelled with and intrigued against other councillors until they finally imprisoned him. He was released by Campbell of Fonab, who had been sent from Edinburgh to bring some order into the unhappy, disease-ridden colony. Whatever else might be said about Drummond, his courage was never questioned, and his jungle expedition against the Spaniards was the only success in the miserable history of the Darien Settlement.

Though they had been the victims, the MacDonalds of Glencoe were less outraged by the massacre than some who used it as a weapon in their political vendettas. Violence and bloody murder are part of the history of the Gael, and there were more terrible slaughters committed by one clan upon another. Raid and reprisal were a way of life, and the MacDonalds must have been aware that one day they might have to pay for their joyous rape of Breadalbane and Argyll. They returned to their valley and they walked with caution. They received no reparation, and to add to their suffering they were threatened with the quartering of soldiers if they did not pay £300 in tax owing to the Goverment. John MacDonald appealed against this cess, and his petition went before the Council and into a pigeon-hole, where it was lost.

Slowly the people flourished, and the old temptations were again strong, though the world was changing. In 1697 they were accused of giving shelter and support to a broken man called Dugal Ban MacKellar, who had cut a traveller's throat with his dirk and robbed him of £800 Scots. He was taken from the valley and hanged. Two years later, two Glencoe men called John MacDonald Mhic Allan and Angus MacAlasdair Mhic Allan, decided to collect an old debt from the Campbells. With three other men from Cameron country, they went down into Lorn and stole cattle, meal, geese, herring-nets, clothes and furniture. They entered Campbell homes and shouted noisy threats, waving "drawn swords and bended pistols". Only one of them was caught, a Cameron, and he was hanged on the Doom Tree of Inveraray.

The Glencoe men were out in the Rebellion of 'Fifteen, a hundred swordsmen under Alasdair Og, and there is no evidence that he or they refused to fight beside the son of the man who had killed their kinsmen. In 1745, the clan again joined the hapless

Stuarts, sending as many men as had once gathered behind
MacIan the Twelfth at Dalcomera. They were led by John
MacDonald's son, who had been carried from the massacre by
his nurse. It was said that during the advance on Edinburgh the
Glencoe men asked for the honour of protecting the Earl of
Stair's house against pillage and burning. The story is probably
the product of the 19th-century romanticism that anaesthetised
the terrible hurt of the clearances and evictions, no more true,
perhaps, than the Black Colonel's curse of Glencoe.* It does not
sound like the men whose fathers and grandfathers burned
Achallader, stripped Glen Lyon, laid Kilbride waste, and emptied
the byres and kitchens of Rosneath.

The little clan stood on the left wing of the Jacobite Army at
Culloden with others of its name, with the MacDonalds of
Clanranald, of Keppoch and of Glengarry. Some died there,
under grapeshot and sabre, others were driven into the hills by
the harrying that followed the Rebellion, and once more their
homes were burnt and their cattle taken. What the red soldiers
began in February, 1692, sheep finished one hundred and fifty
years later, and the people of John of the Heather were gone from
the Valley of the Dogs.

John Hill continued to serve the King at Inverlochy until he
was beyond age and use. Now that there was no great need of
the garrison, the Government was even less inclined to maintain
it, and Hill fretted unhappily about broken palisades, crumbling
earthworks and rotting wood. The foundations slipped, and he
had no carts to carry fresh materials, all that had to be brought
was carried by men's hands alone. The comparison between this
weakening fort and his own body could not have eluded him.
The memory of the massacre was always in his mind, and he was
distressed when he heard that Hamilton proposed to publish a
pamphlet in Holland, putting all the blame on him. He paid the

* It first appeared in Howell's *State Trials* in 1810 and later in General David
Stewart of Garth's *Sketches of the Highlanders*, published in 1822. Stewart and
Walter Scott, with their imitators, created a Highlander who was an amalgam
of Knight Templar and Paladin.

doubts of his conscience with generous concern for the Mac-Donalds and other Lochaber clans, protesting on their behalf when the Tax Collectors were arrogant and pressing. "The imprudent way which the Collectors take," he said, "alienates the hearts of many from the Government, when a little forbearance would do much better." His letters were often written for him by a clerk now, but his tired hand could still put a plain and bold signature at their foot.

Year by year more of his men were taken from him, and he had no strength to object. He looked down the length of his years and they were many. He was at last given a knighthood, but the honour was empty in his loneliness. "I think you begin to forget me," he chided Duncan Forbes, "or to think I live too long, for it's once in a small age that I can have the favour of a line from you. But so you be well and happy, it makes me so too."

His regiment was disbanded at Whitsuntide, 1698, and he was relieved of the Governorship and discharged with half-pay of £168 a year as a Colonel and Captain of Foot. He was replaced by a brigadier.

He died somewhere in England, and in death Glencoe may also have been seen in his face.

ARGYLL, GLENORCHY, GLENLYON AND GLENCOE

Sir Duncan Campbell, *1st Lord Campbell*
Baron of Lochow, d. 1453

ARGYLL

- Colin, 2nd Lord Campbell *1st Earl of Argyll, d. 1494*
- Archibald, 2nd Earl *d. Flodden 1513*
- Colin, 3rd Earl *d. 1535*
- Archibald, 4th Earl *d. 1558*
  - Archibald 5th Earl *d. 1575*
  - Colin, 6th Earl *d. 1584*
    - Archibald, 7th Earl *d. 1638*
      - Archibald, Marquis of Argyll *8th Earl, beheaded 1661*
        - Archibald, 9th Earl *beheaded 1685*
          - ARCHIBALD CAMPBELL *10th Earl, 1st Duke of Argyll, d. 1703*
          - Mary m. SIR JOHN CAMPBELL *11th Laird, 1st Earl of Breadalbane. 1635–1716*

GLENORCHY

- Sir Colin Campbell *1st Laird of Glenorchy, d. 1480*
- Duncan, 2nd Laird *d. Flodden 1513*
- Sir Colin, 3rd Laird *d. 1523*
- Duncan, 4th Laird
  - John 5th Laird
  - Colin, 6th Laird "The Grey" *d. 1583*
    - Sir Duncan, 7th Laird, "The Black" *d. 1631*
      - Sir Colin 8th Laird d. 1640
      - Sir Robert 9th Laird d. 1657
        - Sir John 10th Laird d. 1686

GLENLYON

- Archibald, 1st Laird of Glenlyon
- Duncan. 2nd Laird "Red Duncan of the Hospitality" *d. 1580*
- Colin, 3rd Laird "Mad Colin" *d. 1597*
- Duncan, 4th Laird "Red Duncan son of Colin" *d. 1640*
- Archibald, d. 1640
- ROBERT CAMPBELL *5th Laird of Glenlyon 1632 – 1696*

Jean *married 1. Archibald*
2. Patrick Roy MacGregor
3. Duncan Stewart of Appin

a grand-daughter Sarah married ALASDAIR *son of MacIain of GLENCOE*

Appendix

PRINCIPAL CHARACTERS

BARCLAY, Sir George, Jacobite agent. Went to France in August, 1691, with Menzies of Fornooth to persuade James II to release the chiefs from their oath. Involved in an assassination plot against William III, 1696.

CAMERON of Lochiel, Sir Ewen (1629-1719). Chief of Clan Cameron. Jacobite leader with powerful influence in the Highlands. Submitted to William within the time set. Friend of John Hill, cousin to Breadalbane.

CAMPBELL of Barcaldine, Alexander. Chamberlain to the Earl of Breadalbane. Offered to secure the Glencoe men remission and restitution if they exonerated the Earl.

CAMPBELL, Archibald, 10th Earl and 1st Duke of Argyll (d. 1703). Colonel of the Argyll Regiment which he raised from his own people. Accompanied William to England, offered him the Crown of Scotland, secured the return of the titles and estates forfeited by his father. Chief of Clan Campbell.

CAMPBELL of Ardkinglass, Sir Colin. Sheriff of Argyll before whom MacIain took the oath in January, 1692. His property was ravaged by the Lochaber Men in the Atholl Raid, 1685.

CAMPBELL of Carwhin, Colin. Writer to the Signet in Edinburgh. Law agent for the Earl of Breadalbane.

CAMPBELL of Dressalch, Colin. Writer to the Signet and Sheriff-Clerk of Agryll. In Edinburgh in January, 1692, and was sent the certificate of submission containing MacIain's name. May have scored it out.

CAMPBELL, Sir John, 11th Laird of Glenorchy, 1st Earl of Breadalbane (1635-1716). "Grey John". Submitted to William 1689 and offered to treat with the Rebel chiefs after Killiecrankie. Met them at Achallader in June, 1691. Signed Private Articles with them. Probably gave Stair the idea for the massacre, but his full involvement is unlikely. Imprisoned by the Scots Parliament and released on William's order. Half-heartedly joined the Jacobite Rising of 1715. A cousin of Campbell of Glenlyon.

CAMPBELL of Glenlyon, Robert (1632-1696). 5th Laird of Glenlyon. Captain of the Earl of Argyll's Regiment, and commander of the two companies sent to Glencoe in February, 1692. A bankrupt and a drunkard. His lands raided by the Glencoe and Keppoch MacDonalds. Condemned by the Commission of Enquiry. Died at Bruges.

DALRYMPLE, Sir James, 1st Viscount Stair (1619-1695). Lawyer and statesman. Supporter of the Covenanters, driven into exile by the hostility of Dundee and the Duke of York (later James II). Returned with William, created Privy Councillor and Viscount. Father of

DALRYMPLE, Sir John, 2nd Viscount Stair, 1st Earl of Stair (1648-1707). "The Master of Stair". Advocate. Suffered under the hostility of Dundee and James II. Offered the Crown of Scotland with Argyll to William 1689. Lord Advocate. Joint Secretary with Melville, sole Secretary 1691-92. Responsible for the massacre of the MacDonalds. Accused of excess by the Scots Parliament, 1695, resigned his office. One of the principal supporters of the Act of Union, 1707.

DRUMMOND, Captain Thomas, commander of the grenadier company of Argyll's Regiment, and present with it in Glencoe on the morning of the massacre. A Tayside man. Condemned by the Commission and Parliament in 1695. Served bravely with his company in Flanders.

DUNCANSON of Fassokie, Major Robert (d. 1705). Member of a

Stirlingshire family, adherents of the Campbells of Argyll. A major in the Argyll Regiment, 1691, and its lieutenant-colonel 1695-98. Took four hundred of his men to Fort William, December, 1691, and planned the details of the massacre with James Hamilton. Issued Glenlyon's order on February 12. Prosecution demanded by Parliament, 1695. Killed at the siege of Valencia de Alcantara.

ELLIOTT, Sir Gilbert, Lord Minto (1651-1718). Writer to the Signet and judge. Helped to organise the Argyll Rising on 1685, was condemned to death but pardoned. Clerk to the Privy Council, 1692, and refused to accept MacIain's name on the certificate sent by Campbell of Ardkinglas.

FORBES of Culloden, Duncan, 3rd Laird (1644?-1704), supporter of the Revolution. His lands ravaged by the Jacobites 1689. M.P. for Nairn county. A friend and ally of John Hill during the latter's second Governorship of Inverlochy.

FORBES of Culloden, John, 2nd Laird (fl. 1650-1688), M.P. and Provost of Inverness. Supporter of the Commonwealth. Befriended John Hill during the latter's first Governorship of Inverlochy.

FORBES of Culloden, Major John, brother of the 3rd Laird. Captain in the Independent Company of Grants in 1689, resisted Dundee at Ruthven. Posted to Hill's Regiment at Fort William. Carried dispatches from Edinburgh to Inverlochy. Marched to Glencoe with Hamilton, February 13, 1692. Gave evidence at the Enquiry. Later lieutenant-colonel of Maitland's Regiment and Strathnaver's. Acquired the property of Pittencrieff in Fife. Hill's "dear child".

HAMILTON, Lieutenant-Colonel James. Second-in-command of Hill's Regiment, and Deputy-Governor of Fort William, 1691-95. Origins unknown, could have been Irish. In Stair's confidence and used by him to plan and execute the massacre. Prosecution demanded by Parliament, but fled to Flanders.

HAY, John, 2nd Earl and 1st Marquis of Tweeddale (1626-1697). Lord Chancellor of Scotland. Supported the Revolution, and then plotted against William, imprisoned but released upon confession. As High Commissioner, led the Enquiry into the Massacre of Glencoe. Signed the pass by which Hamilton escaped to Flanders.

HILL, Colonel Sir John. Governor of Inverlochy 1656-60, and 1690-98. A soldier of the Commonwealth. Constable of Belfast 1688. Sent to the Highlands in 1690 to pacify the Rebels. A friend of the clans. Signed Hamilton's order for the massacre. Exonerated by the Commission of Enquiry. Retired 1698.

JOHNSTON of Warriston, James (1655-1737). "Secretary Johnston". Son of Archibald, Lord Warriston, who was hanged after the Restoration. Exiled, studied law at Utrecht. Returned to Scotland to prepare the way for William's invasion. An enemy of Stair with whom he was Joint Secretary of State for Scotland 1692-95. Sole Secretary 1695-96. Helped to bring down Stair by supporting demand for an Enquiry into the Massacre.

JOHNSTONE, William, 3rd Earl and 1st Marquis of Annandale (d. 1721). Nominally supported the Revolution, later joined The Club and was imprisoned for plotting against William. Fully confessed and was released. Created extraordinary Lord of Session, 1693, and a Lord of the Treasury. Pensioned for his services on the Commission of Enquiry.

LESLIE, Charles (1650-1722), non-juror and controversialist. Son of the Bishop of Raphoe, deprived of his curacy when he refused to take the oath to William. Pamphleteer. Published one of the first accounts of the massacre, 1692, and later *Gallienus Redivivus*, 1695. Interviewed Argyll soldiers at Brentford.

LIVINGSTONE, Sir Thomas, 1st Viscount of Teviot (1652-1711). Born in Holland, came to England with William. Commanded Government troops at Cromdale. Later Commander-in-Chief. Transmitted Stair's orders to Hamilton.

MACDONALD of Achnacone. Tacksman of Glencoe, brother of MacDonald of Achtriachtan. Escaped from massacre when about to be shot.

MACDONALD of Inverrigan. Tacksman of Glencoe. Killed by Glenlyon who was his guest. He had a letter of protection from Colonel Hill.

MACDONALD of Glencoe, Alasdair (MacIain), 12th Chief of Clan Iain Abrach (1630?-1692). Also known as The Red. Educated in France, brought his clan out for Dundee in 1689. Took the oath five days late before Sir Colin Campbell of Ardkinglas in Inveraray. Killed at his bedside, perhaps by Lieutenant Lindsay.

MACDONALD of Glencoe, Alasdair Og. Second son of MacIain above. A captain under Buchan at Cromdale. Fought at Killiecrankie and Dunkeld. Married to Sarah Campbell, Glenlyon's niece. Escaped from the massacre.

MACDONALD of Glencoe, John, 13th Chief of Clan Iain Abrach. First son of MacIain above. Escaped from the massacre, later submitted and took the oath on behalf of his clan. Received John Hill's protection.

MACDONALD of Achtriachtan, John. Tacksman of Glencoe and brother-in-law of John MacDonald, 13th of Glencoe. Accused with MacIain the 12th of the slaughter of several MacDonalds. Took John Hill's protection in 1691, but killed by Sergeant Barber's men during the massacre.

MACDONALD of Keppoch, Coll. (b. 1670?) 15th Chief of Keppoch. Leader of the Lochaber Men with MacIain. Bitter feud with Mackintoshes. Fought at Killiecrankie and Dunkeld, raided Glen Lyon with the Glencoe men in 1689. Submitted and took the oath, January 1692. Asked for a Commission in William's army. "Coll of the Cows".★

MACDONALD, Iain Lom, the Bard of Keppoch. (1724?-1710?). One of the most famous Highland poets. Champion of Clan Donald, and violent opponent of William. Wrote a poem on the massacre.

★ Toward the end of the 17th century, the Keppoch and Glengarry branches of Clan Donald began to spell their name Mac Donell. For simplicity's sake, I have used the one spelling of MacDonald throughout this book.

MACDONALD, Ranald, of Achtriachtan. "Ranald of the Shield." Glencoe Bard. Fought at Inverlochy and Worcester. Believed to have been killed in the massacre, but there is no evidence that he was still alive then.

MACKAY of Scourie, General Hugh (1640?-1692). Commanded the Scots Division which landed with William 1688. Commander-in-Chief in Scotland 1689-90. Defeated by Dundee at Killiecrankie. Rebuilt the fort at Inverlochy 1690. Killed at Steinkirk 1692.

MACKENZIE, George, 1st Viscount Tarbat, 1st Earl of Cromarty (1630-1714). Statesman. Founder member of the Royal Society, writer on literature, science and philosophy. James II's chief minister in Scotland. Dismissed at the Revolution. Joined with Melville in a scheme for treating with the Rebels and buying off the chiefs. Scheme later adopted by Breadalbane. Became Secretary 1702, strong supporter of the Union.

MACPHAIL, Big Archibald, one of MacIain's clansmen. Legendary figure long remembered. Stories of his exploits preserved in the Dewar Manuscripts. May have been dead by the year of the massacre, but no evidence.

MATHESON, Murdoch (167?-1757), *Bhard Mathanach*, the Matheson Bard. Believed to have been in Glencoe as a guest of MacIain on the night of the massacre. Was probably the author of a long poem on the event usually attributed to the *Bhard Mhucanach*, the Muck Bard, about whom little or nothing is known.

MELVILLE, George, 4th Baron, 1st Earl of Melville (1634?-1707). Staunch Presbyterian, fled to Holland during reign of Charles II and returned with William in 1688. Appointed Secretary of State for Scotland with task of pacifying the Highlands. Worked with Tarbat. Was joined in the Secretaryship by Stair, and later unseated by him. Deprived of all offices 1702.

MENZIES, of Fornooth, Major Duncan. Jacobite officer. Led some of his clan to join Dundee against the wishes of his chief, who supported William. Was present at the Achallader Meeting in June 1691. Went to France with Barclay to secure James II's discharge for the chiefs. Returned just before Christmas, 1691. In January 1692 unsuccessfully appealed for time to persuade the chiefs to come in.

STEWART of Appin, Robert (167?-1730?), 9th Chief of Appin. Hastened from college to join his clan in 1689, when it was led by his Tutor, John Stewart of Ardshiel. Said to have been present at Killiecrankie. Involved with Alasdair Og MacDonald in an assault on troops from the garrison at Fort William. Came in to take the oath after the massacre, but did not finally submit until two years later.

STUART, James, James II of England and VII of Scotland (1633-1701). As Duke of York was High Commissioner in Scotland for his brother Charles II, and was responsible for repressive measures against the clans. Became King, 1685. Fled to France when William landed, December 1688. Defeated by William at the Boyne in Ireland, 1690. Retired to St. Germain in France. Devoted himself to religious studies.

WILLIAM, Prince of Orange, Stadholder of the United Provinces, William III of England and II of Scotland (1650-1702). Son-in-law of James II. Accepted invitation to undertake an armed invasion of England 1688. Offered thrones of England and Scotland. His anxiety for the pacification of the Highlands, and the release of troops there, made him a party to Stair's plan for the slaughter of the Glencoe men. Reigned jointly with his wife Mary.

CHRONOLOGY

1645
Dec. The MacDonalds of Glencoe and Keppoch raid Breadalbane on their way home from Montrose's army.

1646
June The young men of Glencoe and Keppoch again raid Breadalbane and fight the Campbells at Sron a' Chlachain. Thirty-six Campbells killed.

1655 Glencoe men and Keppoch MacDonalds raid Glen Lyon and Breadalbane in strength. The raid of "Colin's Cows".

1674 MacIain a prisoner in the Tolbooth at Inveraray. He is charged, with John MacDonald of Achtriachtan, with the slaughter of several people named Mac-Donald. MacIain escapes.

1678 The Highland Host is quartered on the Western Lowlands of Scotland.

1683 A Special Commission for Pacifying the Highlands goes on tour. Establishes itself at Achallader and is invited to visit MacIain at his house in Glencoe.

1685 The Marquis of Atholl leads the clans into Argyllshire after the failure of the 9th Earl of Argyll's Rising against James II. The Glencoe men ravage Kilbride, Cowal and Rosneath.

1688

Nov. 5   William of Orange lands at Torbay.

Dec.

22/25   James II flees to France.

1689

Mar.   James lands in Ireland.

Apr.   Convention of Estates in Edinburgh resolves that James has forfeited the Crown. William and Mary proclaimed King and Queen of Scotland.

May 11   The 10th Earl of Agryll and the Master of Stair offer William the Crown of Scotland in the Banqueting Hall at Whitehall.

13   The Earl of Melville appointed Secretary of State for Scotland.

18   The Jacobite clans, Glencoe among them, gather at Dalcomera under John Graham, Viscount Dundee.

July 27   The Battle of Killiecrankie. The Jacobites victorious over General Hugh Mackay of Scourie, but Dundee is killed.

Aug. 18   Sunday. The Jacobite clans are held at Dunkeld by the Cameronian Regiment commanded by William Cleland.

24   Muster of the first companies of the Earl of Argyll's Regiment of Foot.

The Jacobite chiefs enter into a bond for their mutual protection and to support James II. They then depart for their homes.

On their way home the Glencoe men and the Keppoch MacDonalds strip Glen Lyon from one end to the other.

1690

Mar.   Colonel John Hill arrives in Edinburgh from Belfast, offers his services in the pacification of the clans.

The earl of Breadalbane is given a commission to treat with the chiefs.

May   Thomas Livingstone routs Major-General Thomas Buchan's Jacobite forces at Cromdale.

Hugh Mackay sends Captain Scipio Hill to the King at Chester, with plans for his fort at Inverlochy.

Breadalbane also leaves for Chester to urge his proposals upon the King.

William authorises the building of a fort at Inverlochy. John Hill to be its Governor.

June 18   Mackay marches north with an army to establish the garrison at Inverlochy.

July 1   James's Irish army defeated by William on the River Boyne.

3   Mackay and Hill arrive at Inverlochy. Work on the fort commences.

18   Mackay marches his army south, leaving Hill in command.

Dec. 6   First mustering of Hill's Regiment of Foot.

1691

Jan.   The Master of Stair appointed Joint Secretary of State for Scotland with the Earl of Melville.

Apr.   Major Robert Duncanson appointed to the Earl of Argyll's Regiment at Crieff.

Robert Campbell of Glenlyon and Thomas Drummond receive commissions in the Argyll Regiment. Their companies mustered at Stirling.

May   Hill is given orders to reduce the rebel clans by force. Does nothing. Order later withdrawn. The Chiefs agree to treat with Breadalbane.

June   The Achallader Meeting between Breadalbane and the chiefs. His quarrel with MacIain. Treaty signed on 30th, also Private Articles.

July   Alasdair Og MacDonald of Glencoe, Robert Stewart of Appin, and others, raid two supply-boats on Loch Linnhe. Are imprisoned in Fort William and later released on the Queen's orders.

23   In an order from Flanders, William gives Mary full power to ratify the treaty between Breadalbane and the chiefs.

Aug.   Duncan Menzies of Fornooth and Sir George Barclay leave for France to obtain James II's permission for the chiefs to take the oath to William.

17   William offers pardon and indemnity to all those who take the oath provided they do so by January 1, 1692. Those who do not are threatened with "the utmost extremity of the law".

20   MacIain of Glencoe and his tacksman MacDonald of Achtriachtan are freely acquitted of the "slaughter" charged against them (the killing of several persons named MacDonald).

26   The Privy Council issues a Proclamation declaring the King's offer of pardon and indemnity provided the oath is taken before January 1.

28   Major John Forbes delivers a letter to Thomas Livingstone from John Hill, in which the Governor gives details of the Private Articles between Breadalbane and the chiefs.

Sept. 18   Stair writes to Breadalbane from Flanders, assuring him of the King's favour and that he does not believe the gossip against Breadalbane.

Dec.   The Earl of Melville is removed from the Secretaryship. The office is now held by Stair alone.

Stair writes to Breadalbane and to Lieutenant-Colonel James Hamilton at Fort William, exposing his intention to make an example of some of the clans, particularly the MacDonalds.

15   Orders issued for troops to march from the Lowlands to Inverness and Fort William.

Breadalbane arrives in London from the Highlands.

21   Duncan Menzies of Fornooth arrives in Edinburgh, carrying James's permission for the chiefs to do as they think best. He is too exhausted to travel farther, sends word to the Highlands. It reaches Lochiel some seven or eight days later.

29   Four hundred men of the Argyll Regiment under

Major Duncanson march to Dunstaffnage and there take boats for Fort William.

30 Sir Ewen Cameron of Lochiel travels to Inveraray to take the oath to William, and probably leaves word at Ballachulish for MacIain.

30/31 MacIain comes to Fort William to take the oath before John Hill, who tells him that he must go to Inveraray. He leaves at once, is arrested and held at Barcaldine Castle for twenty-four hours by Captain Thomas Drummond.

1692

Jan. 2 MacIain arrives in Inveraray and discovers that the Sheriff is away.

5/6 MacIain takes the oath of allegiance to William.

7 Stair writes to Livingstone, saying that he will soon be ordered to ravage the lands of Lochiel, Keppoch, Glengarry, Appin and Glencoe, and orders him not to trouble the Government with prisoners.

Stair and Argyll dine at Breadalbane's lodgings.

9 Stair hears a false report that MacIain has taken the oath in the time set, and says he is sorry to hear it.

11 Stair sends Livingstone the King's orders to proceed against those who have not taken the oath. He has now heard that MacIain has not taken the oath by January 1, "at which I rejoice". He says it will be a great work of charity "in rooting out that damnable sept".

The King's order to Livingstone is "to cut off these obstinate rebels".

16 Stair sends Livingstone the King's Additional Instructions, with particular orders to extirpate the MacDonalds of Glencoe. He writes also of this to Colonel Hill.

21/22 Major John Forbes, in Edinburgh, opens and reads Stair's letters and orders of January 16, with their instructions to extirpate the MacDonalds of Glencoe.

He sends them on to Fort William, and leaves for Inverlochy himself a day or so later.

29/30   Duncanson's troops arrive at Fort William.

Stair's letters and the King's Additional Instructions reach John Hill. Hamilton and Duncanson plan details of the massacre.

In London the news that MacIain has taken the oath, five days late, is now known. Stair writes to Livingstone saying he is glad that the chief did not come in within the time prescribed. He writes to Hill telling him he can expect no more instructions than those of January 16.

Feb. 1   Two companies of Argyll's Regiment are seen at Ballachulish by John Forbes.

Under Campbell of Glenlyon they march to Glencoe, where they ask for quarters, and are welcomed.

11/12   Stair's letter of January 30, telling Hill there can be no further instructions, arrives at Fort William.

12   Hill orders Hamilton to carry out the instructions he has received from the Commander-in-Chief. Hamilton writes to Duncanson, now at Ballachulish, telling him to begin the killing at seven o'clock the next morning.

Duncanson writes to Glenlyon in Glencoe, ordering him to begin the massacre at five o'clock the next morning, and to spare none under seventy.

13   THE MASSACRE OF GLENCOE is begun at five o'clock in the morning. At seven, approximately, Duncanson arrives with his command from Ballachulish, and at eleven James Hamilton comes over the Devil's Staircase with four hundred men of Hill's Regiment.

14   John Hill writes to the Earl of Tweeddale. "I have ruined Glencoe."

27   News of the massacre reaches London.

Mar.   Argyll's Regiment now quartered on Leith. In Edinburgh, Glenlyon's boasting makes it public knowledge.

Copies of Duncanson's order are circulated in the coffee-houses.

James Johnston of Warriston is now Joint Secretary with the Master of Stair, and begins his intriguing against his colleague.

Apr. 12 Copies of the *Paris Gazette*, containing a brief report of the massacre, have reached London and Edinburgh.

May Charles Leslie publishes *A Letter from a Gentleman in Scotland*, a long account of the massacre.

June Argyll's Regiment is quartered on Brentford. Leslie interviews some of the soldiers.

Aug. John MacDonald of Glencoe brings his people down from the hills, and takes the oath to William.

The Argyll Regiment arrives in Flanders to reinforce William's army after the battle of Steinkirk.

1693

The Duke of Hamilton, as Royal Commissioner to Scotland, is ordered to enquire into the circumstances of the massacre. His orders are found to be inadequate, and little is done. He dies the next year.

1695

Apr. The Marquis of Tweeddale tells the Scots Parliament that the King had ordered a Commission of Enquiry into the Massacre of Glencoe.

June 20 The Commission of Enquiry sends its Report to William.

'MAJOR DUNCANSON'S
CHRISTIAN ORDER''

The order which Robert Duncanson wrote to Glenlyon from
Ballachulish on February 12, 1692, was not given in evidence
before the Commission of Enquiry in 1695. Members of the
Scots Parliament, debating the Report of the Enquiry and
the Massacre, complained that they had not seen it. Although
many copies were circulated in Edinburgh during the spring of
1692, and were still available in 1695, it was never officially
recognised. It was first published by Charles Leslie in the summer
of 1692, and many times later in frequent accounts of the Massacre. Its wording varied with each reprinting, but the substance
remained the same. What Glenlyon did with the order remains a
mystery, but he did not place it with other regimental papers. It
seems to have been in the possession of the Breadalbane family
until some time in the 19th century. It then passed through several
hands before being offered for sale at Christie's in June, 1925. It
was bought by James Ramsay MacDonald who presented it to
the Advocate's Library, prior to its nationalisation. Thus the
order is now in the possession of the National Library of Scotland. At the time of its sale, its authenticity was questioned, but
the signature was compared with others of Duncanson in the
Scottish Record Office, and was declared to be genuine. It is my
opinion that the Glenlyon family jealously preserved this letter
as evidence that Robert Campbell had done no more than obey
orders given him, and that with the extinction of the family it was
kept by the Breadalbane Campbells for the same reason.

GLENLYON'S BATTALION COMPANY
AND DRUMMOND'S GRENADIERS

The last surviving Muster Rolls of the Earl of Argyll's Regiment, previous to the Massacre, are for October, 1691. Since the names of the private soldiers varied little from month to month, it is more than probable that those who follow were present in Glencoe in February, 1692. Lieutenant Millan and Ensign Campbell of Glenlyon's company had been replaced by Lindsay and Lundie. Apart from Drummond, there is no information about the grenadier officers, but it is unlikely that the company would have marched without them

Stirling, October 23, 1691. Mustered there for Robert Campbell of Glenlyon his company of the Earl of Argyll's Regiment of Foot—the Captain, Lieutenant, Ensign, 2 Sergeants, 3 Corporals, 2 Drummers, 57 Sentinels.

Captain	Robert Campbell of Glenlyon
Lieutenant	John Millan
Ensign	John Campbell
Sergeant	Robert Barber
Sergeant	James Hendrie
Drummer	Mungo Dalyell
Drummer	Cuthbert Hunter
Corporal	Archibald Campbell
Corporal	James Macphail
Corporal	Duncan Kennedy

Sentinels Alexander, John
Blair, Archibald
Bruntfield, Thomas
Campbell, Archibald, elder
Campbell, Archibald, younger
Campbell Donald, elder
Campbell, Donald, younger
Campbell, Duncan
Campbell, George
Campbell, James
Dumbar, John
Dyatt, Hugh
Fergusson, John
George, John
Gray, Archibald
MacCallom, John
MacCalloume, Donald, elder
MacCalloume, Donald, younger
MacCallum, Duncan, elder
MacCallum, Duncan, younger
MacCallum, Malcolm
MacChessag, Archibald
MacClewan, Donald
MacClewan, John
MacClewan, Malcolm
MacDiarmid, John
MacDugald, John
MacEacher, —
MacHinbin (?), Martin
Macintyre, Patrick
MacIvackeder (?), —
MacIvor, David
MacKechirn, Patrick
MacKenthor (Macintyre?), John
Mackinlay, John
Mackinlayroy, Duncan, elder

Mackinlayroy, Duncan, younger
Maclean, Archibald
MacNachton, Duncan
MacNicolas, John
MacPholl, Duncan, elder
MacPholl, Duncan, younger
Macray, Adam
Milne, Alexander
Morrison, Archibald
Nicoll, Gillies
O'Breyan, Terence
Patrick, Robert
Robertson, Donald
Robertson, Duncan
Robertson, Ludovick
Scott, Thomas
Sinclair, Archibald
Sinclair, Malcolm
Stewart, John
Tillery, Walter
Turner, John

Stirling, October 23, 1691. Mustered there for Thomas Drummond his company of the Earl of Argyll's Regiment of Foot—the Captain, 2 Lieutenants, 3 Sergeants, 3 Corporals, 2 Drummers, 57 Sentinels.

Captain	Thomas Drummond
Lieutenant	John Kilpatrick
Lieutenant	Robert Campbell
Sergeant	Walter Purdie
Sergeant	Walter Buchanan
Sergeant	Walter Bruss
Drummer	John Mitchell
Drummer	George Lyon
Corporal	Lauchlan Sinclair

Corporal	William Ross
Corporal	James Mackinlay
Sentinels	Alam, William
	Alexander, Adam
	Black, Duncan
	Blair, Donald
	Brown, William
	Buchanan, Patrick
	Campbell, Archibald
	Campbell, John
	Campbell, Malcolm
	Carmichael, Walter
	Dawson, George
	Duncan, William
	Duncanson, Duncan
	Erroll, John
	Fergusson, Donald
	Fergusson, John
	Fisher, Donald
	Forester, Alexander
	Fraser, James
	Graham, Richard
	Grey, Patrick
	Grey, Rorie
	Hossack, William
	Howatt, John,
	Jameson, Hugh
	Johnston, William
	Kerr, James
	Lamont, Walter
	Loudon, Abraham
	MacCallum, Gilbert
	MacArter, Donald
	MacEadam, John
	MacElbrid, Hugh
	MacEwan, John

MacFarland, Walter
MacFinn, Donald
MacIntailer, Donald
MacKellar, Duncan
MacKellar, Patrick
MacKellar, William
Maclean, Hugh
MacNeill, Thomas
MacNish, Duncan
MacNickoll, Archibald
MacRie, John
MacSimon, Donald
MacVurich, Neil
Monss, John
Morrison, Duncan
Mulliken, John
Muirhead, James
Scott, John
Sim, David
Smith, Neil
Taylor, John
Taylor, Thomas

Acknowledgements

I am greatly indebted to the many people who have made this book possible. Mostly they are the men and women of Scotland, Highland and Lowland, who always make me feel welcome, and whose pride of race is complemented by courtesy and hospitality. I love their country, I return to it with delight, and I am glad that I can record some of its history. Among those who have given me advice and guidance I would particularly like to acknowledge my gratitude to the following:

Ian Douglas Campbell, 11th Duke of Argyll, for his hospitality, the freedom of his family's papers at Inveraray, and his knowledge of his clan. Sir William Arbuckle, for making his own great knowledge of the subject available to me, and for his unflagging interest in my work. John Imrie, of the Scottish Record Office, who unknowingly saved me from the mistakes of my own enthusiasm. Dr. James Robertson-Justice, a bonnet laird of Sutherland, for his friendship and his truly Highland welcome. J. R. Ker for particular advice on avenues of research. J. D. MacAlpin, the Warden of the National Trust property in Glencoe. Donald J. MacDonald, of the Clan Donald Society of Edinburgh. Mrs. Jean MacDonald Clark, a descendant of MacIain. Miss Edith MacGregor of Fort William. John MacInnes, of the School of Scottish Studies, for his literal translation of the Muck Bard's verses, and the direction of my interest to Murdoch Matheson. Thomas I. Rae, of the National Library of Scotland, for his generous assistance. W. A. Thorburn, of the Scottish United Services Museum, Edinburgh Castle, whose advice is always invaluable. And also, the staffs of the British Museum Reading Room, the London Library, the Public Record Office, the Scottish Record Office, and the Coulsdon and Purley Public Libraries.

Finally, my special thanks are once again due to my friends Iain Cameron Taylor and Rory Mackay.

Sources and Bibliography

The Report of the Commission of Enquiry is still the main source for this or any book on the subject. It first appeared in print in 1703, in a pamphlet called *The Massacre of Glenco, being a true narrative of the Barbarous Murther of the Glenco-men in the Highlands of Scotland, by way of military execution, on the 13th Feb. 1692*. It was printed, published and sold by the bookseller B. Bragg, at the sign of the Blue Ball in Ave-Mary-lane, London. Prefixed to it was an anonymous letter from Edinburgh, in which the writer said that he had hoped the matter could be forgotten, but since the printer had assured him that a full account was both necessary and longed for, he was glad to supply it.

Until now, it has been generally believed that the manuscript original of the Report, signed by the members of the Commission and sent to King William, was long ago lost. The claim that it was missing was first made in 1845 by the editor of The Maitland Club's *Papers Illustrative of the Political Conditions of the Highlands of Scotland from the Year 1689 to 1696*. Subsequently there were melodramatic speculations on whether or not it had been deliberately destroyed.

However, the original manuscript of the Report not only exists, but is easily accessible. It is in the Public Record Office, Chancery Lane, in King William's Chest 15, Number 84. Bragg's version is an almost exact copy of it, and differs in matters of spelling only, and here and there an omitted phrase. I have used the manuscript for the purpose of this book. I have been unable to find the depositions of the witnesses, which were sent with the Report to London, but I have no doubt that they, too, exist somewhere.

The Maitland Club's *Highland Papers* (above) contain most of the relevant documents that are important, but they give only the skeleton of the story, and the flesh has to be found elsewhere, in the Breadalbane and the Barcaldine Papers, in the Tweeddale and the Leven and Melville Papers. All these are in the Scottish Record Office or the National Library of Scotland· The Breadalbane and the Barcaldine Papers are of particular importance for the picture they give of Grey John, and the light they throw on his real or imagined responsibility for the Massacre. I think they rightly prove that, whatever his many faults, he has taken more blame than he deserved. William Gillies' book *In Famed Breadalbane*, published in 1938, is the best account likely to be published on Breadalbane and Glen Lyon. His sources were principally the Breadalbane and Barcaldine Papers.

John Hill's history and character, his part in the affair, have been pieced together from his letters and from letters to him. These are scattered through many manuscript and published papers—Culloden, Tweeddale, Melville, Menzies, Annandale and Breadalbane Papers. There is much about him, perhaps, that will never be known now, but what we do know is to the old man's credit.

The Argyll Papers at Inveraray Castle were a valuable source of information, and had hitherto not been consulted on the subject of Glencoe. The most important discovery among them was the 9th Earl of Argyll's memorandum on the "slaughter" committed by MacIain and his tacksman of Achtriachtan. The charge that MacIain had killed some of his people who offended him had not before been substantiated, and usually disbelieved by Clan Donald's sympathisers. But this single sheet of paper in the Inveraray archives is now an important piece of evidence.

The strong-room below Inveraray Castle also contains some fascinating material on the early years of the Argyll Regiment. Some of the Muster Rolls of the Regiment are in the Scottish

Record Office and the Public Record Office, and a skeletal account of its service was published in 1906 by Lt.-Col. Robert Mackenzie Holden in the *Scottish Historical Review*. Brief references to its service in Flanders are also to be found in Dalton's *History of the British Standing Army, 1660-1700*. But I could find no information of how this first Highland regiment was clothed and armed until I saw the indents and receipts at Inveraray. These papers also include the sad story of Quartermaster MacUre's imprisonment for debt, and the similar fate later of Duncanson.

The Glencoe MacDonalds' long history as cattle-thieves and troublesome raiders is well documented in the Register of the Privy Council of Scotland.

Finally, there is the valley of Glencoe itself. When one brings knowledge to it, it gives understanding.

MANUSCRIPTS

Argyll Papers	Inveraray Castle
Balhaldie MSS	National Library of Scotland
Barcaldine Papers	Scottish Record Office
Bighouse Papers	Scottish Record Office
Breadalbane Papers	Scottish Record Office
Burnet MSS., Harl. Coll.	British Museum
Choice Collection of Several Scots Miscellanie and Modern Poems (*c.* 1713)	National Library of Scotland
Cromartie MSS, Letters IV	Cromartie Muniments
Culloden Papers	National Library of Scotland
Inverawe Papers	National Library of Scotland
James Johnston's Letter Book	Scottish Record Office
John MacGregor MSS	Scottish Record Office
Leven and Melville Papers	Scottish Record Office
Misc. MSS 2671	National Library of Scotland
Misc. MSS 3134 f. 12	National Library of Scotland
Regimental Rolls 1689-91	Scottish Record Office

Regimental Rolls 1691-98   Public Record Office

Register of the Privy Council   Scottish Record Office
of Scotland, 1691-5 (MSS. and
typescript)

State Papers (Dom). Report of   Public Record Office
the Commission of Enquiry
into Glencoe. King William's
Chest 15 No. 84

Tweeddale or Yester Papers   National Library of Scotland

PUBLISHED PAPERS

An Account of the Depredations committed on the Clan Campbell and their followers during the years 1685 and 1686. A Report drawn up by Ewing of Bernice, 1690. Edited by Alexander Kincaid. Edinburgh, 1816.

An Account of the Proceedings of the Estates in Scotland, 1689-90. Edited by E. W. M. Balfour-Melville. Scottish History Society, Edinburgh 1954-55.

Annals and Correspondence of the Viscount and the 1st and 2nd Earls of Stair. Edited by John Murray Graham. 1875.

The Annandale Family Book, edited by Sir William Fraser. Edinburgh, 1874.

Calendar of State Papers, 1689-96.

Culloden Papers, 1625-1748, 1815.

More Culloden Papers, 1626-1704, Edited by Duncan Warrand, 1923.

The Dewar Manuscripts, Volume I. Scottish West Highland Folk Tales, collected originally in Gaelic by John Dewar for the 8th Duke of Argyll, translated into English by Hector Maclean of Islay, edited by the Rev. John MacKechnie. Glasgow, 1964.

Historical Manuscripts Commission Reports, 15, Appendix Part IX.

Howell's State Trials, Vol. XIII. Thomas Bayley Howell, 1809-15.

Judiciary Reports of Argyll and the Isles, 1664-1705. The Stair
Society, 1949.

Leven and Melville Papers, letters etc., addressed to George,
Earl of Melville, Secretary of State for Scotland, 1689-91.
Bannatyne Club, Edinburgh, 1843.

Original Papers containing the Secret History of Great Britain
from the Restoration to the Accession of George I. Edited by
James Macpherson, 1775.

Papers illustrative of the Political Condition of the Highlands of
Scotland from the year 1689 to 1696. Maitland Club, Glasgow,
1845. (Also known briefly as "Highland Papers".)

Register of the Privy Council of Scotland, 1681-91.

Somers Tracts, John Baron Somers. London, 1748.

JOURNALS

Blackwood's Edinburgh Review, Volume LXXXVI, July, 1859.

Notes and Queries, Second Series, Vol. VIII, July-December, 1859.

The Scottish Historical Review, Volume III, 1906, "The First
Highland Regiment, the Argyllshire Highlanders", by Lt.-Col.
Robert Mackenzie Holden.
Volume XVI, 1916, "The Revolution Government in the
Highlands," by Audrey Cunningham.

Transactions of the Gaelic Society of Inverness, Volume XLI, 1953.
"Gleanings from the Dornie Manuscripts", by Angus Matheson, M.A.

MEMOIRS

Memoirs of Great Britain and Ireland, 1681-92, Vols. I and II,
by Sir John Dalrymple of Cranstoun, 1771.

Memoirs of Hugh Mackay. Maitland Club, Glasgow, 1833.

Memoirs of Secret Services, by John Macky. London, 1733.

Memoirs of Sir Ewen Cameron of Lochiel, edited by John
Drummond. Edinburgh, 1842.

CLAN AND FAMILY HISTORIES, ETC.

MacDonald

The Clan Donald, by Angus J. MacDonald and Archibald M. MacDonald. 3 Volumes. 1896-1904.

The MacDonells of Keppoch and Gargavach, by Josephine M. MacDonell of Keppoch. Glasgow, 1931.

Historical and Genealogical Account of the Clan or Family of MacDonald, from Somerled to the present period, etc., by Hector MacDonald Buchanan. Edinburgh, 1819.

History of the MacDonalds of Clanranald, by Alexander Mackenzie, 1881.

History of the MacDonalds and Lords of the Isles, by Alexander Mackenzie, 1881.

Campbell

The Argyll Papers, 1640-1723, edited by James Maidment. Edinburgh, 1834.

The Black Book of Taymouth, edited by Cosmo Innes. Bannatyne Club, 1855.

The Book of Garth and Fortingall, by Duncan Campbell, 1888.

Glenlyon, some historical reasons why Campbell of Glenlyon and the Earl of Breadalbane hated the MacDonalds of Glencoe, by Duncan Campbell, 1912.

In Famed Breadalbane, by William A. Gillies, 1938.

The Lairds of Glenlyon: historical sketches of Appin, Glenlyon and Breadalbane, by Duncan Campbell, 1886.

The Lairds and Lands of Loch Tayside, by John Christie, 1892.

Dalrymple

Genealogical Account of the Dalrymples of Stair, Earls of Stair, by the Hon. Hew Hamilton Dalrymple. 1909.

The Life of John, 2nd Earl of Stair, by A. Henderson. 1750.

Memoirs of Sir James Dalrymple, 1st Viscount Stair, by A. J. G. Mackay. 1873.

GENERAL BIBLIOGRAPHY

ATHOLL, Katharine, Duchess of. *A Military History of Perthshire, 1660-1902.* 1908.

BUCHAN, John. *The Massacre of Glencoe.* 1933.

BURTON, John Hill. *History of Scotland, 1689-1748*, Vol. I. 1853.

CAMPBELL, Donald. *A Treatise on the Language, Poetry, and Music of the Highland Clans.* 1862.

CAMPBELL, J. L. and THOMSON, Derick. *Edward Lhuyd in the Scottish Highlands, 1699-1700.* 1963.

CUNNINGHAM, Audrey. *The Loyal Clans.* 1932.

DALTON, Colonel Clifford. *History of the British Standing Army, 1660-1700.* 1894.

DONALDSON, M. E. M. *Wanderings in the Western Highlands and Islands.* 1920.

ELDER, John R. *The Highland Host of 1678.* 1914.

FIRTH, C. H. *Scotland and the Protectorate.* Scottish History Society 31. 1899.

FOUNTAINHALL, Sir John Lauder, Lord. *Chronological Notes on Scottish Affairs, 1680-1701, chiefly taken from the diary of Lord Fountainhall.* Published by Sir Walter Scott. 1822.

GRANT, Mrs. Anne. *Superstitions of the Highlanders.* 1811.

GRANT, I. F. *Highland Folk Ways.* 1961.

KILGOUR, W. T. *Lochaber in War and Peace.* 1908.

LANG, Andrew. *History of Scotland.* 1897.

LESLIE, Charles. *Gallienus Redivivus, of Murder will out etc., being a true account of the De-Witting of Glenco.* 1720. *Also published in the Russell Press Stuart Series.* 1903.

MACAULAY, Thomas Babington, Lord. *History of England.*

MACDONALD, Donald. *Comh-Chruinneachadh Orain Ghaidhealach*, Gaelic Poems including the Muck Bard's elegy on the Massacre of Glencoe. 1809.

MACGREGOR, Alasdair Alpin. *Wild Drumalban, or The Road to Meggernie and Glen Coe.* 1927.

MACGREGOR, Edith. *The Story of the Fort of Fort William.* 1954.

MACTAVISH, Duncan. *Inveraray Papers.* 1939.

MENZIES, D. P. *The Red and White Book of Menzies.* 1908.

MARTIN, Martin, of Skye. *A Description of the Western Islands of Scotland, c. 1695, including a voyage to Saint Kilda.* 1703.

NAPIER, Mark. *Memorials and Letters illustrative of the Life and Times of John Graham of Claverhouse.* 1859-62.

NORIE, W. Drummond. *Loyal Lochaber.* 1898.

PAGET, John. *Paradoxes and Puzzles.* 1874.

PHILIP, James, of Almerieclose. *The Grameid,* an Heroic Poem descriptive of the Campaign of Viscount Dundee in 1689. Scottish History Society. 1887-88.

RAMSAY, A. A. W. *The Arrow of Glenlyon.* 1930.

SACHEVERELL, William. *An Account of the Isle of Man, with a Voyage to I-Columb-kill.* London. 1702.

SKENE, W. F. *The Highlanders of Scotland.* 1837.

STEWART, John H. J., and STEWART, Lt.-Col. Duncan. *The Stewarts of Appin.* 1880.

TERRY, Charles Sanford. *The Chevalier de St. George and the Jacobite Movement.* 1901.

THOMSON, Edith E. B. *The Parliament of Scotland, 1690-1702.* 1929.

Index

Where possible, Highland chiefs and lairds are listed in order of precedence within their particular families, and not in alphabetical order of their Christian names. Place-names in Glencoe, and also the names of ordinary members of Clan Iain Abrach, are indicated thus (G).

to Fort
William

GLENRIGH FOREST

North
Ballachulish

Invercoe

Ballachulish

Carnoch

From Inveraray

Brecklet

Laroch

Inverrigan

Pap of
Glencoe

Cliff of
the Feinn

Aonac

Leacantuim

Signal Rock

Meall
Mòr

Achnacone

GLENDOUR FOREST

Bidean
nam Bian

APPIN

N

Miles

0   5

E.W.